Character Education Connections

FOR SCHOOL, HOME AND COMMUNITY

BY DIANE STIRLING
with Linda McKay, Georgia Archibald & Shelley Berg

A COLLECTION OF FIELD-GENERATED, FIELD-TESTED IDEAS FOR INTEGRATING CHARACTER EDUCATION INTO DAILY LEARNING

csd COOPERATING SCHOOL DISTRICTS • ST. LOUIS, MISSOURI

CHARACTER EDUCATION CONNECTIONS

Copyright ©2000 Cooperating School Districts
published by National Professional Resources, Inc.
25 South Regent Street
Port Chester, New York 10573
Toll free: (800) 453-7461
Phone: (914) 937-8879 Fax: (914) 937-9327
Visit our web site: www.nprinc.com

Stirling, Diane
    Character education connections for school,
    home and community : a guide to integrating
    character education / by Diane Stirling ; with
    Linda McKay, Georgia Archibald & Shelley Berg. --
    3rd ed. 2002
        p. cm.
    Includes bibliographical references and index.
    ISBN: 1-887943-28-5

    1. Moral education--United States.
    2. Character--Study and teaching--Activity programs.
    3. Values--Study and teaching--Activity programs.
    I. Title.

    LC311.S74 2000   370.11'4
                                      QBI99-1350

TABLE OF CONTENTS

HIGH SCHOOL LEVEL (9-12)

VARIATIONS ON A THEME

ENRICHING CHARACTER EDUCATION

COMMUNITIES OF PEACE & RESPECT

CONFRONTING THE REALITY OF BULLYING

RESOURCES

ACKNOWLEDGMENTS

Things of worth often begin with the vision of one and the efforts of many. *Character Education Connections* is no different. I express my heartfelt thanks to

. . . the individuals cited as the source of inspiration at the close of each unit. They are teachers, counselors, students and administrators who have imagined and implemented character education. Their concepts are innovative and grounded in experience. They work within the school districts listed on the right. These districts are members of **CHARACTER***plus*.

. . . ***Bob*** and ***Helene Hanson*** of National Professional Resources for the vision and resources to deliver this book to a national audience.

. . . the team who developed this resource, including ***Diane Stirling,*** who combines the diligence of research and writing into clear portraits of character education as it unfolds in classrooms and schools; ***Georgia Archibald***, who draws from a lifelong career in education and staff development as she extends the reach of the concepts presented into the home and community; ***Shelley Berg***, the educator who envisioned such a resource and produced the first edition; ***Mary Schiller*** for her incisive and insightful guidance during the publishing process; ***Mary Daniels Brown, Nan Starling*** and ***Kristin Pratt*** for their thorough editing; ***Sharon Boranyak*** for the development of the index and ***Doug Abbott*** for the symbols that visually express the interconnections between school, home and community.

In closing, I come full circle to acknowledge the vision of one that drives the work of many. **CHARACTER***plus* itself resulted from the vision and commitment of ***Sandy McDonnell,*** chairman emeritus of McDonnell Douglas Corporation, who initiated partnerships and a process of character education not only in the St. Louis community but throughout the country. It is to Sandy that we dedicate *Character Education Connections.*

— *Linda McKay,*
Director of Character Education, Cooperating School Districts

SCHOOL DISTRICTS:
AFFTON
BRENTWOOD
CLAYTON
FERGUSON-FLORISSANT
HAZELWOOD
JENNINGS
KIRKWOOD
LADUE
LINDBERGH
MAPLEWOOD-
  RICHMOND HEIGHTS
MEHLVILLE
NORMANDY
NORTHWEST R-1
PARKWAY
PATTONVILLE
RITENOUR
RIVERVIEW GARDENS
ROCKWOOD
SPECIAL DISTRICT
ST. CHARLES
ST. LOUIS PUBLIC
UNIVERSITY CITY
VALLEY PARK
WASHINGTON
WEBSTER GROVES
WELLSTON

FOREWORD

We must guard our children's growth as carefully as a gardener looks after the crops that will provide his wealth. We must shelter them from the wind of neglect, we must cull the weeds that choke their brains with rubbish, we must water and feed their minds with a sound education.

> *Take care of our children.*
> *Take care of what they hear.*
> *Take care of what they see.*
> *Take care of what they feel.*
> *For how the children grow so will be the shape of [the world].*
> *We must all be diligent gardeners.*
> *– Dame Whina Cooper*
> *Shared Values in a Troubled World*

Once, in talking to my teenage daughter, I shared my concern about her "memory tapes." I was talking about the messages she absorbs from her cultural environment. I wasn't worried about Molly alone, but about all of our youth. When I was growing up, I watched movies and read books peopled with characters who showed courage and moral strength. They did the right thing when it was hard to do. I lived in a community in which respect, integrity and responsibility seemed synonymous with adulthood. These elements created memory tapes, a wealth of images that I've drawn upon throughout my life. These images have inspired high expectations, commitment, a willingness to confront obstacles and persevere, a belief in the goodness of people and a sense of responsibility to myself, my family and my community.

As the mother of four adult daughters, I am acutely aware of the forces contributing to their memory tapes. The same conduits that delivered such positive messages to me have sent mixed or negative messages to our children. Movies, television and popular music imprint images of violence, injustice, dishonesty, infidelity and disrespect. Bad behavior is rewarded with fame and riches while few heroes survive the scrutiny of time. The pursuit of personal goals eclipses the needs of our families and communities. The concern for "I" is rarely balanced by an active concern and empathy for others. The security of the home is betrayed by the prevalence of divorce, shaking the trust our youth once invested in their most intimate community—their families.

The combination of these forces has had a devastating impact. And our children are not immune to it. Many experience a meaninglessness and lack of purpose to their lives. Far too many contemplate suicide and seem unable to value themselves or others. Recognizing a crisis among our youth and the dramatic difference between my memory tapes and those of my daughters, I committed myself to finding ways to pass on positive values to our children. I discovered I was far from alone. I've had the privilege of working professionally with hundreds of local and national educators, parents and business and community leaders as the director of **CHARACTER***plus*. With a 15-year history and the voluntary participation of more than 400 schools, **CHARACTER***plus* has collected a wealth of responses to the challenge of integrating character education into academic lessons and daily living. *Character Education Connections* shares this wealth.

My hope is that everyone—parents, educators, civic leaders, public servants and business people—will seize the opportunity to bring these lessons to children. For when such traits as caring, respect, responsibility and cooperation are experienced, they not only form positive memory tapes, but fuel the decisions and actions of a lifetime and create memory tapes for the next generation.

—Linda McKay

September 2001

We began our journey in character education to counter the negative messages surrounding young people. In recent years we learned, sadly, that we must also counter the negative and violent actions of some of our youth. Our community took up the challenge. We raised the bar, moving from the "talk" to the "walk." The results have been powerful for students and, we discovered, for the adults who walk the walk with them.

Students aren't talking about peace, they are apprentice peacemakers motivated by their work with Nobel Laureates (page 280). They aren't talking about caring, they are buddies who get to know and look out for their younger partners (page 285). They aren't passive in the face of taunts and bullying, they are "bullying-busters" (page 299), effective members of a peace posse (page 282), middle school students who can break down barriers of bias (page 305) and fifth-grade performers who can shape and deliver an unforgettable message (page 302).

The stories behind these realities are told in two new sections: ***Creating Communites of Peace & Respect*** starting on page 279 and ***Confronting the Reality of Bullying,*** starting on page 294. We are proud to share them with you in our third reprinting of *Character Education Connections*.

How to Use This Book

The graphic design (left) symbolizes a school-home-community partnership committed to character education. When these separate forces come together in a process that builds consensus and fosters *thoughtful action,* the result is a message for our youth that helps them connect and understand their strengths, responsibility and respect for themselves and others, and their ability to make decisions that are moral and just.

THOUGHTFUL ACTION PRESENTED IN 50 UNITS

Fifty *thoughtful actions* are presented in these pages. They have a pragmatic creativity that comes from people who implement what they develop and test it in public classrooms and schools. The concepts are varied in design, scope and developmental levels. They range from prekindergarten to 12th grade, and from half-hour lessons to schoolwide events to yearlong courses.

CHARACTER TRAITS

The units share a common reference point, however. They focus on particular character traits that are identified in bold print on the first page of each unit. These traits are not randomly selected. Each school district represented in this book (see page v) invested in a consensus-building process that involved educators, students, parents and members of the local community. Together they agreed upon a list of traits that were important to emphasize and reinforce. The number and nature of the traits vary from district to district, but this composite list suggests the values supported by these communities. Those in bold print are emphasized by 10 or more districts.

Accountability	Goal-setting	Positive work ethic
Abstinence	Healthy lifestyle	Problem-solving
Assertiveness	**Honesty**	Reliability
Attitude	Humanity	**Respect**
Belonging	Initiative	**Responsibility**
Caring	Integrity	Rewards
Citizenship	Justice	Sharing
Commitment	Kindness	**Self-control**
Compassion	Loyalty	Self-discipline
Confidence	Motivation	Self-esteem
Cooperation	Ownership	**Service**
Courage	Patience	Time management
Decision-making	Peacemakers	Unselfishness
Discretion	**Perseverance**	Value
Equality	Positive self-concept	Volunteerism
Freedom	Positive self-communication	Wellness

HOW TO FIND WHAT YOU NEED

The grid on pages x and xi identifies features of each unit to help readers sort and select those that match their interests. Character traits appear in the index in bold print with the appropriate units listed by name under the headings of "elementary," "middle" and "high school." While grade levels are clearly noted, we encourage people to explore beyond the limits of these recommendations. The concepts in this book invite imaginative adaptations.

WHAT TO EXPECT IN EACH UNIT

The first page of each unit includes a quick guide to its application and contents. The example shown here explains the headings and notations. The text of each unit includes its **objectives** and a **description** of the concept. Lesson plans, exercises and handouts accompany many of the units and can be reproduced for use with students. The concept itself serves as a springboard for extensions into the **home** and **community.** If the unit is formatted for use in the classroom, a section labeled **school** or **school & district** appears. The ideas contained under these subheads are suggested as ways to engage other members of the family, community, school or district in the learning experience. Unlike the basic concepts, not all have been field-tested. The **source of inspiration** refers to individuals, partners or teams who developed and implemented the primary concept. They are recognized with the school and/or district they served at the time they initiated their plans. These are not static relationships, nor are the ideas left untouched by time. While the majority of the concepts have been in active use for three to five years, they are subject to change.

Grades most applicable to the level of learning involved → **GRADES** 3 – 5

Self-contained in a classroom → **FORMAT** Classroom
Involves all students in a school **or** students from several classes → Schoolwide

Academic learning → **DISCIPLINES** Math Language arts

Skills are noted when academic disciplines are not applicable → **SKILLS** Listening Leadership

Time estimates refer to what is covered in the **description,** not additional applications. → **TIME** One hour

Titles of exercises and handouts included → **MATERIALS INCLUDED** Character Web

Materials or equipment required → **MATERIALS NEEDED** TV/VCR Newspapers

SPECIAL SECTIONS; WELL WORTH YOUR TIME

Variations on a Theme proves there is more than one way to accomplish the goal whether it is mentoring, positive reinforcement or a schoolwide approach.

Enriching Character Education answers the question "What is character education" and outlines a community-based approach.

Creating Communities of Peace & Respect: These programs, complete with resources and handouts, offer fresh ways to create meaningful connections between students, parents, school staff and the world.

Confronting the Reality of Bullying: Three unique approaches engage our youth in this issue and empower them to respond effectively.

UNIT	Page	Grades	Adapts to Grades	Disciplines	Within a Lesson	Outside a Lesson	Extracurricular	Community Service	Cooperative Learning	Experiential	Parental Involvement	Community Involvement
Character Plays	3	Pre-K	1, 2	L.A., R, Math	✔	✔	✔		✔		✗	
Story of Jumping Mouse	11	1–3		R, Sci	✔							
S.H.A.R.E.	15	K, 1	2	R			✔				✗	
Garden Party	21	K–2		R, Sci	✔	✔				✔		
Service in Bloom	25	2–5		Math, Sci, L.A., S.S.	✔		✔	✔			✗	✗
Rhymes & Reasons	29	K–5	6	Com, L.A.	✔	✔					✗	
You Can Be a Star	33	2–4	1, 2	Sci, Art, L.A.	✔	✔			✔			
Walk in My Shoes	39	4, 5	6	R, L.A.	✔	✔			✔	✔		
Cooperation	43	3–5					✔		✔	✔		
Respect	47	K–5		L.A., S.S., Art			✔		✔	✔		
Responsibility: Me Today . . .	53	K–2		R, L.A.,S.S.			✔				✗	
Lessons In Honesty	61	1–5		R, L.A.	✔							
Be a Goal-Setter	67	2–5		L.A., S.S.			✔		✔		✗	
Puppet Problem-Solvers	75	4–5		L.A., S.S.			✔	✔	✔	✔		
Exercising Character as We Exercise	77	3–5		P.E.	✔					✔		
Lessons for Success	79	K–5	6	S.S., L.A., P.E.	✔	✔						
A Million Pennies	81	K–5		Math, L.A., Art	✔	✔		✔				
Wackadoo Zoo	83	1–4		Music	✔	✔			✔	✔		
Musical Definitions	85	K–5	6–8	Music	✔			✔	✔	✔		
Power of Responsibility	89	2, 3		L.A.	✔	✔						
Statistics, Surveys and Personal Responsibility	93	5	6–8	Math	✔				✔			
Getting Ready	99	5, 6						✔	✔	✔		
School Tools Store	101	6–8		Math, L.A.	✔		✔		✔	✔	✗	
Responsibility on the Job	103	6–8		Math, L.A.	✔	✔	✔					
Exploring the Future	107	6–8		All		✔	✔		✔			
Peer Mediation	109	6–8	9–12			✔	✔	✔	✔	✔		
License to Lead	117	6–8	9–10			✔	✔		✔			✗
Lit Sets with Character	125	6–8		L.A., S.S.	✔							✗

UNIT	Page	Grades	Adapts to Grades	Disciplines	Within a Lesson	Outside a Lesson	Extracurricular	Community Service	Cooperative Learning	Experiential	Parental Involvement	Community Involvement
Dollars & Sense-Ability	129	6–8	9, 10	Math, L.A. Com	✔				✔	✔		✗
Creating Meaning	139	6–8	4, 5	Art, Com L.A.		✔			✔			
Movie Matinee	143	6–8	4, 5 9, 10	L.A.		✔						
Character Education Commercials	147	6–8	5 9, 10	L.A.		✔	✔		✔	✔		✗
Character in Motion	151	6–8	5, 9	Sci	✔				✔	✔		
Healthy Self-Esteem	155	6–8		Health, F&CS	✔							✗
Adopt-A-Student	157	6–8	Elem.				✔					
P.R.I.D.E.	159	6–8	Elem.				✔			✔		
Building Decision Skills	163	9–12	6–8	L.A., S.S.		✔			✔			✗
The Right Ingredients	171	10–12		L.A., S.S.	✔			˙	✔			
Romeo & Juliet	177	9, 10	8	Eng. Lit, L.A.	✔				✔			
S.T.A.R.S.	183	9–12				✔	✔	✔	✔	✔		
Grow a Row	189	9–12		Sci, Math, L.A., Bus		✔	✔		✔	✔		✗
French Cuisine	195	9–12		French, Com	✔	✔	✔		✔	✔	✗	
Senior Citizen Prom	203	9–12					✔	✔		✔		✗
S.M.I.L.E.	205	9, 10	6–8	L.A., Art, S.S.			✔		✔	✔		
Assembly Team	209	9–12	6–8	P.A., Music	✔	✔	✔		✔	✔		✗
Credit Union Practicum	211	11, 12		Math, Bus	✔	✔	✔		✔	✔		✗
Ethical Decision-Making	215	12	11		✔				✔	✔		✗
Character Studies	217	12		Eng. Lit., L.A.	✔							
Ethics in Science & Technology	223	12	11	Sci, S.S. Bus, Chem, Bio, Tech	✔				✔	✔		✗
Character Councils	235	9–12,	6–8				✔		✔	✔		
Project H.A.R.T.	239	9–12	6–8	Health, F&CS	✔				✔	✔		
Service Learning	249	9–12	6–8	Civics, S.S.	✔		✔	✔	✔	✔		✗

KEY

Bus   Business
Com   Computer
Eng. Lit   English Literature

F&CS   Family & Consumer Science
L.A.   Language Arts
P.A.   Performing Arts
P.E.   Physical Education

R   Reading
Sci   Science
S.S.   Social Studies
Tech   Technology

ELEMENTARY

EARLY CHILDHOOD (PRE K)

PRIMARY (K-3)

ELEMENTARY (1-5)

Evaluating Character Education in the Elementary Grades

Do your lessons help students understand the meaning and importance of good character? Can students go beyond basic understanding and apply what they have learned to their own lives? How do you know? Here are a few hints for evaluating the effects of your character education lessons on student learning and behavior.

PRESCHOOL - PRIMARY (P-2)
Ask students to respond to simple discussion questions based on a poem, story, fairy tale or fable that was read in class. (Understanding)

Have students draw a picture of the character trait(s) based on a poem, story, fairy tale or fable that was read in class. (Understanding)

Ask students to share a real story from their experience that shows the character trait(s). This could be something that involved their family, neighbors, friends, scout troop, sports team, etc. (Understanding)

Send a brief questionnaire home to parents to get their feedback on whether or not students understand and apply their learnings at home. (Understanding/ Application)

Have students conduct simple role-plays that show, for example, how a new student would want to be treated or how good friends would treat one another. (Application)

Have students work together in small groups on bulletin boards, posters and other projects that require collaboration and cooperation. (Application)

INTERMEDIATE GRADES (3-6)
Have students read and discuss literature addressing one or more character traits. (Understanding)

Have students keep a daily or weekly journal on the importance of having good character, character development objectives and ways in which behaving with good character (or not) has affected their daily lives. (Understanding)

Have students write stories, poems and essays about the importance of good character and its role in our democratic society? (Understanding)

Have students develop and perform in dramatic presentations illustrating positive character traits. (Understanding)

Have students create and display banners and posters illustrating one or more character traits. (Understanding)

Send a brief questionnaire home to parents to get their feedback on whether or not students understand and apply their learnings at home. (Understanding/ Application)

Have students conduct role-plays illustrating behaviors related to both positive and negative character development. (Application)

Have students engage in small- and large-group cooperative projects such as community service efforts. (Application)

CHARACTER PLAYS

Class performances offer rich learning experiences in character education for very young children.

OBJECTIVES
1. Promote the character traits of **commitment, cooperation, courage, goal-setting, kindness, respect** and **responsibility.**

2. Provide common experiences that integrate reading, language arts, music and math with character education.

3. Present a program for family members.

DESCRIPTION
Early childhood educators teach character lessons as they produce their "Winter Carnival," a program of short plays, carols, rhythm band numbers and dances performed by students for an audience of family members.

As students prepare for the performance, they express and experience many positive traits. Teachers and parents help them by naming the traits, defining them in age-appropriate terms and relating them to the children's learning and actions.

The performance is introduced as a project which takes:
- cooperation, *working with others,*
- commitment, *starting something and finishing it,*
- courage, *trying new things and performing in front of people.*
- goal-setting, *choosing what you want to do and taking steps to do it,*
- respect, *treating others with kindness,* and
- responsibility, *doing your part.*

Stories that amplify these traits are part of the reading curriculum. See page 18 for books that present responsibility in a way young children can understand. The question of how each student will participate in the program becomes a goal-setting exercise.

GRADES
Early childhood
Preschool
Early elementary

FORMAT
Classroom &
after-school

DISCIPLINES
Reading
Language arts
Math

TIME
12-20 hours of
preparation
One hour performance

MATERIALS INCLUDED
I Can Set a Goal...
Sample: I Can Set...
The Land of Respect

GOAL-SETTING

Once the selections for the performance are determined, they are divided into individual tasks and roles for the students. These roles are described to class members and listed on a large chart.   Symbols—such as ☆ for acting, ✂ for making costumes or ♩ for singing—help young children identify the activities. Students' names are listed next to a task after they work through the goal-setting exercise described below. Character traits are added as they are experienced in the process of reaching the goal.

	Name of Task	Name of Student	Positive Trait
♩	Sung "Jungle Bells"	John Mary Joe Susan	Cooperation Courage Perseverance Respect

The teacher takes time to describe the tasks and roles available in the production. A field trip to see a children's play can help young students visualize the parts they can play. As students react to the possiblity of being on stage, they may experience how they are alike and how they are different from others. One may be in competition with three other students for the lead role while another is terrified of standing up in front of an audience. The first student learns to respect others as she is guided through a process of conflict resolution. The shy student chooses a role that helps him work with his fear. Perhaps he joins the chorus so he can perform in front of others, but not alone. These discussions are a valuable part of the learning process and allow such character traits as caring and respect to be introduced. They take adult attention, a requirement that opens an avenue for meaningful parent involvement.

Parent volunteers work with the students throughout the production. They start by helping each child identify a goal—something he or she would like to do as part of the performance. In one-on-one conversations with students, adult volunteers explain the goal in simple terms and check for understanding. The handout on page 6 is designed to guide these conversations toward steps that help the student reach the goal. The sample on page 7 illustrates one way to divide a goal into smaller, intermediate steps. As students choose their goals, their names are printed on the chart next to the corresponding task.

Goal-setting is further reinforced as preschool students participate in planning and preparing refreshments for the program. Cookie recipes are selected and rewritten to show the instructions as a series of steps, the first being the collection of all ingredients. The students check off the steps as they complete them.

COOPERATION

The cooking experience also teaches the value of cooperation. Students are asked to contribute the specific ingredients needed and work together in teams to make the cookies. They measure the ingredients and watch as the teacher shows how to double the recipe using addition (math).

COMMITMENT

Following the performance, all participating students receive a certificate that celebrates their commitment, their willingness to finish what they started.

The Show Must Go On

The following resources can be combined to create a program around character education themes.

THE LAND OF RESPECT   **PAGES 8, 9**
This short play takes its motif from the *Wizard of Oz*.

PUPPET PROBLEM-SOLVERS   **PAGES 75-76**
This unit uses puppets to explore character traits in a way young children can understand.

MUSICAL DEFINITIONS   **PAGES 85-88**
This unit suggests songs that relate to cooperation and respect and might provide ideas for musical numbers.

This approach is especially appropo for performances that celebrate character education. The script of a short play is included with this unit. Entitled "The Land of Respect," it takes its bearings from the *Wizard of Oz* and works well with very young children when adults assume the speaking parts of the narrator and Dorothy. Other resources are noted in the box at the left.

HOME

"Ethics Come in Child-Sized Servings," an article reprinted on page 272, reinforces the role of parents as their children's first and lasting teachers with effective ways to integrate character education into daily activities and situations. It can be part of a training session for parent volunteers or copied and sent home with students.

COMMUNITY

Teachers can invite such public servants as firefighters or police officers to talk to class. They can illustrate goal-setting by defining one of their goals and the intermediate steps they take to acheive it.

SOURCE OF INSPIRATION

The team of early childhood teachers from Normandy Early Childhood Center, Normandy School District

I can set a goal and reach it!

Name _____

My Goal: I will _____

I will take these steps to reach my goal:

1. _____ ☐

   _____

2. _____ ☐

   _____

3. _____ ☐

   _____

4. _____ ☐

   _____

I will check off each step when I have completed it.

I can set a goal and reach it!

Name: _John_

My Goal: I will _sing Jungle Bells on December 3_

I will take these steps to reach my goal.

1. I will have someone read one line of the song.

2. When I can say that line by myself, I will go on to the next one.

3. I will practice saying all the words to Jungle Bells at home.

4. I will practice singing them with the other members of the chorus at school.

I will check off each step when I have completed it.

The Land of Respect

Narrator: You all know the story: The Wizard of Oz. You remember Dorothy *(enter Dorothy)* and the big storm *(music)* and how she whirled around *(Dorothy spins)* and landed in Oz. You remember a Scarecrow *(enter Scarecrow)*, a Tin Man *(enter Tin Man)* and a Lion *(enter Lion)*. And probably you remember that each character wanted something. Dorothy wanted to go home; Scarecrow wanted a brain; Tin Man wanted a heart; and Lion wanted courage. Remember how these characters worked together to get what they wanted?

Well, boys and girls, let me tell you the real story! Dorothy did whirl about in the storm *(spins)* but when she landed, she wasn't looking for a way to go home. She was looking for the Land of Respect. So we take up our story just as Dorothy meets the Scarecrow.

Dorothy: I'm looking for the Land of Respect, you know.

Scarecrow: I haven't got a brain, so I can't show you respect.

Dorothy: Can't show respect???!!! Can't show respect???!!! But of course you can show respect. You know how to listen to what other people have to say, don't you? *(Scarecrow nods)*. You know how to treat people the same way you want to be treated, don't you? *(Scarecrow nods)*. Well then, you really do know what respect is and you have the brains to use what you know.

Both: We're off to see Respect, Respect. The wonderful Land of Respect. (Sung to the tune of "We're Off to See the Wizard.")

Dorothy and Scarecrow come upon the Tin Man.

Dorothy & Scarecrow: We're looking for the Land of Respect.

Tin Man: But I haven't got a heart, so I can't show respect.

Dorothy: Can't show respect???!!! Can't show respect???!!! But of course you can show respect. You know how to care for people by smiling and being kind, don't you? *(Tin Man nods)*. You know how to be polite and call people by their name, don't you? *(Tin Man nods)*. Well then, you really do have a heart and you use it when you show respect.

All Three: We're off to see Respect, Respect. The wonderful Land of Respect.

The Land of Respect (continued)

Narrator: Who do you think they meet next? You're right! They meet the Lion.

All Three: We're looking for the Land of Respect.

Lion: But I haven't any courage, so I can't show respect.

Dorothy: Can't show respect???!!! Can't show respect???!!! Of course you can show respect. You have the courage to do the fair thing toward other people, don't you? *(Lion nods).* You have the courage to follow all the rules, don't you? *(Lion nods).* You have the courage to take care of other people's property, don't you? *(Lion nods).* Well then, you really do have courage and you use it when you show respect.

All Four: We're off to see Respect, Respect. The wonderful Land of Respect.

Narrator: So you see, boys and girls, Dorothy, the Scarecrow, the Tin Man and the Lion realized they already had what they were looking for. Dorothy was really in the Land of Respect. The Scarecrow had the brains to know respect. The Tin Man had the heart to feel respect. And the Lion had the courage to act with respect. And if you just remember to follow the same yellow brick road that they followed with the steps to respect . . . *(Each character picks up a sign that shows one of these four steps and says the step out loud.)*
SHOW RESPECT FOR YOURSELF
SHOW RESPECT FOR OTHERS
SHOW RESPECT FOR AUTHORITY
SHOW RESPECT FOR PROPERTY

. . . you can be in the Land of Respect with Dorothy, Scarecrow, Tin Man and Lion, and you can all live with respect happily ever after!

THE STORY OF JUMPING MOUSE

This Native American legend launches an exploration of wildlife, habitats, landforms, ecosystems and several character traits. It also reinforces community-building and helps at the beginning of the school year when the class is developing a sense of community.

OBJECTIVES

1. Reinforce the character traits of **compassion, cooperation, goal-setting, honesty, initiative** and **perseverance.**

2. Enhance vocabulary and introduce aspects of a temperate biome and its animal habitats.

DESCRIPTION

The Story of Jumping Mouse introduces an array of wildlife and environmental aspects that complement Earth Science studies. At the same time, the tale suggests goal-setting and step-by-step growth within the scheme of a journey. The protagonist, a young mouse, expresses determination, cooperation, perseverance and selflessness as he ventures toward the Far Off Land.

The following discussion questions guide an exploration of wildlife, habitats, landforms, the importance of one's name or self-identity, interdependence, compassion, selflessness and sacrifice.

COMPREHENSION AND DISCUSSION QUESTIONS

1. In this story, Jumping Mouse is determined to reach the Far Off Land. Why do you think he wants to go there? pp. 1, 2

2. The Old Ones warn Jumping Mouse that the journey will be perilous. How does courage help someone face a perilous journey? p. 2

3. Were you ever determined to do something? What does that word mean? Discuss a time you showed determination.

4. Who is Magic Frog? What name does he give Jumping Mouse? pp. 7, 8

GRADES
1 - 3

FORMAT
Classroom

DISCIPLINES
Reading
Science

TIME
One hour

MATERIALS NEEDED
The Story of Jumping Mouse
by John Steptoe,
37 pages

5. Magic Frog tells Jumping Mouse not to despair, to keep hope alive within you. What does that mean? p. 8

6. Describe Fat Mouse in two good sentences. pp. 11, 12

7. Why does Jumping Mouse decide to leave Fat Mouse and go on with his journey? p. 13

8. What happens to Fat Mouse? p. 14

9. Jumping Mouse meets Bison. Describe Bison's problem. pp. 15, 16

10. How does Jumping Mouse help Bison? What does that show about Jumping Mouse? pp. 17, 18

11. Jumping Mouse has given up his sense of sight. Predict how he will now reach the Far Off Land.

12. Bison live on the Plains. Describe the landscape and animals of the Plains.

13. Tell how Bison repays Jumping Mouse for his kindness. pp. 19, 20

14. Jumping Mouse has reached an area of cool breezes blowing down from mountain peaks. Where is he? What kind of habitat? What animals will he find? pp. 21, 22

15. Why is the sense of smell important to an animal like Wolf?

16. How does Wolf repay Jumping Mouse? pp. 23, 24

17. Jumping Mouse has mixed feelings the next day. Why is he happy? Why is he sad? pp. 25, 26

18. Who appears to Jumping Mouse? What does he say?

19. Look at the pictures on pages 31 and 32. Write two sentences to describe the pictures.

20. Read pages 33 and 34. Magic Frog gives Jumping Mouse a new name. How does this new name change Jumping Mouse?

21. What character traits does Jumping Mouse display? Does he show compassion? Does he show perseverance? Is he honest?

ADDITIONAL CLASSROOM LESSONS

The characters in folk tales, fables and fairy tales often portray positive traits. Students can read several tales and use the Character Web handout on page 66 to match characters to specific traits. In class discussions they can identify people in their own lives (parents, teachers, friends, coaches, sports figures) who exhibit certain character traits.

SCHOOL

Students can create a mural depicting Jumping Mouse's journey. Class members can work with the teacher or parent volunteers in developing a skit based on the story. They can commit to certain responsibilities, such as painting scenery or memorizing the lines to a part.

HOME

Send a note home to parents explaining the topics raised by the story. Suggest that they talk about family experiences—vacations, trips to parks, zoos or wildlife sanctuaries—that reinforce the student's awareness of different animals and their habitats. Suggest that they identify positive character traits that may have made the excursion memorable. For instance, a child's patience at a petting zoo may have been rewarded as a shy animal came closer.

COMMUNITY

The Story of Jumping Mouse invites a hands-on introduction to wildlife and landforms. The chance to walk in prairie grass and touch a snake can bring this legend to life. Call on the educational resources of the zoo, conservation department, parks and wildlife sanctuaries to explore animal behavior, habitats and ecosystems that support various wildlife in your area.

> **Vocabulary from *The Story of Jumping Mouse***
> brush
> exhausted
> content
> perilous
> journey
> peered
> gravelly
> encounter
> dismay
> reflection
> spanned
> boulder
> enormous
> bison
> rhythm
> cautiously
> despair
> misused
> scornfully
> rustling
> unselfish
> compassion
> commanded
> wondrous

SOURCE OF INSPIRATION

Marilyn Conrad, Valley Park Elementary School, Valley Park District

S.H.A.R.E.

SUPPORTIVE HOMES ARE READING ENRICHED

Selected students and their parents are invited to participate in S.H.A.R.E,
a reading support program organized around positive character traits.

OBJECTIVES

1. Promote the character traits of **caring**, **commitment**, **cooperation**, **goal-setting**, **honesty**, **perseverance**, **respect**, **responsibility**, **self-discipline** and **service.**

2. Promote reading for fun.

3. Develop a strong connection between home and school.

DESCRIPTION

S.H.A.R.E. adds a new twist to the concept of a lending library. Primary
students who are identified as needing reading-improvement support take a
S.H.A.R.E. tote bag home once a week. The distinctive bag contains:
- a book with content that relates to a character trait
- pre- and post-reading questions to stimulate conversation between parent and child
- instructions and supplies for an activity or project related to the story
- a comment sheet to be completed by the parent

The bag is sent home on the same day each week and returned within two or
three days with all contents except the supplies used to make the project.
Parents commit to spending one hour each week with their child in reading,
going over the questions together, talking about the character trait and
guiding the activity.

S.H.A.R.E. resources, researched by elementary-level reading specialists
throughout the district, include a bibliography of 10 to 20 books for each
trait. The number of traits included is determined by the number of reading
specialists involved, for each one takes responsibility for one trait. The
books are developmentally appropriate. Experience has shown that the most
popular ones are those the students can read aloud or follow closely as their
parents read the words.

GRADES
K, 1

FORMAT
Home-based

DISCIPLINES
Reading

TIME
One hour a week

MATERIALS INCLUDED
Bibliography for
Responsibility
S.H.A.R.E. Sewing
Bag Instructions

MATERIALS NEEDED
S.H.A.R.E. bags
Books
Activity sheets
Supplies

PREPARATION

S.H.A.R.E. bags can be sewn by volunteers during the summer before the project begins and according to directions on page 18. The rest of the preparation tasks are divided among the reading specialists by character trait. For instance, a reading specialist at School A does the following for the trait of responsibility:

- researches books, finding 10 to 20 that are developmentally appropriate and that relate to the trait
- develops pre- and post-reading questions and a related activity to go with each book
- writes instructions for each activity that are designed to be read by the parent and relayed to the student
- collects and assembles supply kits to complete the activity

The bags circulate among roughly 12 to 20 students in each of the schools. The reading specialist prepares enough supply kits to restock the bag for each student. For example, *Alexander's Terrible, Horrible, No Good, Very Bad Day* by Judith Viorst is on the "Responsibility" list. The emphasis of the book and the pre- and post-questions focus on being responsible for one's own feelings. The activity involves making a two-sided stick figure. Two paper plates and one wooden craft stick are included in the supply kit. Enough materials are collected to make 13 supply kits because each S.H.A.R.E. bag will circulate among 12 students at that school and a sample kit will go with the bag to the next school. The reading specialist there will make kits for the students of that school based on the sample.

Reading specialists at Schools B and C follow the same procedure for different traits, perhaps cooperation and courage. When the preparation is complete, the bags circulate among the students in each specialist's home school for eight to 10 weeks. The bags are collected, filled with a sample kit and traded with the bags from another school.

A bibliography for the trait of responsibility, a sample activity and a comment sheet are included with this unit on pages 18-20.

CLASSROOM REINFORCEMENT

Students who have worked through a S.H.A.R.E. bag take 5 or 10 minutes to tell fellow reading students about the experience. They describe what they liked or disliked about the story, show a favorite picture from the book and display their activity.

HOME

Families of identified students are introduced to the S.H.A.R.E. program during the first parent-teacher conference or at a special evening meeting. After discussing the concept, goals and process, parents sign a contract. They commit to spending one hour a week with their child reading, reviewing the discussion questions and helping with the activity. They receive a sample "Comment Sheet" and agree to complete the evaluation as part of the contract. This intentional and early communication between family and teacher strengthens a partnership that is vital to student success.

COMMUNITY

Libraries throughout the district and the surrounding community can display a sample of the completed S.H.A.R.E bag, with an accompanying book, activity and explanation of the project. These libraries might post the reading lists prepared for each trait.

SOURCE OF INSPIRATION

Elementary reading specialists of the St. Charles School District

S.H.A.R.E.

18 inches

—18 inches—

S.H.A.R.E. SEWING INSTRUCTIONS

Select a blue denim or canvas fabric. Pieces are cut approximately 18 inches wide and 36 inches long. Material is folded in half. Two sides are sewn together with 1/2-inch seams.

A 1-1/2-inch casing is made at the top of the bag. On each side, an opening is left for a drawstring. Two white athletic shoe laces are used for the drawstring.

S.H.A.R.E. is handwritten on each bag in three-inch letters in washable fabric paint.

Bibliography for Responsibility

The following list of books were chosen because they amplify the trait of responsibility in a way that young children can understand.

My Mom Made Me Go to School	Judy Delton
Alexander's Terrible, Horrible, No Good, Very Bad Day	Judith Viorst
Ira Sleeps Over	Bernard Weber
The Broody Hen	Olivier Dunrea
Happy Miss Rat	Peter Firmin
Beast & The Halloween Horror	Patricia R. Giff
Wake Up Baby	Joanne Oppenheim
Trash Bash	Judy Delton
The Fight	Betty Boegehold
Lost in the Museum	Miriam Cohen
Harry in Trouble	Barbara Ann Porte
Fish Face	Patricia R. Giff
Hucklebug	Steven Cosgrove
Dinner's Ready: A Pig's Book of Table Manners	Jane Gedye
Rabbit's Birthday Kite	MaryAnn MacDonald

S.H.A.R.E. Activity

Book: *Don't Forget the Bacon*
by Pat Hutchins

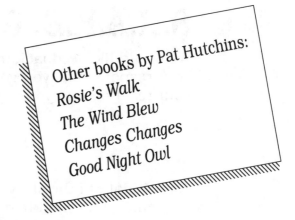

Other books by Pat Hutchins:
Rosie's Walk
The Wind Blew
Changes Changes
Good Night Owl

Character Trait: Responsibility
A willingness to be accountable for your own
actions without blaming others.

Discussion Questions
1. What could the boy do to help him remember?
2. What do you do?

Activity: Reminder Tag
1. Cut out pattern.
2. Punch a hole in the top with a paper punch.
3. Place the yarn that is in your S.H.A.R.E. bag through the hole and tie it, leaving enough space to slip it over a door handle.
4. Put it on your bedroom door or a door of the house that you can see as you leave.

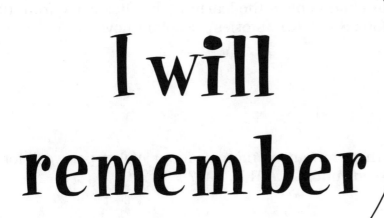

I will remember

S.H.A.R.E. Comment Sheet

We would like feedback from you and your child. Please talk about your responses as you go through the questions and record both your reaction and your child's reaction.

1. What did the story tell you about the character trait? Please ask your child to draw a picture of the character trait based on the story. Use the back of this sheet.

2. Does the content of the story and the additional materials provide a clearer or broader understanding of the trait?

3. Has your child applied the learning that has come from this or previous S.H.A.R.E. stories? Explain how.

4. Should there have been more or fewer nights per week for you to keep your S.H.A.R.E. bag? Why?

GARDEN PARTY

A garden can teach many things: scientific observation, alphabetizing, an appreciation of differences, patience and respect for the environment.

OBJECTIVES

1. Reinforce the character traits of **caring, cooperation, initiative, patience, reliability** and **respect.**

2. Learn through scientific observation.

3. Strengthen reading, vocabulary, alphabetizing and reasoning skills.

DESCRIPTION

The following activities integrate academic instruction and the classroom's physical environment (bulletin boards, displays) with the learning of specific character traits.

ACTIVITY I: ALPHABET GARDENS

- Cut pictures of plants from seed, vegetable and flower catalogs. Make sure each clipping includes the name of the plant.
- Place a group of these clippings, representing plants that begin with several different letters of the alphabet, into separate envelopes for each student.
- Pass out the envelopes and instruct students to dump them out on the desk and order them alphabetically.
- Encourage students to develop their own methods of remembering and ordering.
- Reflect! Discuss how they decided which plant came first, the dandelion or the daisy? Ask about their methods of ordering. Was it difficult to stack paper that was cut into different shapes and sizes? How many marked a number on each clipping? What other ways did students have of ordering? Perhaps they made a list of all the plants in the packet and worked from that list. Discuss the character trait of initiative. Define it. Ask the students if and how they showed initiative in completing the assignment.
- Have students work cooperatively as a class to create an alphabet garden on a bulletin board by combining the individual sets into one large set, starting with plants that begin with the letter "A."

GRADES
K - 2

FORMAT
Classroom

DISCIPLINES
Reading
Science

TIME
Several class sessions

MATERIALS NEEDED
Seed catalogs
Envelopes
Newsprint
Charcoal

ACTIVITY 2: BARKING UP THE RIGHT TREE

- At the beginning of the school year, ask students to identify their favorite tree as they tour the grounds of the school. This becomes their "adopted" tree, which they visit and observe throughout the year. Their awareness of one tree helps to foster a connection to and respect for the environment.
- Provide newsprint and charcoal or colored chalk to make a tree rubbing. Rub charcoal or chalk over the paper as it is held against the bark.
- Discuss these rubbings, comparing textures, patterns, width of the grain and distinguishing markings.
- Just as fingerprints are unique to people, bark is unique to each tree. Pass an ink pad around the room. Ask each student to press their right thumb onto the pad and then onto their rubbing. Compare their fingerprint with their neighbor's. Provide a magnifying glass for closer examination.
- Use the magnifying glass on an identifying expedition, observing the bark of the tree at close range. Measure the width of the trunk and estimate the height of the tree. Sketch or note characteristics of the leaves and seeds. Record these observations in a tree journal that is updated throughout the year. Include the tree rubbing in the journal.
- Plan a series of field trips to the students' adopted trees throughout the year. Ask them to note seeds, berries, nuts, pods and such variables as weather conditions, observable changes in leaf size and color, as well as the absence of leaves.
- Ask students to select one reachable branch and measure it each time they visit, then record these measurements and any visible changes in their journals. Encourage them to sketch such characteristics as the shape and size of leaves and seeds.
- Add a personal dimension to this exercise by asking students to measure and record such statistics as their height, the length of their shoes and the length of a strand of their hair. Near the end of the year, review the changes they note in themselves and the changes they have recorded in their adopted tree.
- Expand the theme of change and growth through literature. Read *The Giving Tree* by Shel Silverstein. Trace the changes that occur in the boy and the tree as the book progresses.

HOME

As a homework assigment, students are asked to notice the plants growing inside and around the outside of their home. They are to ask their parents about the care that is given the plants: How often do they need to be watered? Do they need fertilizer or other kinds of treatment? Do they need pruning, trimming, weeding, transplanting? Who is responsible for the care of the plants in and around the home?

COMMUNITY

Students can plant gardens or tubs of plants around the school or central office. They can start plants in the classroom and, when they are mature, take them to people in nursing homes or hospitals. The local media might report on students' "adopted" trees, emphasizing the academic skills involved in their yearlong observations. The local park services might provide volunteer opportunities for students that would reinforce their learning about plants, gardens, trees and the value of character traits such as care, patience, reliability and respect for the environment.

SOURCE OF INSPIRATION

Bertha Richardson, University City School District

SERVICE IN BLOOM

The student body participates in an activity that provides a tangible, visible service to the community and many lessons in math, science and character education.

OBJECTIVES

1. Promote the character traits of **cooperation, goal-setting, perseverance, respect** and **responsibility.**

2. Provide a **service** experience for students that brings their work into a partnership with the business community and local government.

3. Provide an experience in planning and implementing a community project that integrates math, science, language arts and social studies.

DESCRIPTION

Bruce Elementary developed a unique beautification and service project involving more than 200 second- through sixth-graders. Students worked in teams with parents, teachers and school staff members as they planted petunias and alyssum in existing flower boxes along the sidewalks of the local business district.

In language arts classes, fifth- and sixth-graders drafted letters of invitation and instruction to vendors and merchants along the streets involved. In science, they researched the characteristics of various annuals to select the plants most amenable to the climate and conditions, (e.g., hardy, low-maintenance, colorful). In math classes, they measured the flower boxes, calculated the number of plants needed to fill each one and determined the total cost from the individual price per plant. Students in lower grade levels became familiar with the parts of plants, their growth cycles and needs.

The event started with a parade as the students walked from the school to the business district. They carried banners and posters indicating they felt responsible for their community. The planning and perseverance of all those involved came to fruition in a project that lasted well beyond the school year.

GRADES
2 - 5

FORMAT
Schoolwide

DISCIPLINES
Math
Science
Language arts
Social studies

TIME
Planning: 10 hours
Planting: 6 hours

MATERIALS INCLUDED
Matrix & Venn Diagram

MATERIALS NEEDED
Plants, soil, gardening tools

CLASSROOM CONNECTIONS: MATH

Several mathematical functions are involved in determining the number of plants needed for the endeavor. A lesson focused on practical problem-solving allows students to see the result of applied academic skills.

Problem 1: How many plants do we need?
Measure planters. Determine length and width. Multiply to determine the area. Multiply by the total number of planters to be filled.
Determine the number of plants required for each planter if the plants are placed 6 centimeters apart. Determine the number of plants required if they are placed 8 centimeters apart. Multiply by the total number of planters. Divide by 36, the number of individual plants in each flat. Check this number for the specific plant. Some flats include eight 6-packs or 48 plants.

Problem 2: Knowing the number of flats needed, the next step is to determine their cost and make a purchasing decision. The class develops a list of plant sources and questions to ask: How many plants are in a flat? What size is the plant? What is the cost per flat including tax and shipping (if from a catalog)? Are quantity discounts or coupons applicable? Students volunteer to call and collect information. They report their findings. Class members work with this information individually or in small groups to determine the price per plant from each source. They must factor in taxes and such variables as discounts. They make purchasing recommendations based on their calculations and, as a class, they decide on where to buy the plants.

Problem 3: If plants are donated by a local nursery, students calculate the dollar value of the donation. This figure is used in press releases and notes of appreciation.

CLASSROOM CONNECTIONS: SCIENCE

Activity 1: Observe and compare similarities and differences in two different types of plants. Look at characteristics such as size, color, leaf, shape, blossom and roots. Use the Venn diagram and matrix on page 28 to record these observations.

Activity 2: Observe, compare, chart, graph and illustrate the changes that occur as a plant grows from seed to maturity.

Activity 3: Examine and label the different parts of a plant. Each part has cells and a specialized role in the life of the plant. Describe the function(s) performed by each part and its cells.

Activity 4: Design an investigation that will place two similar plants in different habitats. Consider the variables that exist between the two habitats and predict what adaptations the plant will make as it attempts to survive. Observe and chart those adaptations. Draw conclusions about which variables helped and which hindered the plant's growth.

CLASSROOM CONNECTIONS: SOCIAL STUDIES

Students learn at developmentally appropriate levels the interrelatedness of various business, community and government entities within their community and how vital each is to the success of the community. In this way they can begin to see themselves as part of a larger social group and to recognize the qualities of good citizenship and responsibility.

If the decision about color schemes is open to the students, each class can experience and contrast the processes of consensus and democratic voting as they determine the colors of the flowers for their assigned planter.

HOME

Students can use the planting and care techniques they learn to start a planter at home.

COMMUNITY

Fifth- and sixth-grade students design, write and produce a booklet with background about the project and instructions for the care and feeding of the plants. They include a comment page that is to be completed and returned to the school. The booklet is given to those responsible for the planters.

Students from all grade levels can revisit the planter sites throughout the summer and again in the fall to note the results of their efforts. Were the flowers maintained as had been agreed upon? Class discussions can focus on the value of follow-through and responsibility.

SOURCE OF INSPIRATION

Judy Owens and Carolyn Birge, Bruce Elementary School, Maplewood-Richmond Heights School District

MATRIX

PLANT	ROOTS	LEAVES	BLOSSOMS	HEIGHT	COLOR

Note differences between the two plants selected for comparison.

VENN DIAGRAM

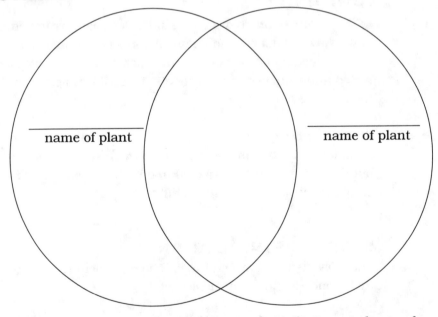

name of plant   name of plant

Note characteristics the plants have in common in the area where the two circles overlap.
Note characteristics that are unique to each plant in the remaining space of each circle.

RHYMES & REASONS

When students write about character, they translate the traits into the language of their lives. This language is active, imaginative and publishable! Their works have a ready market in the student body and the families of the young authors. This unit explores two different approaches: (1) a school-wide collaborative effort and (2) a classroom project that produces individual books written by each child.

OBJECTIVES

1. Promote the character traits reinforced by the school community, which could include **caring, compassion, confidence, cooperation, goal-setting, honesty** and **initiative.**

2. Reinforce the writing process through a Writing Workshop.

3. Increase student experience with computer word processing.

4. Interest and inform others outside the school of character traits. Generate discussions among others about these concepts.

DESCRIPTION: SCHOOLWIDE EFFORT

Claymont Elementary School collected student poems written about character over a two-year period and published them in a professionally printed, 72-page book called *Reach for the Stars.* The brainchild of the Character Development Poetry Committee, the book includes student illustrations throughout and student artwork on the cover.

Logistics: Students write on their own prose, in response to class assignments, on schoolwide Poetry Days and in their One-Room Schoolhouse groups (see box on page 30). They type and edit their work during their computer lab time. Parent volunteers often work with very young students in recording and editing their poems. Teachers accumulate poems throughout the year and submit them to a selection committee. The committee includes the work of as many different students as possible within its space limitations. A teacher or volunteer experienced in computer layout produces camera-ready pages for a professional printer. (Claymont's Book Fair profits covered the cost of printing.)

GRADES
K - 6

FORMAT
Classroom
Schoolwide

DISCIPLINES
Language arts
Computer lab

TIME
Intermittent

MATERIALS NEEDED
Laminator
Spiral binder
Copy machine
Computers

Every author and school family receives a book. A copy is included in welcome packets for new students.

DESCRIPTION: CLASSROOM PROJECT

Students in a second grade classroom at Mason Ridge Elementary respond to 14 different character traits during separate 40-minute sessions called "Writing Workshop." These sessions, held once every two weeks, are complemented by regularly scheduled computer labs (50 minutes each).

One-Room Schoolhouse

A large student body becomes friendlier in small doses. Each teacher and counselor works with a Schoolhouse Group which includes two students from grades 1-6. These groups meet once every two weeks and students remain in their group throughout their career at the school.

Advance work: Lesson preparation involves advance communications with parents about the topic, asking them to talk with their child about their concept of the trait, where they see it and how they express it and experience it differently from others.

Rap session: Students gather on the floor around an easel for a 20-minute discussion of one of 14 traits posted throughout the room. The teacher:
- defines the trait in words the children understand.
- introduces brief scenarios that illustrate it and asks students what these situations have in common.
- relates it to recent stories the class has read, if applicable.
- talks about experiences when students have expressed the trait and experienced the trait in others.
- talks about how people show it, how it benefits them as individuals, friends, family members and community members. For example, when your best friend shows you respect, you feel good about yourself and safe enough to share feelings that you don't want everyone to know about, such as being scared, worried, uncomfortable or sad.

Writing workshop: Students return to their desks and write a paragraph about the trait, often starting with a topic sentence provided by the teacher, and moving through the Writing Workshop process.

Computer lab: During regularly scheduled lab time, students "typeset" what they have written and enhance their computer skills by:
- finding the correct software and activating it
- selecting a new document and saving it
- selecting font styles and sizes
- typing content
- indenting paragraphs

The author's chair: When the paragraphs are complete, students are invited to read their work to the class. They receive caring, thoughtful feedback from fellow students who understand the responsibility of their role as reviewers.

Published works: These individual paragraphs, collected and preserved through the year, combine to become a book for each student. Students create their own covers with computer drawing programs or other artistic media. The covers are laminated and, with the inner pages, are spiral bound into a book.

Comments: Blank pages are included for comments. Students are encouraged to ask members of the schools staff, parents, coaches, scout troop leaders and others to read their book and write their comments.

SCHOOL & DISTRICT

The school library can maintain copies of the collected poems and lend them out. School libraries in other buildings should receive bound copies of the poetry collection. Copies can be displayed in the reception area of the district's central office so that visitors may read while waiting.

HOME

Parents are crucial to the project. They work with young students in recording their poetry or expressions about particular traits. They may input, format, copy, collate or bind in the process of producing the books. They are encouraged to use the content of the book as a springboard for one-on-one talks and family discussions of the character traits. Parents provide meaningful feedback when asked to write comments about the poems in the back of their student's book or in response to the schoolwide collection.

COMMUNITY

Copies of the books can be distributed in nearby doctors' or dentists' offices, coffeehouses, barber and beauty shops, libraries and other places where people tend to sit and read. Links with area associations for writers and poets might produce guest speakers who can inspire and validate the students' creative efforts. A local bookstore might be willing to host a "book signing" or "reading," inviting the young authors and their parents to an event that focuses on the character traits and applauds the students' creative efforts.

SOURCES OF INSPIRATION
Poetry Book: Patty Roe, Claymont Elementary, Parkway School District
Class of Authors: Susan Heigel, Mason Ridge Elementary, Parkway School District

Stop the Hate

Peace,
Sharing,
Things we have in our world today.

Prejudice,
Hate,
Also what we have in our world today.

Black and White
Why all the hate?
Skin doesn't tell who you are.

Killing and War.
Who needs it?
A bad way to settle a score.

Peace,
Sharing,
Things we need more of in our world today.

Be a Goal-Setter

"To be or not to be,"
Said Shakespeare long ago.
His goal was to write plays,
He reached his goal in many ways.
This just goes to show you
If you put your mind to it,
You can be your very best
And soar above all the rest.

Honesty is the Best Policy

Honesty is the best policy
It makes a friendship grow,
If you want a good friendship,
You must keep it so.
Do not lie,
You could make people cry,
It would not make you feel good,
Or feel as you think you should.
Always be honest,
And friends will have trust.
If you want that,
Do this,
You must.

Source of poems and art: *Reach for the Stars*

You Can Be a Star

This lesson looks beyond the glamour of stars to their substance, whether they are celestial bodies or people who have earned star status.

OBJECTIVES

1. Promote the character traits of **commitment, goal-setting, initiative, perseverance, responsibility** and **self-discipline.**

2. Learn the nature of stars and identify major constellations.

3. Discuss the definition of *star* that as it relates to fame and outstanding performance. Relate the qualities of these stars to character traits.

DESCRIPTION

Students examine the nature of stars in a mini-astronomy lesson.

* They define a *star* as a body in the sky that shines by its own light. They also define a *star* as a person who is well known because of outstanding performance or position.

* In class lessons, they learn that a star is made of many gases and held together by its own gravity. They identify major stars visible in the night sky, recognizing how they are grouped in constellations. They also recognize the sun as a star. They review facts about the sun, including its distance from and effect on Earth. They imagine what would happen to life on Earth if the sun vanished.

* They explore the second definition of star through such questions as "What do the stars of the night sky share in common with the stars we see in sports, on the stage, in the movies, on television and in our community?" They might recognize that both kinds of stars shine. Famous performers and athletes, for instance, shine on stage, stand out and draw people's attention.

* They suggest other words that define famous people, such as *celebrity, famous, popular, superstar, hero.*

* They fill in the Star worksheet on page 36 and share their responses with the class.

GRADES
2 - 4

FORMAT
Classroom

DISCIPLINES
Language arts
Science
Art

TIME
Four 30-minute sessions

MATERIALS INCLUDED
Name the Stars
Starmakers (pattern)
Starmakers (sample)

* They discuss how people become stars.
  * *effort* — You can shine by your own light.
  * *goal-setting* — Wishing on a star won't get the job done.
  * *desire* — What do you want to be able to do?
  * *study* — What do you need to learn to be able to do this?
  * *action* — What do you do to achieve your goal?

* They make their own star by cutting out the pattern on page 37. In the center of the star, they write their name or initials and a short phrase to suggest a goal they have set. In each point, they jot down an intermediate step or action that will bring them closer to their goal.

* In small groups or as a class, they discuss how people give support to and receive support from others. Students recognize the personal responsibility one has in defining, setting and working toward goals. They recognize the responsibility of friends, classmates and family members in helping others move toward their goals. They discuss the importance of active support and how it is expressed in attentive listening, checking in, empathizing when one faces difficult obstacles and celebrating successes.

* In small groups, students think of things that get in the way of achieving goals. The teacher can offer a personal example:

  To become a teacher, I knew I had to pass a certification test. I had a fear of this test and it was making me put off studying for it. As the date got closer, I became more worried and anxious and the studying I needed to do seemed overwhelming. I told a friend about these feelings and that is when I realized I was afraid. She helped me organize all my notes and books in one study area, then sat down with me and started asking questions about the material. I was so focused on coming up with the answers for her that I stopped feeling overwhelmed. She got me started and after that session I kept going on my own.

* They ask a "recorder" from each group to report the results of their discussion to the rest of the class. Students return to the small groups to consider these questions: What could another do to help me move toward my goal? What does it feel like when another person is aware of what I am trying to do? What is the difference between nagging and checking in? As they brainstorm ways that people can show support, the students arrange their individual stars with those of the other group members in a constellation. They name the constellation and display it.

SCHOOL

A school council comprising of students and staff can meet monthly or quarterly and review nominations for *Star* status. The basis for becoming a *Star* may be high grades, a good deed, volunteer service, outstanding performance or impressive improvement in some behavior or study, A bulletin board visible to all students and visitors can display pictures of the school's *Stars*.

HOME

Family members can complete a copy of the chart on page 36. Who are the stars in each of these categories? Why? Do members of the family have different reasons for choosing the stars they did? Do qualities of character such as perseverance, initiative, responsibility or honesty influence their choices?

Family members can scan local newspapers together and determine the people who are named as stars, heroes or outstanding people in some way. Why are these people being recognized? What character traits helped them achieve their goals? Did they need commitment, responsibility or self-discipline? Does service or care for others play a role in their stardom? Are there people who qualify as stars but have never received public attention? Who are they? How do you recognize and support these everyday stars? A discussion about personal "stardom" and the importance of recognizing each other's efforts and achievements within the family can flow from this activity.

COMMUNITY

A search of the community for stars, past and present, can be conducted. Are there statues of historic figures? Are places, streets or buildings named after famous people? Are residents of the community noted for outstanding achievement? Students teamed in small groups can research or interview three community stars, trace their life history and identify when particular character traits helped them to acheive their success.

SOURCE OF INSPIRATION

Sherry Kaiser, Forder Elementary School, Mehlville School District
"You Can Be A Star." *St. Louis Public School Fourth Grade Curriculum,*
St. Louis Public Schools Career Education Office, 1988.

★Name the stars you know★

Write down the names of any stars or constellations you know in the first column.
Write the names of the stars (famous people) you know under each of the categories.

Stars & Constellations	Sports Heroes	Performers*	Leaders**

*Performers can include actors, actresses, musicians, band members and others who perform before audiences.
** Leaders can include a range of people from such world leaders as the President to community or school leaders.

Starmakers

1. Write your name or initials on the line shown.
2. Write a goal in the center.
3. Write a word or phrase in each of the five points that suggests a step that will help to reach the goal. See the sample.

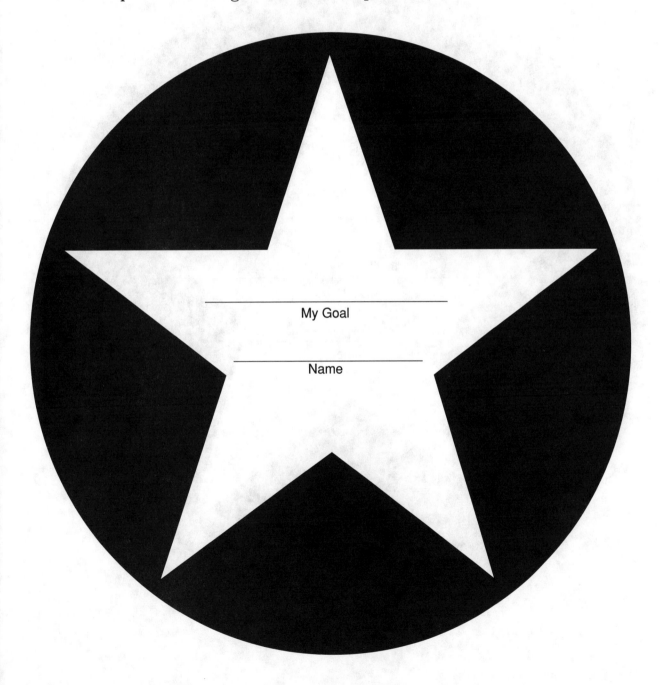

My Goal

Name

Starmakers

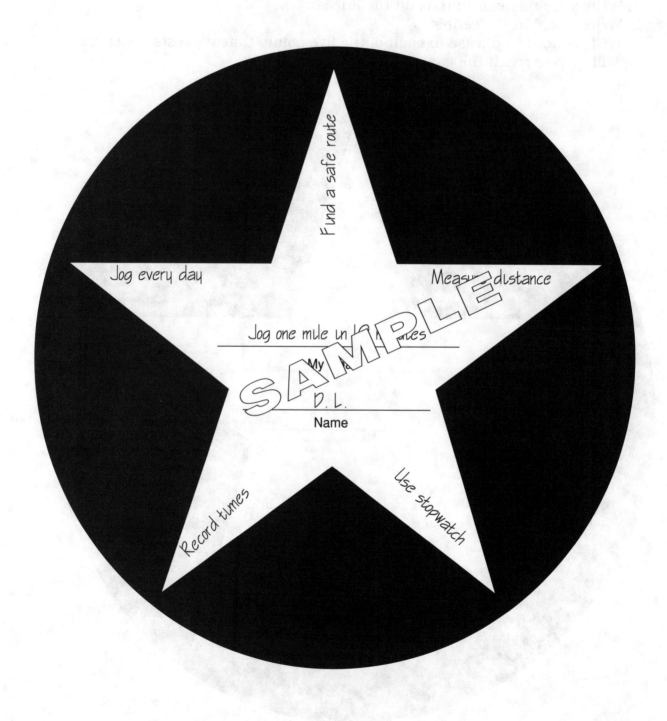

WALK IN MY SHOES

The story of Helen Keller and her teacher, Annie Sullivan, becomes even more meaningful when students simulate the experience of blindness. In this experiential lesson, students also learn to be responsible to another.

OBJECTIVES

1. Promote the character traits of **caring, compassion, cooperation, goal-setting, kindness, patience, perseverance, reliability, respect** and **responsibility.**

2. Communicate verbally with another student in a manner that is clear and effective.

3. Reflect on the experience.

DESCRIPTION

Preparation: Assign the reading of the story of Helen Keller. Refer to the list of books on the next page if the story is not readily available. Ask students to bring a dark scarf, bandana or strip of material to serve as a blindfold. Before class, weave roughly 50 feet of rope through a course on the playground that moves around, up, over, under and through the equipment.

Class session: After discussing the story of Helen Keller, students simulate the experience of blindness. They pair off. One partner closes his or her eyes. The other partner issues a command such as "sharpen your pencil" and proceeds to guide the sightless student through the task by giving verbal directions and cues to the surroundings. The partners then exchange roles.

Outdoors: The class moves to the playground. Students "walk in the shoes of Helen Keller" as they move, blindfolded, through an obstacle course prepared by the teacher. Students line up single file. Each one places one hand on the shoulder of the student in front. Students are responsible for communicating with and helping the one immediately behind them to locate the guide rope and to follow it as they move through the playground. If the lead student must duck under the jungle gym, she tells the person behind her what she has done so he can follow in her footsteps. The progression continues until all students have completed the course.

GRADES
4, 5

FORMAT
Classroom

DISCIPLINES
Language arts
Reading

TIME
Three class sessions

MATERIALS INCLUDED
Compare & Contrast

MATERIALS NEEDED
Helen Keller
The Miracle Worker
50 feet of rope
Playground
TV-VCR

Class members return to their room and take time to respond in their journals to reflective questions such as:

How did it feel to be blind?

How did it affect your other senses?

What did you hear?

How did it affect your relationship to the person who guided you?

What was it like to rely on someone so completely?

Did the guide's touch convey caring and kindness?

Did the voice sound patient?

Were the directions clear and reliable?

What helped you to trust your guide?

As the guide, did you feel a sense of responsibility?

What would you imagine as your most difficult challenge if you were blind?

Does your experience change the way you respond to the story of Helen Keller?

Compare and Contrast: View a video of *The Miracle Worker* and compare it to one of the biographical or autobiographical accounts of Helen Keller. Were there episodes, scenes or events that appeared in the book and not in the film? Use the Venn diagram on page 42 to note the similarities and differences between the book and movie version. Do you think the screen-writers represented the story honestly as they adapted it to a movie?

SCHOOL & DISTRICT

Invite people who are visually impaired to speak to students. Ask them to share their ways of accomplishing everyday actions, how they learned to use their other senses to help them and how other people have interacted with them in positive and negative ways. Finally, ask them to talk about the character traits they have developed in response to their challenges.

At the district level, ask students to research the district's inclusion policies for extra credit or as part of the assignment. How are students who are visually impaired involved in the district's schools? How are decisions regarding their educational needs made?

Viewing

The Miracle Worker (1979) Melissa Gilbert as Helen Keller; Patty Duke as Anne Sullivan. Warner Home Video Running time: 98 minutes

Further Reading

The Story of My Life
An excerpt from this auto-biography is reprinted in *Wind By the Sea,* a 6th-grade reader published by Silver, Burdett Ginn, 1993.

The Story of My Life
by Helen Keller
Doubleday, 1905

The Helen Keller Story
by Catherine Owens Peare
Crowell, 1959

The Silent Storm:
Annie Sulivan Macy
by Marion March Brown
Abingdon, 1963

HOME

Repeat the activity described under the heading "Class session" on page 39 with family members. Discuss feelings provoked in both the guide and the person who simulates blindness. In a second experience, consider the importance of familiar surroundings. Most people can move about their home in the dark or when blindfolded. Now create unfamiliar surroundings by moving furniture and objects to different locations. Repeat the activity. Discuss the heightened need for interdependence, trust and cooperation when someone with limited sight is in unfamiliar surroundings. The importance of putting things where they belong becomes clear from this experience. Family members talk about these issues: How do you feel if people use something of yours and don't put it back in the place they found it? Have you ever looked for something in its usual place and found it missing? What were your reactions? Imagine how much more anxious you would be if your search was compounded by limited vision or blindness. These considerations help people to empathize with others.

COMMUNITY

Locate organizations that serve the visually impaired. Foster a link between the agency and students through a club activity, leadership training, service learning or a class field trip. For instance, students might read short stories, articles or books onto tapes. They might create awareness of volunteer opportunities with posters, P.A. announcements and fliers.

SOURCE OF INSPIRATION

Kathy Steinmann, Commons Lane Elementary, Ferguson-Florissant
School District

Compare & Contrast

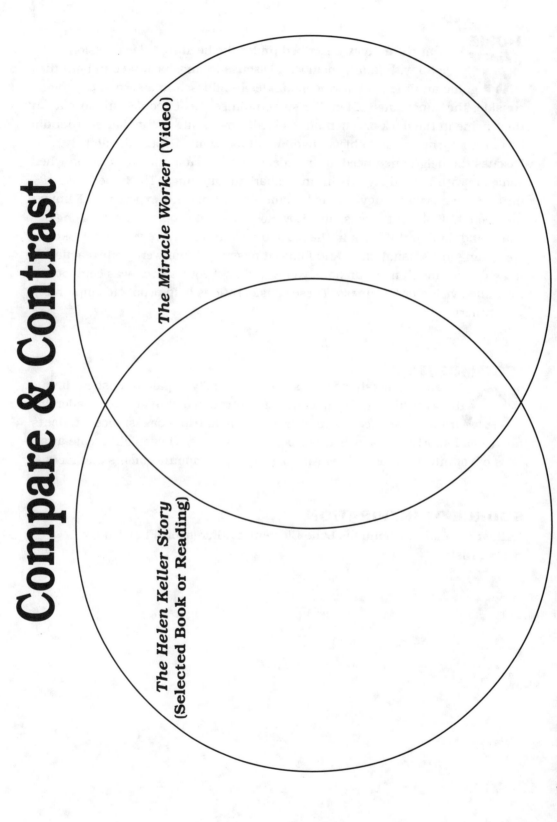

The Miracle Worker (Video)

The Helen Keller Story
(Selected Book or Reading)

Instructions: Note characters and scenes (situations or events) that appear **only** in the written version of the Helen Keller story on the far left, beneath the heading *The Helen Keller Story*. Note characters and scenes that appear **only** in *The Miracle Worker* on the far right. In the center area where the two circles overlap, note the characters and scenes that appear in the written story and the video.

COOPERATION

This lesson emphasizes the relationship between sensitivity, caring and cooperation.

OBJECTIVES

1. Promote the traits of **caring, cooperation** and **self-esteem.**

2. Strengthens listening skills and awareness of others.

DESCRIPTION
ACTIVITY I: MIRRORING

Ask class members to form a circle with one student in the center. The center student moves in slow and exagerrated movements so that the other students can follow the exact motions. Students take turns leading the group in mirroring the movements of others. This activity also can be done in pairs as student partners take turns in leading each other through mirroring movements.

Ask questions about the experience. Where was their attention focused? What gave them cues to a change in movement: facial expressions, body posture, other aspects?

Brainstorm the meaning of cooperation. Put a few words on the board that suggest the trait: teamwork, partners, etc. Ask students to give a word or instance that best describes the trait: sharing, supporting, listening, compromising, getting along, talking things out, asking someone for ideas, sharing credit for the job, being on a team, being part of a volunteer crew.

Discuss self-worth. Each student has something valuable to contribute to this group. When people appreciate their own abilities and ideas, they have a strong sense of self-worth. This makes them more willing to speak up, offer their thoughts and opinions, volunteer for tasks and invest more of themselves in the group. This, in turn, makes the group stronger and more successful. Ask students to think about gifts and talents they bring to class. Model this process by identifying your talents and those of others in the school community. Describe an instance when one's particular gift has come to the rescue. Ask students to brainstorm different ways to show that a

GRADES
3 - 5

FORMAT
Classroom

SKILLS
Listening
Communication

TIME
One hour

MATERIALS NEEDED
Chalkboard
Colored marshmallows
Colored toothpicks

person is valued, such as awards, honors, certificates, ribbons, compliments or applause.

One values another by identifying positive ways a person contributes. Compare these two comments. The one on the right recognizes the character traits of initiative and responsibility and shows how these qualities made a difference.

Good job. Thanks for your help.

If you hadn't double-checked the date, we would have printed it wrong on the posters. You saved us a lot of work and time.

ACTIVITY 2: BUILDING BLIND

1. Brainstorm about situations when students have followed directions.

2. Explain that they will practice giving and following directions.

3. Each student works with a partner. One is the communicator and the other is the listener. The partners sit back-to-back on the floor.

4. Each student receives a kit which includes colored marshmallows (not mini-marshmallows) and colored toothpicks.

5. The goal is to build identical structures. The communicator builds a structure using materials from the kit. At the same time, the communicator gives clear directions to the listener. The listener tries to build a matching structure from these directions. The partners, still seated back-to-back, are not allowed to turn around during the activity.

6. Explain expectations for noise levels. Each communicator needs to use a low tone of voice and speak distinctly while giving directions.

7. Set a timer for 5 minutes. When it rings instruct the partners to look at their structures to see how close they came to the goal of identical structures.

8. Instruct the partners to switch roles. Reset the timer for 5 minutes. Repeat the steps in 5-7.

Reflection and Closure: Invite students to discuss ways they cooperated with their partners to build their structures. Ask each one to communicate something specific about the partner's abilities that helped the process. Have the class review the words generated on the board earlier and see how many of those were used during the activity.

SCHOOL

A schoolwide cooperation-cluster chain can literally trail through the halls of the school. The chain is a symbol of strength, each link connecting to the other. Students realize that they, too, are stronger when they connect and work together. Each time a group (two or more students) works together in some way that is valuable to the school as a whole, the names of group members appear on separate pre-cut strips of colored paper. The activity or task is written on another strip. The students link the strips together, forming a closed circle. This "chain cluster" is added to other clusters to create an ever-growing chain. By doing this, students become aware not only of specific ways in which they cooperate, but also of their worth in the school community.

HOME

Working together requires sensitivity and cooperation, especially when group members cannot talk! Enlist the family in a cooperative chore, assigning coordination to one of the children. Once the members involved are clear about the task and its desired outcome—a clean garage, for instance—they begin the work. *No one* may speak while working. They must express directions, questions, concerns, agreement, disagreement and support without words. Each becomes sensitive to the actions and nonverbal communications of the others. At the end of the task, the participants discuss how they felt during the activity. Were they more aware of each others' actions? Did they become frustrated when they did not agree with what others were doing and couldn't express their feelings? Was the level of cooperation different than if they had been talking while working? If so, how?

COMMUNITY

Invite members of a business or community organization where cooperation is an obvious part of their work—paramedics, firefighters, builders, symphony musicians, restaurant staff—to share the systems and methods that help them work together effectively.

SOURCE OF INSPIRATION

Laura Bishop, Meramec Elementary School, School District of Clayton

RESPECT

This lesson develops self-respect and respect for others through activities that enhance relationships.

OBJECTIVES
1. Promote the character trait of **respect** for self and others.

2. Involve students at different grade levels in the activity, allowing older students to help younger ones and thus experience **caring, cooperation, initiative, kindness, patience, reliability** and **responsibility.**

DESCRIPTION
ACTIVITY: PARTNERS (GRADES 2-5)
Pair class members with someone they do not know well and give each pair a copy of the Partners handout on page 50. Allow 5 to 10 minutes to complete the sheets, then invite students to come together as a class and share some of the things they noted. List on the chalkboard some of the responses students wrote under "ways we are alike" and "ways we are different." Ask students to reflect on their brief exchange. What helped them to gain a better understanding and sense of respect for their partner?

ACTIVITY: PATCHWORK QUILT (GRADES K-3)
1. Ask students if they have ever seen a patchwork quilt. Discuss how many different smaller pieces add to the uniqueness of the larger quilt.
2. Explain that they will create a paper quilt from squares which represent the individuality of each student. These squares, when pieced together, will reflect the uniqueness of the class as a whole.
3. Give each student a quilt square, a 6" x 6" piece of colored construction paper. Include squares cut from wallpaper sample books or stiffened fabric for added variety.
4. Instruct them to write their name on their square and decorate it to illustrate qualities, talents and experiences they respect in themselves. Drawings, pictures clipped from magazines, words and photographs can be incorporated. Art supplies, including tissue paper, foils (gold and silver), glitter, sequins, markers and fabric, add dimension and variety.
5. Glue these pieces together on poster board or a long stretch of white craft paper. Hang on the door or on a wall within or just outside the classroom.

GRADES
K - 5

FORMAT
Classroom

TIME
1 hour

DISCIPLINES
Language arts
Social studies
Art

MATERIALS INCLUDED
Partners
A Great Group

MATERIALS NEEDED
Art supplies
Quilt pieces

One of the quilts at Meramec Elementary School is mounted on white craft paper and covers the entire door. Yellow squares designed by individual students reveal favorite pets, soccer balls, baseballs, hockey sticks, books, paint brushes and ballet shoes. These squares are interspersed with green squares that feature a teddy bear, heart, or schoolhouse.

CLOSURE: THE GREATEST GROUP (GRADES 2-5)
1. Divide students into five groups.
2. Give each group a copy of the script on page 51. Members practice saying their parts together. They think of an accomplishment of the group and select a spokesperson to share it during the reading.
3. After roughly 5 minutes, bring the groups together to present the script. Close by sharing things you think the group has accomplished.

SCHOOL

Publish a *Respect Gazette* and distribute it throughout the school and to parents of students. The *Gazette* contains stories and interviews written by student reporters. Photographs, cartoons and charts may accompany the articles. Reporters can watch for examples of respect—student to student, student to staff, staff to student—and write about these incidents. They can develop survey questions about respect and chart the results. Other students participate cooperatively by editing the copy, formatting the publication and coordinating distribution.

HOME

Members of the family write one way they will show respect to each of the other family members and one way they would like others to show them respect. They then share their lists aloud. As they describe situations in which they will show respect, the person to whom they are talking responds by saying "'thank you." As they tell the family the way they would like to be respected, they say "please."

SAMPLE LIST: PLEASE AND THANK YOU
I will help mom clear the table after meals without being asked. (Mom: "Thank You.")

I will ask dad if he needs to use the telephone or is expecting any important calls before I make my calls. (Dad: "Thank You.")

I will not interrupt my sister while she is talking, no matter how long she takes to tell a story. (Sister: "Thank You.")

I would like people to stay out of my desk and dresser drawers unless they ask me first, *please.*

COMMUNITY

Communities are naturally diverse, including people of varying age groups, ethnicities, abilities, lengths of residency and interests (pet lovers, gardeners, walkers). Have students explore and report on indicators of respect for different groups and individuals. Are streets and sidewalks wheelchair accessible? Are there places that welcome pets? Do pet owners respect others by using leashes? What special activities or accommodations are there for senior citizens? Are there welcoming committees for new people moving into the community? Student investigation may result in suggestions that can be sent to community newspapers, city hall and other appropriate places. Students may want to act on one of their suggestions to show their respect for others in the community.

SOUCE OF INSPIRATION

Cathy Ely, Meramec Elementary School, School District of Clayton

PARTNERS

NAME _____   **NAME** _____

WAYS WE ARE ALIKE	WAYS WE ARE DIFFERENT

SOME QUESTIONS YOU CAN ASK EACH OTHER:

1. What is your favorite food?
2. What are two things you like to do?
3. What is your favorite color?
4. Do you have any brothers or sisters?
5. What is your favorite subject or activity in school?
6. What is something you learned to do during the last year?

A Great Group

All: Now listen to the scoop on a really great group! We'd like to tell what we've done well!

Group One speaker steps forward and shares an accomplishment

Group 1: So give a cheer for the whole group here.

All: Hip, hip hooray!

Group Two speaker steps forward and shares an accomplishment

Group 2: Now take a pause, for a little applause!

Everyone claps

Group Three speaker steps forward and shares an accomplishment

Group 3: Let's say it loud, we're feeling proud.

All: We're feeling proud!

Group Four speaker steps forward and shares an accomplishment

Group 4: For all this drive, please give me five!

Everyone gives each other a high five.

Group Five speaker steps forward and shares an accomplishment

Group 5: For this special hand, let's all shake hands!

Everyone shakes hands with one another.

R ME TODAY, ME TOMOROW
RESPONSIBILITY

This lesson builds a bridge to the future as it explores how people make career decisions and assume the responsibilities that go with their jobs.

OBJECTIVES

1. Promote the character traits of **decision-making** and **responsibility.**

2. Increase awareness of available careers and professions. Recognize how one's interests and abilities become part of the career-planning process.

DESCRIPTION

Invite a discussion of careers by identifying positions within a school community: principal, administrator, teacher, cook, clerk, receptionist, bus driver, custodian, nurse, counselor, coach. Talk about the education, skills, responsibilities and tasks required of each job. Make a chart on the chalkboard or large sheet of paper with four columns as shown:

GRADES
K - 2

FORMAT
Classroom

DISCIPLINES
Language arts
Reading
Social studies

TIME
1 hour

MATERIALS INCLUDED
Me Today,
Me Tomorrow
Parts I, II, III

JOB	RESPONSIBILITIES	PROVIDES GOODS	PROVIDES A SERVICE
Veterinarian	Takes care of pets		✓

Read the riddles on the next page. As students guess the occupation, write it on the chart. Discuss the job's responsibilities and indicate these tasks in the second column. Check either the "Provides Goods" or "Provides a Service" column, whichever is appropriate.

Rhyming Riddles

Read these riddles, substituting **this person** for the job shown in bold print.

A **zookeeper** cares for his animals with food and tender care.
The animals feel safe and sound to know he's always there.

By sanding and painting and nailing, a **builder** can make quite a lot.
A home or a barn or an office. We're glad for the talent he's got.

A **bus driver** has a very big job, transporting so many to school. We can help make her job so much simpler by remembering to obey every rule.

The **sanitation workers** are helpful, we know. They pick up our refuse and trash. They drive trucks all over our neighborhood and clean up the mess in a flash.

When our most favorite pet's feeling ill, the **veterinarian's** the one that we call. For puppies, cats, birds and bunnies, she does her best for them all.

The **hairdresser's** someone who gives us a haircut, a trim or shampoo.
For ladies or men or for children, they help us look fresh and feel new.

The **grocer's** the person we go to for food and small things for our home.
This person's so nice, and we thank him for each little kindness he's shown.

The **bank teller** is a good friend. She works at the bank every day. When we're spending or saving our money, she's there to help show us the way.

A **pharmacist** fills our prescriptions and helps us when we need advice about medicine that we might be taking. She's real busy, but nice.

Whether you go to a church or a temple, a synagogue or a hall,
your **clergy** is right there to help you and to help each of us, one and all.

When you go to our favorite library in search of a real special book,
the **librarian's** the one who shows you just where to look.

A **truck driver** brings us so many things from places far and near. He brings his goods to neighborhood stores. He's important to us, and that's clear.

The **farmer** gives us vegetables and milk and grain and meat. And eggs and butter and whipping cream and most of the things that we eat!

The head of our own community is the person who's called the **mayor.**
We count on this person that we voted in to be honest, upstanding and fair.

The **baker's** a community helper we'd hate to be without. It's his cakes and pies and cookies that we're always dreaming about.

A **reporter** gets a story, a scoop, a line or the news.
For radio, TV or newspaper, whichever you like, you choose.

A **nurse's** job is aiding the doctor in taking good care of the sick.
A good nurse is very important, you see, to help us be better real quick.

When we are ill or need a checkup, our **doctor's** the one that we see.
When she can make us feel better, we're as thankful as we can be!

When we walk to school in our community, it could be dangerous and quite hard. But there's someone who makes it easy and safe and this is our **crossing guard.**

Someone who helps in a special way is the person who cleans our street.
The **street cleaner** is the one to thank for keeping our avenues neat.

Ambulance drivers and paramedics have important jobs, we know.
One drives us safely to the hospital, one cares for us as we go.

A **firefighter's** job, they say, takes courage, strength and speed.
They put out fires and protect us in our greatest times of need.

A **police officer** is someone on whom we can depend
to keep our community safe and sound, we know he is our friend.

The **dentist** helps us keep our teeth so strong and pearly white.
When he says to brush and watch our sweets, we know that he is right.

The **mail carriers** are special helpers who bring us all our mail.
They deliver almost every day; they do it without fail.

If you had a tough legal problem, or a simple one would even do,
A **lawyer's** the community helper who will give assistance to you.

Teachers are very special helpers, they teach us all how to do
each of these special occupations. Soon you'll choose one, too.

Activity: Talk about how people match themselves to their careers. Their interests, strengths, abilities, talents and personalities influence the choice. Introduce the two activity sheets: Me Today, Me Tomorrow Parts I and II (pages 57 and 58). Ask students to complete the forms individually. Talk about the kinds of jobs that correlate with different interests. For instance, somone who likes being outside might consider the outdoor aspects of these positions: builder, mail carrier, firefighter and crossing guard. Someone who likes to be with people might consider these jobs: hairdresser, bank teller, reporter and teacher.

HOME

Parents talk with their child about their work experience as they complete the "Me Today, Me Tomorrow Part III" take-home questionnaire on page 59. A trip to the office or work site complements these conversations with concrete images.

COMMUNITY

Elementary students are not too young for career days. Students can make a list of the jobs, professions and careers they would most like to explore. Faculty members and parents plan the event, involving students whenever possible. For instance, students can draft letters inviting guest presenters as part of a language arts assignment, create posters and flyers in art, use math skills to estimate the average number of participants for each session. Primary students learning about community helpers in social studies can meet firefighters, police officers and paramedics in person and perhaps get a close-up look at their vehicles.

SOURCE OF INSPIRATION

Sharon Snell, Meramec Elementary, School District of Clayton

ME TODAY, ME TOMORROW

PART I

Make a list of the jobs you do at home. Start the list with your favorite job. End the list with a job you do not like to do.

1. _____

2. _____

3. _____

Make a list of the things you do in school. Make the first thing the one you like the most.

1. _____

2. _____

3. _____

Now pretend you are at home and can do what you like to do. Make a list of the hobbies you like to do.

1. _____

2. _____

3. _____

ME TODAY, ME TOMORROW

PART II

Using the lists you prepared in Part 1, color in this chart. If your favorite job is indoors, color in the square under "Indoors." If it is outdoors, color in the square under "Outdoors." Do this for your school work and hobbies, too. Color in either the square "With People" or "Alone" for each activity.

	Indoors	Outdoors	With People	Alone
Home Job				
Schoolwork				
Hobby				

Draw a picture or write a paragraph describing one job that you would enjoy doing that includes most of the choices that you made.

ME TODAY, ME TOMORROW

PART III

Note to Parents: Please take a moment to answer these questions with your child. Talk about your work experience in concrete terms, describing what you do and how it helps the organization reach its goals. Reflect on the education, skills and character traits that help you do your job. For instance, structural engineers need calculus. They prepare for calculus by learning math in elementary school, then algebra, geometry and trigonometry in high school. It takes perseverance, which is the opposite of quitting, to prepare for calculus. After discussing the questions, have your child record short answers on the blanks below.

What is your job or title?

_____

Does your job help to:

☐ produce goods

☐ provide services

What are three of your responsibilities?

_____

_____

_____

What character trait helps you in managing your responsibilities? (Perseverance, honesty, initiative, courage, reliability, respect, caring, commitment, etc.)

_____

LESSONS IN HONESTY

This unit explores the trait of honesty through three delightful books that show how to look at a situation from more than one point of view.

OBJECTIVES

1. Promote the character traits of **honesty** and **respect**.

2. Identify the parts of a story that define and describe its main character.

3. Look at a situation from more than one point of view.

DESCRIPTION

Honesty is examined in three stories. The first two involve familiar tales told from the hero's perspective and from the other side.

LESSON 1: ROBIN HOOD AND JACK

The books *Robin Hood & The Sheriff Speaks* and *Jack and the Beanstalk & Giants Have Feelings Too* offer the traditional tale up front. When the books are flipped and read from back to front, the stories are retold from another point of view. The sheriff, for instance, recognizes Robin Hood's inherent dishonesty and the giant considers Jack a thief.

Procedure: Discuss either or both of the stories. Talk about different points of view. Identify a common situation in school that looks very different from the perspective of the student and the perspective of the teacher. Ask students to brainstorm other scenarios at home or school that can be seen from two different perspectives. Older students might focus on how people rationalize their decisions so they seem acceptable, even when dishonesty is involved. Have students write about a time when they or someone they know was honest or dishonest and what effect it had.

Activity: Create an honesty T-Chart. Have students identify what honesty looks like and what it sounds like. Use the following questions:
1. What does honesty look like at home? What does it sound like?
2. What does honesty look like in class? What does it sound like?
3. What does honesty look like when you are with friends? What does it sound like?
4. What does honesty look like in the community? What does it sound like?

GRADES
1 - 5

FORMAT
Classroom

DISCIPLINES
Language arts
Reading

TIME
60 minutes

MATERIALS INCLUDED
Character analysis
Character sketch
Character web

MATERIALS NEEDED
Books mentioned
in unit

HONESTY T-CHART

LOOKS LIKE	SOUNDS LIKE
not taking things that don't belong to you	telling the truth

Alternative Activity for Fourth-Graders: The teacher fills in the name of the characters and the traits on the Character Analysis chart shown on page 64. Students work from the chart to write compound sentences about the characters. For example, Robin Hood was courageous, but he was also dishonest.

Alternative Activity for Fifth-Graders: Distribute copies of the Character Analysis chart shown on page 64. Students are to list two characters from each story under "Name of Character." For instance, they might choose Robin Hood, the Sheriff of Nottingham, Jack and the Giant. They then list character traits related to the tales—perhaps honesty, courage, justice—on the slanted lines. They rate the characters with a plus sign if they expressed the trait by the end of the story or a minus sign if they did not express the trait. Using their chart, students write one paragraph comparing the characters based on the traits.

LESSON 2: JAMAICA'S FIND
Jamaica's Find by J. Havill offers a look at honesty and decision-making. A little girl finds a stuffed animal and then must decide whether to be honest and turn it in or keep it. When she realizes the effect that keeping it will have on the child who lost it, she makes her decision.

Procedure: Have students discuss times when they found something and wanted to keep it. Have them also discuss times when they have lost something. Focus on how they feel about losing something valuable in an informal brainstorming session. Write their comments on the chalkboard in one column. Ask them to describe how they feel when they have something returned to them. Note these feelings in a second column.

Activity: Ask students to complete a Character Sketch (see page 65) on Jamaica.

Activity: Have students draw pictures that represent honesty, titling them "Honesty is. . ."

HOME

Enclose samples of the students' responses to the question, "What does honesty look like at home?" in a note to parents. With this, parents can start a conversation about honesty with their children, expanding on the "way it looks" with episodes from their shared experiences. Parents can watch for an incident that lends itself to retelling from different perspectives. Say the cat escaped during an impromtu game of indoor-outdoor tag between two siblings. The parent asks each child to tell the story separately, out of earshot of the other. The parent gathers them together and relays the stories back to them, asking them to note the similarities and differences between the two accounts.

COMMUNITY

Invite a professional mediator, judge or reporter to speak to students about the ability to listen to more than one side of a story. Ask them to share their experiences in concrete terms and images that young students can understand.

SOURCE OF INSPIRATION

Carol Kemper and a team of educators from the Hazelwood School District

RESOURCE INFORMATION

Granowsky, A. *Robin Hood & The Sheriff Speaks.* Austin, TX: Steck Vaughn Publishing, 1993.

Granowsky, A. *Jack and the Beanstalk & Giants Have Feelings Too.* Austin, TX: Steck Vaughn Publishing, 1996.

To order these books, call (800) 531-5015 and ask for the Curriculum K-12 catalog from Steck Vaughn Publishing.

Havil, J. *Jamaica's Find.* Houghton Mifflin, 1990.

MORE BOOKS ON THE SUBJECT OF HONESTY

Andersen, Hans Christian. *The Emperor's New Clothes*

Steig, William. *The Real Thief.*

Ross, Tony. *The Boy Who Cried Wolf.*

Cohen, Miriam. *Liar, Liar, Pants on Fire.*

Carlson, Nancy. *Arnie and the Stolen Markers*

Hillert, Margaret. *Pinocchio*

INTERESTED IN LESSONS LIKE THIS FOR OTHER TRAITS?

This unit is one of more than a dozen imaginative encounters with character traits in "Oh, the Places We'll Go, Travelling through the Year with PREP Themes." (See reprints on pages 64-66.) The booklet was developed by educators from the Hazelwood School District elementary schools. For more information, please write: Dr. Tom Bick, Director of Student Services, Hazelwood School District, 15955 New Halls Ferry Road, St. Louis, Missouri 63031.

CHARACTER ANALYSIS

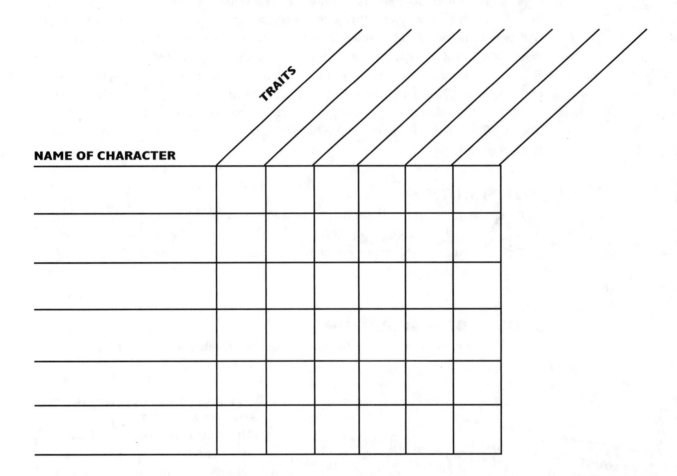

NAME OF CHARACTER

This graphic organizer is an effective way to have students comprehend what they have read by analyzing and comparing the characters of one story or several related stories. They first identify specific characteristics, then rate each character based on those characteristics, assigning either a + or - (or Y=yes or N=no) for each character as an indication of whether he or she exhibits that particular characteristic.

Objectives:
1. Identify the characters to be compared.
2. Identify characteristics to be analyzed.
3. Organize the characteristics.
4. Rate each character based on each characteristic.
5. Discuss and summarize each character in light of his or her characteristics.
6. Write a paragraph about each character describing his or her characteristics or write one paragraph comparing the characters based on the characteristics.

Name_____

CHARACTER SKETCH

Title_____

_____

Author_____

_____

Words that describe the character

Character

Note information from the story that explains the words you used to describe the character.

1._____

2._____

3._____

4._____

5._____

CHARACTER WEB

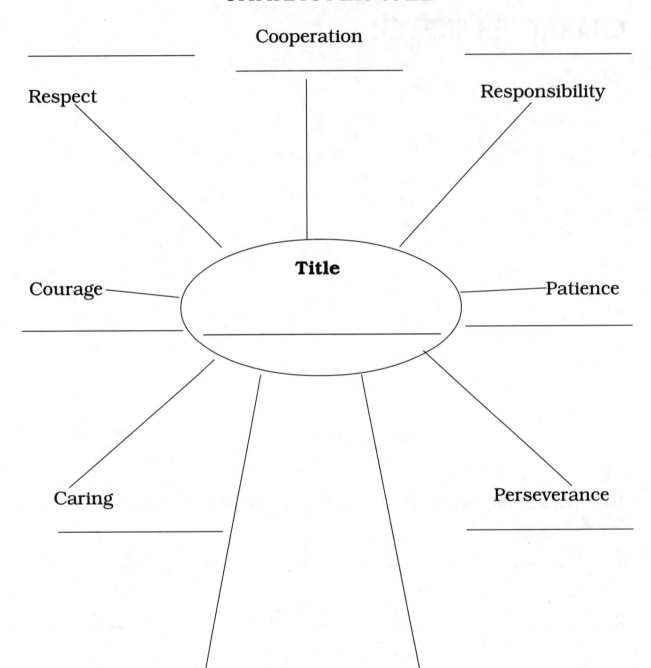

Cooperation

Respect

Responsibility

Title

Courage

Patience

Caring

Perseverance

Self-Control

Honesty

Write the title in the center. Think about the characters. Write the name of a character on the line near the trait that he or she exhibits. If a character expresses more than one trait, the name may be used more than once.

BE A GOAL-SETTER

A skit introduces the concept of goal-setting, while guided practice sessions help students put it into use.

OBJECTIVES

1. Promote the character traits of **goal-setting, perseverance, cooperation, honesty, self-control** and **self-discipline.**

2. Learn and practice a process of **goal-setting**.

3. Develop the ability to visualize and communicate that vision to others through writing and drawing.

DESCRIPTION

Enlist eight students to enact "Julie's Story," the skit starting on page 70. Or read the skit together in the class before the actual lesson.

LESSON PLAN FOR UNIT I: GRADES 2, 3

Part A: As a class, review the steps which Julie took as a goal-setter. Clearly identify the steps on the chalkboard and in handouts. Introduce real-life examples of goal-setters, drawing from historical figures, athletes, actors, local leaders and students. Invite people—perhaps an elected official, a sixth-grade student, a firefighter or policeman, a parent who has coordinated a field trip or a schoolwide fund-raiser—to speak about a particular goal and the steps involved in reaching it.

Ask students to choose a goal they want to illustrate from the ideas that have been discussed and to represent it in a drawing, including the start, intermediate steps and a finish. These pictures can be mounted or laminated and used for reference in future goal-setting experiences.

Part B: Students now decide upon and record their goals, such as getting an A on the next spelling test, setting the table correctly, learning a new word, hitting a baseball 50 feet or sewing on a button. Cooperative groups are helpful at this stage. Upper-grade students or parent volunteers act as guides to small groups of students, helping them to keep their goal specific

GRADES
Unit I: 2, 3
Unit II: 4, 5

FORMAT
Classroom

DISCIPLINES
Language arts
Social studies

TIME
2 hours; easily divided into 30-minute segments

MATERIALS INCLUDED
Julie's Story
Practice the Process of Goal-Setting

and to think through the process: What would you need to do next? What do you need to know? Where would you go to learn it? These guides also act as recorders, writing the students' responses.

SET your goal
UNDERSTAND the obstacles
CLEAR your mind of doubt
CREATE a positive mental picture
EMBRACE the challenge
STAY on track
SHOW the world you can do it!

Post goals in a place regularly visible to the student, for example, taped to a desk top, hung on a bulletin board in the classroom or on the refrigerator at home. Students check off each step they've completed. These check marks provide a foundation for reflective conversations with a teacher or volunteer. Students experience the value of honesty as they assess their gains. Motivation and self-esteem are bolstered by progress recognized with stickers or on a chart. If progress has not met the intended mark, students exercise self-discipline by reviewing the steps and perseverance by trying again.

LESSON PLAN FOR UNIT II, GRADES 4, 5

Part A: After watching the skit, "Julie's Story," review as a class the steps Julie took by answering these questions:

    Start: What was Julie aiming for?

    Plan: What steps did she need to take to succeed? Who helped her?

    Measure: Where was her first "check in" point?

    Write: State her goal in writing.

    Finish: Did she have a target finishing date? How did she celebrate?

Ask students to apply these questions as they analyze the short scenarios on the handout (page 73). Have them generate possibilities for any missing components. This work can be done in cooperative learning groups.

Part B: Ask students to work in cooperative groups to generate one story that includes some or all of the components necessary for reaching a goal. The groups present their stories to the whole class for more analysis.

Part C: Students are now asked to set and write individual goals in story form. Upon completion of their stories, they work in pairs or small groups to analyze the stories to be sure they have included all the steps and components.

Students post their goals in a prominent place, checking off incremental steps as they achieve them. Honesty is important in assessing progress. Self-discipline and perseverance serve to keep students on track. Recognition of goal achievement by fellow classmates provides a sense of accomplishment.

SCHOOL & DISTRICT

Administrators from the district's central office or school board members can visit the class and talk about the goals of the district, comparing the process of goal-setting to the one the students have learned. A focus on a concrete objective, such as purchasing more student computers, is helpful. The speaker can track the development and progress of this goal.

HOME

The teacher might invite family members to a meeting focused on:
- an explanation of the lesson's goal and the goal-setting process
- a tour of the children's goal-setting posters or papers
- an exercise in which parents plot on paper a goal they set, the steps they took to achieve it and the skills and knowledge they learned
- instructions for them to share the exercise with their child, emphasizing such character traits as commitment, cooperation, initiative, patience, perseverance, responsibility and self-discipline.

These same elements could be packaged in a packet as a take-home assignment during the unit.

COMMUNITY

Representatives from civic or service organizations are as effective as district personnel in helping students understand and relate to the larger communities in which they live. They focus on a concrete objective, such as developing a food pantry or building a Habitat for Humanity home, and outline the steps involved in reaching the goal.

SOURCE OF INSPIRATION

Jan Caimi, Spoede Elementary School, Ladue School District

Julie's Story

NARRATOR: Let's peek in on Julie as she uses goal-setting to help her. Julie is in first grade and has just come in from a day at school.

JULIE: Mom, today we started jump rope in P.E. I'm not good at it so I'm going into the basement to practice and I'm not coming up until I can jump 50 in a row without missing.

MOM: That's a pretty big job for a little girl. How do you know that 50 is the number you should shoot for?

JULIE: There's another girl in my class that can already jump 50; she's been practicing with her sister since last year. So, if she can do it, I probably can too if I practice enough. Bye.

NAR: 2 hours later

MOM: *(yelling down the basement stairs)* Julie, time for dinner.

JULIE: I can't come now, Mom. I can't jump 50 yet.

MOM: That's all right. You can take a break. You have to eat dinner.

JULIE: *(coming up the stairs)* Well, I can't do 50 yet but I CAN finally jump rope a few times without missing. I'll go back down after dinner.

(MOM and JULIE walk behind the curtain and re-emerge after NARRATOR talks)

NAR: After dinner

JULIE: *(heading downstairs)* OK, Mom. It's back downstairs for me. I'm going to get to 50 this time.

NAR: One hour later

MOM: *(yelling down stairs)* Julie, come on up, it's time for your bath.

JULIE: I can't now, Mom. I haven't reached 50 yet.

MOM: That's OK. You can work on it again tomorrow. *(Julie comes up the stairs.)* You have to get some sleep so that you can do some other things that are important for school, too. And besides, you need to charge up your energy for some more practice. How are you doing so far?

JULIE: Well, I can't do 50 yet, but I can do about 20 in a row without missing. I'm a lot better than when I started. Goodnight, Mom.

NAR: Next day after school

JULIE: I'm home. Back to the basement for some more practice. I was really proud of myself today. In gym class, I jumped about 25 times without missing and yesterday I couldn't even jump at all.

MOM: That's great, Julie! Even though you haven't reached your goal yet, you're seeing an improvement. Keep up the good work!

NAR: Just before dinner

JULIE: *(yells up the stairs)* Mom, come on down and watch this.

MOM: *(coming downstairs)* Are you ready for an audience?

JULIE: I can do it! I can jump 50 times now. Let's see if I can do it with somebody watching. 47...48...49...50...51...52.

MOM: OK! OK! You were really determined on this goal. Come on upstairs and have some dinner now. We'll celebrate your success with your favorite dessert. All that hard work has really paid off.

JULIE: And tomorrow I'm going down to the basement and practice until I can jump 50 BACKWARDS!

MOM: You are really something, Julie!

NAR: Let's give Julie a hand for setting goals for herself and working toward them.

STUDENT 1: Did you notice what Julie did first?

JULIE: I'm going to jump 50 times in a row without missing. *(She set the goal)*

STUDENT 2: She tried to make her goal reasonable by seeing what others could do.

JULIE: Another girl in class can do it already.

STUDENT 3: Julie knew that the other girl had been practicing for a while, but she was pretty good at things like this, so she set her standards fairly high. Then she decided how she would meet her goal.

JULIE: I'm going to the basement to practice over and over and I'm not quitting until I can get to 50.

STUDENT 4: She knew she had hard work ahead of her but she needed a little help in understanding there would be obstacles in her way. Mom helped her understand that she would need to take breaks for eating and sleeping.

STUDENT 5: It's usually a good idea to tell someone else that you are setting a goal. The other person can be encouraging or give you helpful feedback if you get off the track. Julie didn't seem to need others to keep her going, but it was nice to have her mom talking to her about her goal.

STUDENT 6:   Don't forget to check in with yourself along the way to see how you are doing. Give yourself some credit for improving and getting closer to your goal.

JULIE: I was really proud of myself today. In gym class, I jumped about 25 times without missing and yesterday I couldn't even jump at all.

STUDENT 7:   Don't forget to celebrate when you reach your goal. Share your success with someone else or, at the very least, give yourself a pat on the back.

STUDENT 8:   Then get ready with a new goal!

ALL 8 STUDENT
PLAYERS: *(Each student holds a poster showing part of the phrase or the exclamation point. The brackets indicate how the phrases can be divided among eight students.)*

{SET} {YOUR GOAL}
{UNDERSTAND} {THE OBSTACLES}
{CLEAR} {YOUR MIND} {OF DOUBT} {!}

Practice the Process of Goal-Setting

The following questions guide the process of goal-setting. Try them out on the scenarios below, substituting the name of the main character for "I" in each question.

Start: What am I aiming for?

Plan: What steps will I need to succeed? When will I start?

Measure: Where am I now? How far do I want to go?

Write: State my goal in writing.

Finish: What is my target finishing date? How will I celebrate?

Scenario 1

Lisa wants to understand fractions better. She wrote a goal for herself that said, "I will understand how different size pieces relate to each other. I will practice on this until I can pass the quiz that I failed at the end of the year. I will use measuring cups and spoons to work on some of the basics. I will use the fraction games that I borrowed from school. I will have my mom and sister make up problems with the rods that I have."

Scenario 2

John wants to pass the deep-water test. He said, "I will go to the pool every day. I hope I can pass it by next Friday."

Scenario 3

Jeanine just turned 16. She wants to get her driver's license. She said, "I want to be able to pass this test by the time three months is up. I will ask my parents to take me driving at least 3 evenings each week for about 30 minutes in the neighborhood at first. Then I will start driving when each of them has to run errands, like to the grocery store or cleaners, so that I can get out on to some more busy streets. Then maybe I can practice on the highway on vacation. Last, I'll practice parallel parking. Then I'll take my parents on a pretend driving test and they can tell me what I need to work on. By then, I should be ready."

Scenario 4

Donna wants to go to camp for 6 weeks this summer. It will cost $400 and her parents said that she would need to earn half of the money herself. She has 12 weeks before she needs the payment. She said, "I can baby-sit for my sister after school for $10 each week until then. That will be $120. I still need $80 so I will try to check with the neighbors about baby-sitting on the weekend. If I could just work 8 of the weekends for 3 hours each, I could make more than enough money at $4 an hour. I will make flyers and call them tomorrow to see what I can line up. If I can't get enough jobs like that, I will see if I can help my brother with his lawn service for a little extra money."

PUPPET PROBLEM-SOLVERS

A cast of puppets become known schoolwide for their ability to get into and out of character-based dilemmas. Students write scripts and present puppet shows to classes of younger students and at assemblies.

OBJECTIVES

1. Promote the character traits of **caring, commitment, cooperation, goal-setting, honesty, perseverance, respect, responsibility, self-discipline** and **service.**

2. Involve students in real-life situations in which character traits and choices come into play.

3. Strengthen students' creativity, writing and oral skills.

4. Practice using a problem-solving model.

DESCRIPTION

Members of a class, gifted program or after-school club devote time weekly to the creation of a puppet theater. They
*   design (or purchase) a small cast of puppets
*   design costumes and props
*   script vignettes that amplify character traits
*   rehearse and perform shows
*   improvise or role-play situations and dilemmas

Students work with a particular trait each month, such as honesty, patience, perseverance, responsibility or service. They brainstorm ideas to develop skits cooperatively and work together on props, staging and costumes. They present puppet shows to younger classes and at assemblies. They also videotape their productions. Teachers can request the videos and incorporate them into their lessons. They can also invite the puppet troupe to do some improvisational role-playing about a particular situation that the class is facing, such as bullying, teasing or cheating.

GRADES
4, 5

FORMAT
Classroom or
after-school activity

DISCIPLINES
Language arts
Social studies

TIME
Four 30- to 40-
minute sessions

**MATERIALS
NEEDED**
Costumes
Puppets

SCHOOL & DISTRICT

The puppeteers can visit classes in other schools, perform a vignette at a School Board meeting and talk about the character traits they develop in their scripts. The district's newsletter can feature the work of the puppeteers.

HOME

Families can check out the videos, watch them together, discuss the content and relate the issues to happenings in their lives.

COMMUNITY

The puppeteers can perform as a way of serving audiences in nursing homes, retirement centers, at fund raisers or other community events. Professional puppeteers, actors, playwrights and script writers can speak to the group or class, providing inspiration, tips and techniques.

SOURCE OF INSPIRATION

A staff committee and group of fifth-grade students at Tillman Elementary School, Kirkwood School District

EXERCISING CHARACTER
AS WE EXERCISE

This physical education unit teaches students a spirit of game-playing that encourages fun and care for others rather than competitiveness.

OBJECTIVES

1. Promote the character traits of **cooperation, respect, self-control** and **self-discipline.**

2. Promote team playing.

3. Provide practice in following directions.

DESCRIPTION
COOPERATIVE MUSICAL HOOPS
Teach the class a simple line dance, such as The Electric Slide or Cotton-Eyed Joe. These dances are, by nature, inclusive and cooperative. Once students have learned the dance steps, they dance around the outside of an oblong boundary created by hula hoops laid out on the floor. When the music stops, everyone tries to get both feet inside the nearest hoop. No one is eliminated from the game, but one hoop is removed each time the music pauses. Four or five children fit easily inside one hoop with cooperation. As the number of hoops decreases, the need for individual self-control increases. Students are instructed to achieve their place inside the hoop respectfully, with no pushing, shoving or bullying.

SHUFFLING THE DECK
This activity divides the class into small groups or partners. The teacher gives a playing card to every student and instructs the students to split into two groups by saying, "All those with red cards go on that side of the line; all those with black cards remain on this side." Other combinations include odd or even numbers, clubs and hearts versus spades and diamonds. Call out combinations such as the four suits; even black, odd black; even red, odd red. Subdivide these groups by calling for such combinations as two with the same color, four with the same number, three of the same suit. The calls come rapidly enough that students must choose quickly and work cooperatively with everyone in the class.

GRADES
3 - 5

FORMAT
Classroom

DISCIPLINES
Physical education

TIME
30 minutes each

MATERIALS NEEDED
Hula hoops
Music
Tape or CD player

REFLECTIVE DISCUSSION AND JOURNAL-WRITING

With the class in small groups, the teacher raises these questions: What did you feel as the goal became harder to achieve? Did you feel respected by others? Could you show respect for others? How? If you did not get in the group or with the partner of your choice, how did you respond? Who spoke first? Did your partner put you at ease? How? Did you help your partner to feel at ease? How close can someone get before it is too close? Identify your comfort zone with this exercise: Partner A walks slowly toward Partner B. B repeats the word "comfortable" or "fine" continuously until A moves into the B's discomfort zone. B says "uncomfortable" or "not fine" twice. A stops. Repeat the exercise, reversing the partners' roles. Note if the "discomfort zone" appears at the same or different distances. As a class, brainstorm polite but firm ways to request another's cooperation in protecting one's "comfort zone" from intrusion.

CLASSROOM CONNECTIONS

Shuffling the Deck is a clever way to break into cooperative learning groups and works with any subject.

Integrate physical education, language arts and social studies by asking students to recall what it felt like to be crowded into the hula hoop on the last turn. Express this as a simile. Talk about the effects of crowded environments. Contrast the average number of people per square mile in the U.S., Japan, Russia. Compare New York City with Casper, Wyoming.

Ask the students to name or create another game that requires a character trait. If they create a new game, ask them to write directions and rules for the game. Use diagrams or drawings to help with the explanation.

HOME

Students can take a leadership role, teaching siblings and parents the line dance(s) they've learned. Initiative, patience (as they instruct novices in a new skill), respect and cooperation are involved and worth reflecting as the family talks about the experience.

COMMUNITY

Invite a dance instructor to teach several line dances and speak of their social, physical and community-building value.

SOURCE OF INSPIRATION

Cathy Cunningham and Vicky Stricklin, Wedgwood Elementary School, Ferguson-Florissant School District

Lessons for Success

The Jefferson Center for Character Education's curriculum, *Lessons for Success*, is the foundation for this unit. Banners, posters and weekly character-focused lessons develop a common language and understanding of the traits among the student body. Teachers expand prepared lessons and develop literature sets that complement specific traits.

OBJECTIVES

1. Promote the character traits of **caring, commitment, cooperation, goal-setting, honesty, perseverance, respect, responsibility, self-discipline** and **service.**

2. Provide students with the opportunity to recognize the consequences of their actions, solve problems and resolve conflicts, develop and improve self-confidence, to set and achieve realistic goals, to be punctual and reliable and to treat others with respect.

DESCRIPTION

Monthly themes organize the yearlong exploration of certain traits through posters, banners, weekly character sessions, literature sets, integrated lessons, activities and assemblies.

Setting the stage: Posters, banners, bulletin boards, student artwork and P.A. announcements broadcast a monthly theme, such as "Be Friendly." The staff observes students to catch them in the act of expressing the trait. The entire building is committed to learning about the traits and translating them into action.

Weekly sessions: Designed by the Jefferson Center to introduce common terms and language about the trait, these half-hour sessions are geared to each grade level. They evoke student participation, discussion, brainstorming, cooperative learning, role-playing, problem-solving, writing stories and scripts, performing and carrying out service projects.

GRADES
K - 5

FORMAT
Schoolwide

DISCIPLINES
Social studies
Language arts
Physical education

TIME
30 minutes a week
integrated in classes

MATERIALS NEEDED
Lessons for Success from the Jefferson Center for Character Education

JEFFERSON CENTER FOR CHARACTER EDUCATION
P.O. Box 4137
Mission Viejo, CA 92690
Phone: (949) 770-7602
Fax: (949) 450-1100

Literature sets

Traits and qualities are identified in books selected for literature sets. Coordinated with the monthly theme, these stories become a springboard for discussions, journal entries and writing assignments. They illustrate the many dimensions of character and how they play out in real-life situations. Refer to *Lit Sets in Character*, pages 125-127, for more ideas.

SAMPLE ACTIVITIES

Be Friendly: Students become observers of other students' actions. When they notice a classmate showing respect or care toward others, they note it and make a paper link, showing the name of the individual and some reference to the act. The link is then connected to others to create a Friendship Chain. These chains can be hung around the room or through the halls as they grow.

Being Present: While the class is engaged in a small-group activity that requires cooperation, one member of the group is purposely called away (asked to run an errand, called to the office). The remaining students do not know when or if the student will return and are faced with the dilemma of completing the task without the individual. When the task is finished, the missing student is signaled to return. The teacher leads a discussion asking members of the group to reflect upon their expectations, decisions, feelings and actions. They examine, as if in slow motion, the effect of one's absence and recognize the responsibility each member of the group has to one another.

HOME

Families can focus on the trait of the month at home: post it on the refrigerator, define it and amplify it with examples from their collective experience. ("Remember the patience Allison showed as she waited in line to ride on Dumbo at Disney World.") They can note one another's behavior, keep a tally and celebrate their successes.

COMMUNITY

Invite guest speakers (civic leader, sports figure, service organizer, news reporter, paramedic, firefighter, pilot). Ask them to address the trait of the month with vivid examples from their experiences. Students can also watch for examples of the character trait expressed within the community. They may find examples in local newspapers or on the news. They may see people in stores and at community events using the trait. Their reports can be brought back to class and discussed.

SOURCE OF INSPIRATION

Vivian Delia, Westridge Elementary, Rockwood School District

A MILLION PENNIES

A service goal unites the school in a penny-by-penny fund-raiser that visually demonstrates the concept of one million.

OBJECTIVES

1. Promote the character traits of **commitment, cooperation, goal-setting, honesty, perseverance, responsibility** and **service.**

2. Provide a tangible way of working with the mathematical concept of one million.

DESCRIPTION

The school community commits to collecting one million pennies. Each class brainstorms ways in which the funds can be spent in service to the community and reaches consensus on three ideas. These are combined with suggestions from all other classes and put to a vote. The winning idea is announced and posted.

COLLECTION

The pennies are collected in 5 gallon plastic jugs placed in secure, yet visible places throughout the building. Honesty and responsibility are required as the students work with the pennies. Because the project extends over a year or more, students must remain committed.

Monthly, the jug totals are tallied and reported to the student body. This involves the·coordinated efforts of the faculty as the responsibility rotates among all math classes. The tasks (see box on next page) lend themselves to integration into math curricula at all grade levels, cooperative learning assignments and multi-class teams. Groups of students from several grade levels can work together, united by a goal and a real-life deadline. They learn to set goals, rely on others, care about team members, experience respect for the contributions of each one, value responsible action, take initiative and persevere.

Activity: Students in fifth-grade math classes rotate responsibility for reporting collections each month. The report must be submitted to the newsletter

GRADES
K - 5

FORMAT
Schoolwide

TIME
Intermittent
throughout the year

DISCIPLINES
Art
Language arts
Math

**MATERIALS
NEEDED**
5-gallon jugs

editor by a specific due date and include calculations of the following:

- total amount received during the month,
  - total of the entire fund from its inception,
  - amount available in cash,
  - amount available in savings account, and
  - average collected per day.

MATHEMATICAL TASKS

counting
addition
subtraction
multiplication

weight/volume
percentages
estimating
mean and average

Students must also add the current income to the chart and graph and calculate the percentage of increase recorded in the last month.

The team meets to discuss the project, determine the steps to complete it, set intermediate deadlines, delegate tasks by age-appropriate assignments, understand how each person's task helps to reach the goal, and plan a buddy system or ways to exchange information and check in with each other. They meet at the end of the project to reflect on their experience: What worked? What didn't? Did they feel overwhelmed? Confused? Capable? Valued?

PROMOTION

Students promote the program. In language arts, they write power paragraphs, business letters, newspaper ads, news releases and public service announcements for radio. In art, they create posters for the school building and for the wider community. They plan special events, lotteries (25 pennies buys a ticket for "Lunch with Your Favorite Teacher" drawing) and competitions (class with highest contributions wins a pizza party).

HOME

Students contract with their parents to perform chores to earn pennies. Parents discuss long-term goals and the concept of one million. When did they set a goal that took years to achieve? What did they do to keep themselves motivated? How did they feel when they completed it? When have they come across one million (rain drops, grains of sand on the beach, blades of grass on the lawn).

COMMUNITY

The local media can publish or air the story or invite student-authored articles and reports. Local businesses and organizations can be encouraged to participate in the penny drive. Students can sponsor projects that involve the community, such as car washes and bake sales, to earn pennies for the project.

SOURCE OF INSPIRATION

Nancy Jamieson, High Ridge Elementary School, Northwest R-1 School District

WACKADOO ZOO

Students learn the value of diversity and recognize character traits in action as they produce and perform the musical "Wackadoo Zoo."

OBJECTIVES

1. Reinforce the character traits of **caring, cooperation, commitment, kindness, perseverance** and **respect.**

2. Combine language arts and music in an interdisciplinary project.

3. Introduce the medium of chorale singing to young students.

DESCRIPTION

"Wackadoo Zoo" introduces an unusual menagerie: pigs that crow cocka-doodle-doo, cows that meow, goats that bark and monkeys that bray like donkeys. As a frustrated professor attempts to correct each animal's faulty expression, he learns to accept and appreciate the animals as they are. The song "Different Means Special" emphasizes respect for others and an acceptance of differences. "A Smile Can Go a Long Way" focuses on kindness and caring. "Practice Makes Perfect" extolls perseverance.

These character traits are defined in simple, clear terms and illustrated with concrete examples long before the first audition. When fellow cast members gently prompt an actor who has forgotten his lines, they express both respect for the individual and cooperation. As the cast creates sets, memorize lines, rehearse and perform, they come to understand commitment.

CLASSROOM CONNECTIONS

Teachers strengthen the appreciation of differences with literature by selecting and discussing books and stories that increase understanding of ethnic, cultural and individual differences. For third- and fourth-grade students, refer to *Lit Sets in Character*, pages 125-127.

Explore authentic animal behavior, including habitats, predators, movements, mating and the vocabulary of sounds available to each species in

GRADES
1 - 4

FORMAT
Schoolwide

DISCIPLINES
Music

TIME
14 hours

MATERIALS NEEDED
Script and music for "Wackadoo Zoo"
Costumes
Tape player
Scenery & sets

life science. For an additional lesson on the subject, refer to *The Story of Jumping Mouse,* pages 11-13.

The calypso rhythms of "Practice Makes Perfect" invite an exploration of this West Indies musical tradition: its origins, improvisational lyrics and relationship to the country's culture and geography.

HOME

The process of goal-setting and the meaning of commitment become understood in concrete terms with parents' help. The goal-setting form on page 6 can be adapted for use with students involved in the production. Their role or task is filled in near the top. They take the worksheet home to parents who are encouraged to ask questions and talk about the task. Together, they brainstorm steps or intermediary objectives that will help the student reach the goal. These are listed on the form and returned to the the play's director.

COMMUNITY

A zoo tour offers the chance to compare animal facts with "Wackadoo Zoo" fiction. Students might tape record the sounds of various animals and ask their classmates to "Name that Creature."

"Wackadoo Zoo" converts to an entertaining road show for nursing homes, hospital children's wards, elementary classes throughout the school, district and wider community.

SOURCE OF INSPIRATION

Kelly Dismore, Valley Park Elementary, Valley Park School District

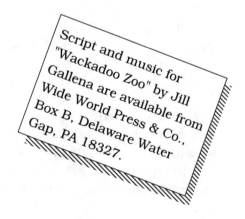

Script and music for "Wackadoo Zoo" by Jill Gallena are available from Wide World Press & Co., Box B, Delaware Water Gap, PA 18327.

MUSICAL DEFINITIONS

Songs create harmonies that continue long after class, especially when they define character traits.

OBJECTIVES

1. Promote the character traits of **cooperation, goal-setting, respect, responsibility** and **service.**

2. Correlate existing music materials with all character traits from cooperation to respect.

DESCRIPTION

A team of teachers identify songs in available music books according to character traits and grade level. The index can be used to focus lessons on a particular quality. For instance, a teacher with a third-grade class and an interest in cooperation might plan this lesson:

Song:	"Make New Friends"
Traits:	Cooperation, Respect
Discussion:	How do you make new friends? What would you do if someone your age moved into your neighborhood? How do you keep a friend? How do you lose a friend? Cooperation is part of getting along. Can you give an example of cooperating with a friend? How do you show respect for someone else? How does a friend show respect for you?
Activity:	This song, performed as a round, demonstrates cooperation. Explain this to students as the lesson proceeds.

The index also can be used to recognize the learning opportunities in songs as they are practiced and performed. The team that developed the index incorporated activities to use at any time, including these suggestions for the theme of cooperation.
- Have students who read music help other students learn the music.
- Have class cooperatively orchestrate sound illustrations for stories.
- Structure activities in which groups of students create rhythm patterns.

GRADES
K - 6

FORMAT
Music room
Classroom

DISCIPLINES
Music

TIME
One class session

MATERIALS INCLUDED
In Tune with Respect
In Tune with Cooperation

MATERIALS NEEDED
World of Music
Music
Piano or other accompaniment

HOME

Teachers alert parents to new songs students have mastered. Notes can suggest home exercises. For instance, the sample letter below describes a project that involves cooperation, goal-setting, personal responsibility and service.

COMMUNITY

A choir specializing in music with a character education theme can become an attraction of its own within a community. The performances can expand on the traits revealed in songs through dramatic readings, mime, a Will Rogers-style monologue, skits, riddles and straightforward definitions. Such a choir could appear at civic functions, music festivals, educational conferences, other schools and district-wide events.

SOURCE OF INSPIRATION

Music teachers from the Ferguson-Florissant School District

Dear Parent,

Your student learned the song "The More We Get Together" in music class. We talked about how we can bring these lyrics to life. Together we set a goal: We will collect food that provides balanced meals for families and donate it to a food pantry. The members of the class felt they could accomplish their individual contribution by working cooperatively with an adult partner. They identified the responsibilities they could handle alone and those that needed adult help.

What I can do

Tell what the goal is
Write down the menu
Make a list
Check off what we do
Find items in store
Load bags in the car
Carry them to class

Please help me with...

What makes a balanced meal?
What foods are nonperishable?
Making sure we have enough
Shopping
Comparing prices
Buying the food
Getting it to school

In Tune with Respect

ACTIVITIES WHICH PROMOTE RESPECT:
• Emphasize the behavior traits of a good audience.
• Teach songs that originate in various countries.
• Structure lessons that teach children to respect the preferences of classmates.

GRADE	SONG TITLE	SOURCE	
K	Hello Everybody	SILVRBUR	p. 106
	We Give Thanks	SILVRBUR	p. 166
1	John the Rabbit	SILVRBUR	p. 46
	I Don't Know Why You Like Me	SILVRBUR	p. 174
	You Like Me	SILVRBUR	p. 174
	Thanks For Food	SILVRBUR	p. 189
2	I Like You Like You Are	SILVRBUR	p. 189
	There Are Many Flags	SILVRBUR	p. 226
	San Severiro	SILVRBUR	p. 35
	Michael Row the Boat Ashore	SILVRBUR	p. 91
	If You Can't Say Something Nice	HOLT	p. 120
3	He's Got the Whole World	SILVRBUR	p. 51
	Make New Friends	SILVRBUR	p. 110
	He's a Clown	SILVRBUR	p. 172
	Thank You for Being You	SILVRBUR	p. 181
	A Place in the Choir	HOLT	p. 34
	Get Onboard	HOLT	p. 50
	Hymn for Nations	HOLT	p. 96
		HOLT	p. 172
4	Getting to Know You		
	I Like You	SILVRBUR	p. 4
	Thank You for Saying Thank You	SILVRBUR	p. 202
	Only Love Is Spoken Here	SILVRBUR	p. 200
	No One Like You	SILVRBUR	p. 182
5	Like It Here	SILVRBUR	p. 222
	The Star-Spangled Banner	SILVRBUR	p. 218
	Say Something Good about America	SILVRBUR	p. 214
6	Asadoya (of other cultures)	SILVRBUR	p. 20
	La Manitas	SILVRBUR	p. 22
	Jamaica Farewell	SILVRBUR	p. 26
	Dundai	SILVRBUR	p. 76
	Long John (soloist)	SILVRBUR	p. 106

SILVRBUR refers to:
Palmer, Mary, et al. World of Music. New Jersey: **Silver Burdett** & Ginn Co., 1988.

HOLT refers to:
Boardman, Eunice, et al., Music. New York: **Holt,** Rhinehart & Winston, 1975.

IN TUNE WITH COOPERATION

GRADE	SONG TITLE	SOURCE	
K	Marty	SILVRBUR	p. 6
	Circus Parade	SILVRBUR	p. 50
	The Carpenters	SILVRBUR	p. 56
	Walk Along John	SILVRBUR	p. 64
	Two Bears	SILVRBUR	p. 75
1	You'll Sing a Song	SILVRBUR	p. 4
	What Shall We Do?	SILVRBUR	p. 17
	Old House	SILVRBUR	p. 28
	Hi-dee-roon	SILVRBUR	p. 150
2	Everybody's Welcome	SILVRBUR	p. 4
	Come and Dance	SILVRBUR	p. 114
	Buddies and Pals	HOLT	p. 131
	I Live in the City	HOLT	p. 10
	You'll Sing a Song and I'll Sing	HOLT	p. 9
3	Daisy Bell	SILVRBUR	p. 54
	Make New Friends	SILVRBUR	p. 110
	The Friendship Song	SILVRBUR	p. 140
	Let's Communicate	SILVRBUR	p. 180
	Let's Make Music	SILVRBUR	p. 182
	Sing about Martin	HOLT	p. 18
	Hey There Neighbor	HOLT	p. 8
	Let's Go Zudie-O	HOLT	p. 54
	The More We Get Together	HOLT	p. 62
4	Getting to Know You	SLVRBUR	p. 4
	Brethren in Peace Together	HOLT	p. 112
	Crawdad Song	HOLT	p. 88
	Songmaker	HOLT	p. 54
5	Down By the Riverside	SILVRBUR	p. 178
	There's a Meeting Here Tonight	SILVRBUR	p. 130
	Harmony	SILVRBUR	p. 128
	Zum Gali Gali	SILVRBUR	p. 116
	When Johnny Comes Marching	SILVRBUR	p. 36
	Erie Canal	SILVRBUR	p. 16
6	Let's Make Music	SILVRBUR	p. 210
	Go My Son	SILVRBUR	p. 34

IF THIS LIST WHETS YOUR WHISTLE
Ask for songs related to other traits. Contact:
Carl Yochum, Fine Arts Coordinator
Ferguson-Florissant School District
1005 Waterford Drive • Florissant, MO 63033

POWER OF RESPONSIBILITY

Students verbally and visually define responsibility in power paragraphs, illustrations and a month-long calendar of actions.

OBJECTIVES

1. Define and extend students' understanding of **responsibility** into real-life situations at school and home.

2. Organize thoughts by using power-writing strategies.

DESCRIPTION

Involve students in a class discussion that leads to a definition of responsibility. Brainstorm ways they can show responsibility at home and school. Record their ideas on the chalkboard or chart paper. Note other character traits suggested by or related to the students' ideas. Ask the students to rewrite each idea in a complete sentence.

Sample:	Do Homework
Related Traits:	Initiative, goal-setting, self-discipline
Sentence:	I do my homework.

LESSON 1: POWER PARAGRAPHS

Explain the 1-2-2 construct power-writing structure for paragraphs.

Step 1: Write *one* (1) topic sentence that states the main idea. This sentence is called the "first power sentence."

Step 2: Write *two* (2-2) sentences that support the main idea and provide supporting detail.

I take good care of my pet cat. I feed her every day, brush her and give her baths. If she gets out, I look for her and bring her home so she will be safe.

Ask students to write two power paragraphs, the first telling how they show responsibility at school; the second, responsibility at home. Ask the students to illustrate each of their paragraphs.

GRADES
2, 3

FORMAT
Classroom

DISCIPLINES
Language arts

TIME
Two 30-minute segments

MATERIALS INCLUDED
Responsibility Calendar

LESSON 2: RESPONSIBILITY CALENDAR

Provide students with a blank calendar (see next page) to reinforce their concept of themselves as responsible people. Review some of the responsibilities discussed in the brainstorming session. Instruct students to draft one short sentence about a responsible action they take and write it in one square. Then follow the same process for the rest of the squares. The teacher may want to write the sentences on a master calendar to be duplicated for younger students.

SCHOOL

Encourage another class to do the same lesson and exchange suggestions that result from the brainstorming sessions. Compare the ideas generated by each class, noting additions, differences and similarities.

HOME

Send a packet home with the student that includes the following items:
- a copy of the student's completed Responsibility Calendar as a sample
- three blank calendar forms
- instructions asking family members to complete the calendars with short declarative sentences that reflect their home responsibilities.
- suggestions for related conversations: Identify tasks that are interdependent and trace how they affect the family. (When you put your dirty clothes in the laundry basket, I can find them to wash them. If they are not there, they don't get washed. When you set the table, we have the silverware we need to eat.) Talk about reliability (doing what you agree to do), self-discipline (making yourself do what needs to be done when you don't want to) and initiative (seeing something that needs to be done and doing it without being asked). Relate examples or situations from daily life to each of these character traits.

COMMUNITY

The school nurse, counselor, district food services or transportation director may be invited to explain the importance of responsibility in his or her job. Extend the invitation to a school board member, superintendent, city planner or mayor.

SOURCE OF INSPIRATION

Vanessa Thomas, Marvin Elementary School, Ritenour School District

RESPONSIBILITY CALENDAR ☑

MONDAY	TUESDAY	WEDNESDAY	THURSDAY	FRIDAY	SAT. & SUN.
☐	☐	☐	☐	☐	☐
☐	☐	☐	☐	☐	☐
☐	☐	☐	☐	☐	☐
☐	☐	☐	☐	☐	☐
☐	☐	☐	☐	☐	☐

STATISTICS, SURVEYS AND
PERSONAL RESPONSIBILITY

This unit examines the surveys and statistical information in daily newspapers and adapts these research techniques to character-related topics.

OBJECTIVES

1. Reinforce the character traits of **commitment, cooperation, goal-setting, perseverance, respect** and **responsibility.**

2. Introduce descriptive statistics and their expression in tables, charts and graphs.

3. Strengthen students' reasoning and problem-solving skills.

DESCRIPTION

Each student needs classroom access to *USA Today* or another daily newspaper. Multiple copies of the same edition or an assortment of dates and publications are equally effective.

LESSON I: SURVEYING THE WORLD
Students scan newspapers for graphs, charts and articles that include survey results. Math concepts related to statistics and surveys are introduced as students analyze these aspects:
  • the kinds of questions asked
  • who is chosen for the survey
  • principles of random samples, representative samples
  • calculations: totals, percentages, ratios, averages, medians, modes
  • reporting results: pie charts, bar graphs, tables, narratives

In small cooperative groups, students develop a survey or research available statistics. Their focus relates to a character trait, directly or indirectly, whether they choose a suggested problem or develop their own topic.

Suggested Topics: Arriving on time reflects commitment, self-discipline and responsibility. Learn how tardiness records are collected and tabluated by the school or district. Use these statistics to compare one of the following:
(a) the number of "on time" arrivals for each grade level in one month;

GRADES
5

FORMAT
Classroom

DISCIPLINES
Math

TIME
Several class
sessions

**MATERIALS
NEEDED**
Daily newspapers
Meter sticks or
tape measures

(b) the "on time" rates between bus riders and walkers; and (c) the number of tardies reported each week (do rates go up around holidays or near the end of the school year?).

More suggested assignments: Develop a survey to determine the causes of tardiness. Do these causes vary by grade level, gender, modes of transportation? Do students feel respected by their peers? Do they feel respected by their teachers? How do these responses vary by grade level? How much time do students spend per week in competitive activities compared to the time they invest in cooperative activities? How many students recycle items at school? How many recycle items at home? How many students participated as a volunteer at some time in the past year? How do these totals compare by grade level?

ACE IT
A deck of cards can divide a class into small groups. Turn to page 77 to find out how it works.

A plan of action: Each group develops a plan of action, including questions to be asked and resources to be researched. Two groups exchange plans and critique them. Are the questions understandable? Do they ask what the survey seeks to find out? Are the answers quantifiable? Can their survey be completed in the time provided? Do they need to use a random or representative sample? Where can they find the data they need? What is the best way to present the results?

LESSON 2: THE PRESENTATION
Students conduct their poll, gather and analyze data, write a narrative description of the process and depict the results in charts, tables or graphs. If computer instructions and software are available, students enter data in spreadsheet formats, then convert the data to graphs. Each group presents its study to the class, including their reflections on the experience: Did the survey confirm their expectations? Did their findings raise new questions?

LESSON 3: A CLOSER LOOK
Surveys can focus inwardly, examining one's own actions and attitudes.
Exercise 1: Students record the positive and negative messages they receive from others and from themselves in one day. They record the feelings, moods and actions of the day. As they review the data, they look for connections and correlations. These are represented graphically in the chart shown on the next page.

MESSAGE	SELF	OTHER	+	-	FEELING, MOOD, ACTION
Can't move fast enough	√	√		√	Frustrated, insecure. Lose or scramble my things.
I am creative in art	√	√	√		Energized, look forward to art class.

In the second phase of this exercise, students count the number of positive messages they receive from others and themselves in one day. After reflecting on their findings, students develop strategies for increasing positive messages and decreasing negative messages.

Exercise 2: Students log their choices for one week. As a class, they brainstorm a sample list: what to wear, what to eat, whether to try out for a team, whether to yell at an annoying sibling, when to start on a long-term assignment, whether to answer the phone. They illustrate choices in their different forms:

deliberate	*I will spend one hour studying science.*
routine	*I will wear jeans and a T-shirt today.*
automatic	*I lock the door when I leave the house.*
reactive	*I talked to Marcy when she called.*

Recognize that personal responsibility means owning all of these choices, from carefully considered goals to knee-jerk reactions. At the end of the week, students review their logs in a class exercise. Working with their individual record, they evaluate their choices, coding each with a *d* for deliberate, *r* for routine, *a* for automatic, or *re* for reactive. They review their list again, marking each choice with a (+) if they are comfortable with the choice they made or (-) if they are uncomfortable with the choice they made. They look for similarities and patterns. Were uncomfortable choices made while under pressure, rushed, hurried, angry? Were the consequences known up front? Were they unknown? Was too much time spent on some decisions? Were some decisions made by default? For instance, if there is no response to an invitation, the choice is "no." This lesson is heightened and complemented by the exploration of choice-making in *License to Lead*, pages 117-124.

Excerise 3: Ask students to think of a long-term goal they want to accomplish. Incorporate material from *Be a Goal-Setter*, pages 67-73, particulary concerning intermediate steps. Their task is to develop a chart or graph that will visually represent their progress toward the goal. For instance, a chart related to "Julie's Story" (pages 70-72) and the goal of jumping rope 50 consecutive times would look something like this:

Steps	No. of Tries	Date Achieved
20 jumps		
30 jumps		
40 jumps		
50 jumps		

SCHOOL & DISTRICT

The class may vote or reach consensus on a question to be asked of all members of the student body. The results of the survey would then be combined, tallied, analyzed and reported. The question should be one that provokes thought about a character trait.

HOME

All of the lessons from this unit can be extended into the homes of students, where families can share in the assignment or in conversations about the assignment. Adults and siblings may want to gather and use their own data as they focus on the same questions.

COMMUNITY

After a classroom discussion on lifestyles, students can develop a set of characteristics that they feel exemplify a positive lifestyle. Based on those characteristics, students can create a "Community Member of the Month" program. Students would research and nominate people that they felt were living positive lifestyles and exhibiting good citizenship and community involvement. The monthly award might include a certificate, a special seat of honor at lunch in the school cafeteria or a news article and picture of the community member displayed in some prominent way.

SOURCE OF INSPIRATION

Terri Moore, Wren Hollow Elementary School, Parkway School District

MIDDLE SCHOOL
INCLUDES GRADES 6-8

Evaluating Character Education in the Middle Grades

Do your lessons help students understand the meaning and importance of good character? Can students go beyond basic understanding and apply what they have learned to their own lives? How do you know? Here are a few hints for evaluating the effects of your character education lessons on student learning and behavior. (Also see hints for evaluating secondary lessons on page 162.)

Have students keep a daily or weekly journal on the importance of having good character, character development objectives, and ways in which behaving with good character (or not) has affected their daily lives. (Understanding)

Have students write stories, poems and essays about the importance of good character and its role in our democratic society? (Understanding)

Have students develop and perform in dramatic presentations illustrating positive character traits. (Understanding)

Have students create and display banners and posters illustrating one or more character traits. (Understanding)

Have students discuss ethical dilemmas and identify alternative courses of action and their potential consequences. (Understanding)

Have students write essays, poems or short stories on character-related themes. (Understanding)

Have students design a community service project to improve a neighborhood or the community. (Understanding)

Have students conduct research projects on historical figures and discuss the role of good character in their lives. (Understanding)

Have students conduct role-plays illustrating character-related situations. (Understanding/Application)

Have students conduct a school-wide survey of students regarding their perceptions of the school climate, and use the results to plan action strategies for addressing negative findings. (Understanding/Application)

Divide the class into several teams and have students engage in team problem-solving to develop a solution to a school or community problem. (Understanding/Application)

Have students plan and teach character-related lessons to younger children. (Understanding/Application)

Have students engage in small- and large-group cooperative projects, such as community service efforts. (Understanding/Application)

TRANSITION TO MIDDLE SCHOOL
GETTING READY

This program smooths entry into middle or junior high school with a week together during the summer preceding the opening of school.

OBJECTIVES

1. Reinforce the character traits of **caring, commitment, cooperation, decision-making, goal-setting, honesty, perseverance, respect, responsibility, self-discipline** and **service.**

2. Help incoming students feel comfortable with their new school, the staff, one another and themselves.

DESCRIPTION

The week-long program is centered around the PIES theme which encompasses the physical, intellectual, emotional and social development of adolescents. The curriculum for much of the week's activity is drawn from *Lions-Quest Skills for Adolescence.* Students are placed in groups of 12 and these groups are matched with teachers they will have throughout the coming year. They learn to navigate through the building with locker drills and beat-the-bell competitions. They navigate the subtler terrain of positive interaction as they learn conflict resolution techniques, anger control and manners. Their discussions and reflections bring the traits of honesty, respect, responsibility and self-discipline into focus. In addition, problem-solving exercises and a mini-ropes course emphasize team-building and the traits of commitment, cooperation and perseverance.

The culminating event is a Carnival, planned as a service project that raises funds for local charities. Again, students work in teams to create booths consistent with a chosen theme (i.e., multiculturalism). They work with art supplies, shipping cartons or corrugated boxes, creating booths that offer puppet shows, games of chance and skill, or exhibits of school and community projects. Team members are scheduled to sell tickets, run the booths and help collect prizes. During the early part of the week, students develop a publicity campaign to draw the community to the Carnival. The funds earned are given to a charity such as the American Heart Association.

GRADES
5, 6

FORMAT
Summer course

SKILLS
Cooperation
Trust-building

TIME
One week

MATERIALS NEEDED
Lions-Quest Skills for Adolescence
Art supplies
Boxes
Prizes
Game equipment

A potluck supper provides closure to the week's activities. Families are invited and the students perform skits exemplifying different traits.

School begins with students and teachers already warmly familiar with one another. The students find that they have a common language with which to discuss appropriate classroom behavior and that the character traits, which they already know and understand, are the foundation of the teachers' expectations. Class lessons continue to include responsible decision-making opportunities and weave character traits into ongoing academic learning.

HOME

During the five-day experience, students can be asked to communicate with their families about the day's activities. They may draw a floor plan of the school and point out the location of their locker, the gym or the cafeteria. They may describe a particularly difficult challenge they faced that day and talk about their feelings during the ordeal. They may discuss one or several of the character traits they are studying and give examples of instances at home when they can practice the traits. These daily communications can take the form of an assignment or they can be encouraged by a note sent home to families at the beginning of the week.

The early positive introduction to the focus and spirit of the school and its staff encourages parents to become involved. They become more effective partners, participating in school activities, volunteering and providing understanding and support to their child.

COMMUNITY

Area merchants and companies can support the Carnival by donating prizes and posting flyers to publicize it.

SOURCE OF INSPIRATION

Administrators of the Hazelwood School District and staff members from the district's junior high schools

LIONS-QUEST SKILLS FOR ADOLESCENCE is available from Quest International P.O. Box 4850, Newark, OH 43058-4850 (800) 446-2700 • Web site: www.quest.edu

SCHOOL TOOLS STORE

This unit originated as a math project that involved extracurricular commitment to a store that operates outside of school hours.

OBJECTIVES

1. Promote the character traits of **commitment, cooperation, honesty, perseverance, respect, responsibility** and **service.**

2. Apply math skills and concepts.

3. Use communication skills to promote the store, transact business operations and serve customers.

DESCRIPTION

Students in a math class or after-school group work with a capital allocation of $50 and the desire to start a school store that serves student needs. They develop a list of potential inventory items (pens, pencils, erasers, notebooks, crayons, colored pencils, markers, paper, locks) and research their cost, comparing prices from several supply catalogues and local stores. They consider volume discounts and figure tax, shipping or delivery charges. They develop a table like the one below that helps them compare cost per item and select the most economic source. In the process, they perform addition, multiplication, division and percentage calculations.

Item: Two-Pocket, Pronged Folders

Source	Price	Qty.	Shipping	Vol. Discount	Cost per item
Office Supply	$5.95	25	$3.50	10% on 100*	.25
Joe's Store	$ .20	-0-	-0-	-0-	.20

* The volume discount of 10% is available on quantities of 100 or more.

Students determine a selling price from the cost per item, providing a net profit. They place orders, stock the store and schedule volunteers to operate it on a rotating basis. They advertise with posters, flyers and announcements over the P.A. system. Cash is collected for sales, recorded and depos-

GRADES
6 - 8

FORMAT
Classroom plus extracurricular

DISCIPLINE
Math
Language arts

TIME
Ongoing

MATERIALS NEEDED
Art supplies
Ledger
Calculators
Cash drawer
Storage space

ited in the school's office. A bank account is established and income deposited until the need to restock supplies. Periodically class time is spent in an analysis of the store's finances, volume of business and general management issues. Decisions concerning the future of the store are made during these class meetings.

The entire operation becomes the students' cooperative responsibility. Other character traits, such as honesty and perseverance, emerge during the course of doing business. Honesty protects the income as volunteers report all monies collected. Perseverance irons out scheduling conflicts, shipping delays, book-keeping balances. Respect is emphasized in all customer interactions.

HOME

Parents can explain the process of stocking supplies for the household. They may have adopted methods from business, such as a first in, first out system of inventory. By dating frozen meats and using them in the order of the earliest date, foods cycle through the freezing process with a minimum of time lapse. The same principle applies to refrigerated items. Is there a system for recording needed menu items or noting stock depletions so the next grocery list is complete? Another complementary area is in balancing accounts. Parents can trace the process of check-writing, bank deposits and balances with their child.

COMMUNITY

This unit invites the participation of retailers, entrepreneurs, small-business owners and accountants. Professionals from these fields can visit the school or invite the class to tour their operation to discuss such practices as inventory control, audits, marketing campaigns and planning for the future.

SOURCE OF INSPIRATION

Sybil Bowen, Bishop Elementary School, Wellston School District

RESPONSIBILITY ON THE JOB

Students' understanding of character traits is applied to the world of work and the use of money in a unit that integrates language arts and math.

OBJECTIVES

1. Promote the character traits of **commitment, cooperation, goal-setting, perseverance, responsibility** and **self-discipline.**

2. Explore goal-setting and decision-making in money management.

3. Become familiar with classified advertising and the responsibilities related to various jobs, careers and professions.

DESCRIPTION

Responsibility is viewed through the lens of successful work experiences. Character traits such as self-discipline, commitment, cooperation, goal-setting and perseverance are involved in responsible work habits. Students discuss these traits in language arts, coming to a common understanding of their meaning. They identify positive applications of these words as they relate to a worker's sense of responsibility. They also list antonyms and discuss their negative implications within the workplace. Students then divide into cooperative groups and scan an assortment of business magazines and the business section of local newspapers. They look for situations, advice, advertisements, employment listings and photographs that relate to the traits and cut them out. Each group reports, one at a time, to the class about their findings.

MATH COMPONENT: AN EXERCISE IN SAVING

Students look at attitudes and practices in money management, such as those expressed in the adages:

> "A penny saved is a penny earned."
> "A fool and his money are soon parted."

The teacher leads a discussion about these statements, asking what they mean, what kinds of actions they suggest, how one "saves a penny" or acts wisely enough to keep one's money. This problem is posed to students: "You earned $250 working part-time during the summer and want to open a bank account." Options are presented, using actual brochures from two

GRADES
6 - 8

FORMAT
Classroom

DISCIPLINES
Math
Language arts

TIME
Several class periods

MATERIALS INCLUDED
Getting the Most for Your Money

MATERIALS NEEDED
Bank brochures
Newspapers
Business magazines

different banks which explain the savings and checking account options available. Make sure the banks selected provide different variables in interest rates, minimum balance requirements and fees. Go through the brochures and explain the information they provide. Distribute copies of the handout on page 106. Set up a similar table on the chalkboard and demonstrate how to organize the information in a way that allows a comparison of options. Pair students with a partner. Ask them to pick one of the financial goals on the handout and develop a plan of action to achieve it, involving some combination of investment in one or both of the banks.

LANGUAGE ARTS

Students become familiar with the language of classified advertising. Individually or in small groups, they analyze a page of employment opportunity listings. They clip two ads and identify grammatical use and abuse, academic disciplines or degrees, job responsibilities and any reference to character traits.

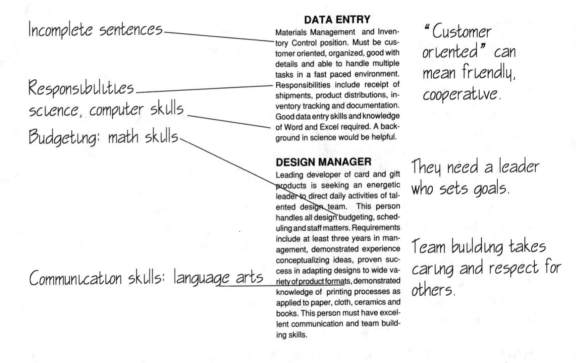

Incomplete sentences

Responsibilities

science, computer skills

Budgeting: math skills

DATA ENTRY
Materials Management and Inventory Control position. Must be customer oriented, organized, good with details and able to handle multiple tasks in a fast paced environment. Responsibilities include receipt of shipments, product distributions, inventory tracking and documentation. Good data entry skills and knowledge of Word and Excel required. A background in science would be helpful.

"Customer oriented" can mean friendly, cooperative.

DESIGN MANAGER
Leading developer of card and gift products is seeking an energetic leader to direct daily activities of talented design team. This person handles all design budgeting, scheduling and staff matters. Requirements include at least three years in management, demonstrated experience conceptualizing ideas, proven success in adapting designs to wide variety of product formats, demonstrated knowledge of printing processes as applied to paper, cloth, ceramics and books. This person must have excellent communication and team building skills.

They need a leader who sets goals.

Team building takes caring and respect for others.

Communication skills: language arts

Discussion focuses on responsibilities for different jobs or professions. Students are asked to identify and list their responsibilities at home, school and in community and extracurricular activities. They use these (not necessarily all of them) as the basis for an imaginary job and write a classified ad, including the job title, academic and experience requirements and responsibilities. When finished, they determine the cost of placing their ad in a local or national publication. Selected students can be assigned the task of calling a publication (daily newspaper, suburban newspaper, *Wall Street Journal, USA Today*, others) for classified advertising rate information. They share this information with the class.

ADDITIONAL OPPORTUNITIES

A program which allows students to take on such jobs as lunchroom helpers, classroom and school monitors, and library or science lab assistants, can reinforce the concept of responsibility. As part of the program, provide students with opportunities to reflect on their work, the responsibilities they manage, the ways their work affects others and their feelings about doing the work.

HOME

Students can interview a working member of the family, an adult friend or a neighbor about particular job responsibilities and the skills, talents, education and character traits necessary to meet those responsibilities. As a class, brainstorm and refine a list of appropriate questions and interview approaches.

COMMUNITY

Teachers or parent volunteers can contact a community organization, perhaps the local chapter of the Lions, Rotary or Kiwanis clubs or the Chamber of Commerce, to plan an evening with students that centers on careers, responsibilities, choices and the community's experience. The format can be one of question and answer, roundtable discussion or a sharing of ideas—adults to students and students to adults. The tone is one of inquiry and respect for one another's thinking. What is the community doing to attract a diverse population of responsible citizens with a variety of abilities and interests? What will this community look like 10 years from now? How can the community support and show cooperation to its young people as they grow and enter the world of work? What advice can these adults give to young people? The session can be video-taped and reviewed later by the students. Did they conduct themselves in a professional manner? What did they learn from the dialogue?

Guest speakers and field trips provide students with real-life examples of work responsibilities. A variety of career paths can be explored. Each presentation or field trip is followed by a discussion asking students what they learned. As mentioned in the lessons, business people and workers can share their work, responsibilities and ethics with the students. More elaborate arrangements can include "shadowing" an employer or employee for a day.

SOURCE OF INSPIRATION

Vallarie Jones, Toussaint L'Ouverture Middle School, St. Louis Public School District

GETTING THE MOST FOR YOUR MONEY

Situation: You earned $250 last summer. Now you want to put this money in a safe place. You brought home brochures from two different banks to study your options. Determine how much money you will place in a checking account and/or a savings account. Determine which bank and which account options you will use based on one of the following goals. Your choices must maximize your interest earnings while fulfilling your needs.

Goal 1: To earn the most money you can by this time next year. In what account and how much of your funds will you invest? How much will you have at the end of one year?

Goal 2: To have ready access to $100 for entertainment expenses for the next three months and, at the same time, to earn the most interest possible. Will you divide the money into different accounts? Different banks? How much will you have at the end of three months when you have spent $100?

Goal 3: You want a $150 CD player, but decide you can wait three months before you buy it. How can you maximize your deposit and still purchase the CD player at the end of three months? How much interest will you earn in that time? How much money will you have after you buy the CD player?

Type of Account	Bank A		Bank B		Bank A		Bank B	
	check	int. check	check	int. check	savings	money mkt.	savings	money mkt.
Amount to open acct.								
Minimum balance								
Service charge								
Charge per withdrawal or check cleared								
Monthly fee								
Compounding and crediting of interest								

check: checking account
int. check: interest-bearing checking account

CAREERS & CHARACTER EDUCATION
EXPLORING THE FUTURE

Careers for the 21st Century videos introduce students to professions with fast-moving, MTV-styled coverage of various fields. The videos, available in different volumes, adapt to several teaching formats: interdisciplinary units, individual classes and college and career planning sessions.

OBJECTIVES

1. Reinforce the character traits of **cooperation, commitment, goal-setting, perseverance, responsibility, service** and **self-discipline.**

2. Heighten student awareness of possible careers and the educational requirements and character traits that contribute to success in these careers.

3. Connect the world of school to the world of work, and show the importance of learning now and in the future.

DESCRIPTION

A video is chosen from among the library of career videos available from Take Off Multimedia (see box on next page). A broad selection of career fields is recommended if the presentation is part of an assembly, homeroom, career day or guidance counseling session. If the exercise is to be part of a science class, videos focused on oceanography, marine biology, chemistry, pharmacy, environmental engineering or zoology might be chosen. The same logic applies to math, English and other disciplines.

Before viewing the videos, students identify their personal career goals, what they think they will need to prepare them for such work, and what character traits will help them to achieve success. Students then watch the videos. They use a worksheet designed by the teacher or counselor that includes space to note the educational needs, potential salaries and working conditions of each vocation. Students also note qualities, such as attention to detail, creativity,

GRADES
6 - 8

FORMAT
Classroom
Extracurricular
Career Day

DISCIPLINES
All

TIME
Variable

MATERIALS NEEDED
Video: *Careers for the 21st Century*
TV/VCR unit

SEND FOR A CATALOG
Careers for the 21st Century
Take Off Multimedia
Educational Excellence Inc.
P.O. Box 6798
St. Louis, MO 63144
(800) 462-5232 (314) 863-0700
Fax: (314) 647-0945

risk-taking, honesty, initiative, self-discipline, responsibility, caring, cooperation and other traits that are part of doing one's best on the job.

After viewing the videos or in a subsequent class, students compare their previewing lists to the information on their worksheet. Career planning is complex and involves many choices throughout middle and secondary school. This unit sets the thinking process in motion.

HOME

Assign students an interview with an adult member of the family (aunts, uncles, grandparents) or an employed friend of the family. A generation ago, many entered their professions with the understanding that they would work for one company and in one area, such as engineering or accounting, throughout their lifetime. Today, people work for several different companies and often pursue multiple careers. Suggest the following questions to be asked during the interview: What attracted you to this particular field? What are the day-to-day responsibilities? How did you think about your career at the time you entered it? Did you intend to stick with it at the same level, advance to higher positions, stay with one company, move from one firm to another, change careers? How did the economy or the times affect your career choice? Were you influenced by a depression, a war, a new invention? What education was needed to enter into the career of choice?

COMMUNITY

Such business organizations as the Chamber of Commerce or Rotary Club can be enlisted to develop a core of sites that are willing to host student visits. These visits allow students to shadow a professional throughout the work day and may evolve into long-lasting mentor relationships.

SOURCE OF INSPIRATION

Jim Boland, Ladue Junior High, Ladue School District

PEER MEDIATION

This approach introduces the concept of peer mediation to the student body in a 30-minute assembly. Students volunteer or are selected for a one-day training session and are then on-call when actual peer mediation is needed.

OBJECTIVES

1. Reinforce the character traits of **commitment, cooperation, decision-making, goal-setting, honesty, perseverance, respect, responsibility, self-discipline** and **service.**

2. Strengthen students' skills in communications, listening and problem solving.

3. Present conflict resolution as an acceptable alternative.

DESCRIPTION

The counselor introduces a peer mediation program to respond to conflicts among students on an as-needed basis. The student body views a video or a live presentation demonstrating conflict mediation. This provides an awareness and, hopefully, an acceptance of the conflict-resolution process. After viewing the video, students are asked to fill out a form if they are interested in being considered as a mediator or to recommend other students they think might be effective in that role.

Seventh- and eighth-graders are chosen for training; Hixson Middle School selected 16 from each grade level. Ten additional eighth graders, returning to the program for the second year, act as aides and small-group facilitators. A one-day off-site workshop is planned. Team-building exercises are used at the start of the workshop and interspersed throughout the day to increase the sense of community among those involved. In one exercise, students complete the "What's Your Opinion" questionnaire on page 112 and discuss their responses. Students learn a step-by-step processs for conflict resolution (see page 111). The character traits are woven into the training along with an emphasis on listening, reflection and empathic skills. Strategies for mainintaining control and a conflict mediation report form are also included on pages 114 and 115, respectively.

GRADES
6 - 8

FORMAT
Schoolwide

SKILLS
Conflict resolution
Leadership
Listening

TIME
30-minute assembly
One-day training
as needed

MATERIALS INCLUDED
Checklist
What's your Opinion?
Role playing
Strategies
Report form

When conflicts arise, students are excused from class and given an office in which to meet. Those involved must meet the following conditions:
- All parties agree to participate fully in peer mediation.
- They recognize that the purpose in meeting is to resolve the issue.

CLASSROOM CONNECTIONS

All teachers know the group's purpose and abilities. They support peer mediation not only by making it available to students in conflict but with class discussions that translate the techniques to everyday situations. The character traits of responsibility and respect for others are part of these discussions.

Social studies lessons lend themselves to discovering the history and use of conflict resolution: labor negotiations, war treaties, U.N. actions. Can countries or groups of people, as well as individuals, demonstrate the use of character traits? How?

Language arts exercises can incorporate hypothetical scenarios of student conflict. Given situations, students discuss and write possible resolutions. They reflect the character traits—honesty, responsibility, self-respect and respect for others—involved in the process.

Posters designed by students remind others of the alternatives to fighting and violence. Self-discipline, honesty and other traits are featured in the posters.

HOME
Students can implement the mediation process when resolving conflicts at home. Parents of peer mediators can be invited to a mini-workshop that introduces the skills of listening, reflection, empathy, brainstorming and conflict resolution. They can role-play situations with the student mediators and discuss the process and its use in other settings.

COMMUNITY

Labor negotiators, professional mediators or other community leaders involved in conflict resolution can be invited to share their experience and wisdom with students.

SOURCE OF INSPIRATION
Dan Mosby, Hixson Middle School, Webster Groves School District

CHECKLIST FOR MEDIATION

PART I: INTRODUCTION
Have everybody introduce themselves ☐
Explain the purpose of the mediation ☐
Explain the ground rules ☐

PART II: TELLING THE STORY
Both parties tell their side of the story ☐
Summarize facts and feelings of both parties' sides of the story ☐

PART III: ROLE REVERSAL
Have disputants summarize facts and feelings of other person ☐

PART IV: IDENTIFYING ALTERNATIVE SOLUTIONS
Ask both parties how they can solve the problem ☐
Write down all solutions ☐
Check solutions both agree to ☐

PART V: REACHING AN AGREEMENT
Write solution both agree to ☐
Sign contract ☐

PART VI: THANK YOU
Thank the people for being there ☐
Sign passes back to class ☐

WHAT'S YOUR OPINION?	AGREE	DISAGREE
1. It's possible to live in a world without conflict.		
2. You can have conflicts without fighting or violence.		
3. All conflicts can be worked out.		
4. People should never fight.		
5. People turn to violence when they refuse to listen to each other.		
6. You can still be a strong person and choose not to fight.		
7. The world would be a boring place without conflict and differences.		
8. Fighting may be the only way some kids know how to deal with their anger.		
9. "Put downs" and "fighting words" can be as violent and hurtful as physical fighting.		

ROLE PLAY: Probe to Discover More About the Situation

Pair students and ask Student A to assume the role of mediator. Student B receives a copy of one of the situations below and presents the problem accordingly. Student B then responds to the mediator's questions using the information in "Response." If the mediator's questions do not allow Student B to reveal the additional information, the pair discusses and formulates the kind of questions that would work.

SITUATION: You were walking down the hall when a student came up behind you and knocked your books out of your hands. She and her friends laughed at you as you scrambled to pick them up.

RESPONSE: If the mediator asks about your relationship or previous encounters with the individual, respond by telling about an incident when you and your friends had snickered about an incorrect answer she gave to a question during class.

AFTER PROBING: You discover you had embarrassed the student in class by laughing with your friends when she answered a question incorrectly.

SITUATION: You got mad while playing basketball and pushed another student, who pushed you back. You've calmed down now and want to come to a settlement but can't admit it.

RESPONSE: You recall that a group of students saw the confrontation and pressured you to fight. You already said you would meet the person after school.

AFTER PROBING: You realize you were caught up in the heat of the moment. You can see how the other player's actions were accidental; he didn't mean to do it. You're confused about what to do next.

SITUATION: A new student came into school and was hanging out with you for a couple of weeks. Recently, you have given the person the "cold shoulder."

RESPONSE: You say you just don't like the person, although you can't say what the person did that bothered you. Upon further questioning, you tell how your friends feel toward this person.

AFTER PROBING: You discover one of the more popular and influential students among your friends is jealous of the person and has been starting rumors.

SITUATION: You yelled at a younger student who made a joke that offended you.

RESPONSE: You are not the bully type and are not sure why you reacted so strongly. If asked about other things going on in your life, explain that it's been miserable. You were grounded last night and your teacher didn't accept late homework that you spent two hours doing.

AFTER PROBING: You discover that you vented your frustrations on the first person who got in your way.

Strategies for Maintaining Control

(When a disputant breaks a rule)

1.   "SHHHH"

2.   Remind them of the rule

3.   "I" message

4.   Warning

5.   End the mediation—report this on form and return it to counselor.

Getting Workable Solutions

When a disputant is asked what she or he could do to solve the problem and responds "I don't know," ask the following sequence of questions:

1.   "What will happen if ..."
      (i.e., "What will happen if you don't solve this problem now?")

2.   "Do you want that to happen?"

3.   "Then what could you do now to solve the problem?"

When a disputant offers a solution that is not likely to work, ask the following questions:

1.   "Will that work?"

2.   "What is a solution that might really work?"

Conflict Mediation Report

Mediator_____   Date _____

Mediator _____

Names of students with conflict:

1._____   Team_____

2._____   Team_____

Purpose: To help students come up with their <u>own</u> solutions, not to decide right or wrong.

AGREEMENT TO GROUND RULES:
1. Agree to solve the problem.
2. No name-calling or put-downs.
3. Do not interrupt.
4. Be as honest as you can.
5. Everything said is confidential.

Getting the Story: Facts and Feelings
Student #1   Student #2

_____   _____

_____   _____

_____   _____

Role Reversal: Stating the other person's feelings
Student #1   ❏ yes ❏ no   Student #2   ❏ yes ❏ no

Brainstorming Solutions
Student #1 Suggests: Student #2 Suggests:

_____   _____

_____   _____

_____   _____

Signatures of Agreement

_____   _____
Student #1   Mediator

_____   _____
Student #2   Mediator

LICENSE TO LEAD

When students complete this unit they no longer ask, "Am I a leader?" but "What kind of leader am I?"

OBJECTIVES

1. Promote the character traits of **cooperation, honesty, respect, responsibility, self-esteem** and **self-discipline.**

2. Develop an understanding of the relationship between values, ethics and leadership.

3. Learn a process for making ethical decisions.

DESCRIPTION

License to Lead is a mini-course that can be done in ten 30-minute segments with an option for four or five follow-up sessions. Students work in groups of five to seven with an interactive curriculum that:
- examines characteristics needed for positive leadership.
- shows how one's leadership is based on personal, chosen values.
- defines values and ethics, distinguishing between the two.
- recognizes how values and ethics are acquired.
- provides several dilemmas to examine.
- guides the development of a school or community creed.
- introduces a step-by-step process for making ethical decisions.
- explores the application of ethical values to school and society.
- encourages students to own and exercise their leadership potential.

The curriculum also adapts to a half-day workshop. The Maplewood-Richmond Heights district used it to prepare their sixth-graders for junior high. The teacher-coordinators moved to an off-school location and combined students from two elementary schools that feed into the junior high.

LICENSE TO LEAD
30-page curriculum, including 15 lessons and 10 handouts available from NASSP.
National Association of
Secondary School Principals
1904 Association Drive
Reston, Virginia 20191-1537
Phone: (703) 860-0200
ISBN 0-88210-309-1 Product No. 6209601

GRADES
6 - 8

FORMAT
Classroom
Homeroom
After-school club
Half-day workshop

SKILLS
Decision-making
Leadership

TIME
Variable depending
on format

**MATERIALS
INCLUDED**
Workshop Outline
Sample Lesson
What's Important to Me?
Value Characteristics
Key Terms Defined

HOME

Parents are invited to complete the surveys—"What's Important To Me?" and "Value Characteristics" from *License to Lead*—and use them to stimulate family discussions.

COMMUNITY

The teacher-coordinators from Maplewood-Richmond Heights district asked area business people to serve as table discussion leaders and enlisted a corporate sponsor to provide lunch. The curriculum guide suggests that students interview, by phone or in person, someone they admire from the community. They are to ask their subjects about their personal values, what they are and how they have made a difference in their lives.

SOURCE OF INSPIRATION

Judy Owens, Maplewood-Richmond Heights School District

ETHICAL DILEMMAS

You and a friend are shopping in a local department store. A very popular CD that you really want is on the shelf. It is the last one and you are short two dollars to be able to buy it. Your friend says, "Go ahead and stick it in your pocket. You buy stuff here all the time and they have made plenty of money from your other purchases." *What do you do?*

Word is circulating through the school that two of your classmates are going to meet in a local park to finish a fight that started earlier in the day at school. More than likely, other classmates will fight also. *What do you do?*

You are invited to a slumber party. Your friend's parents are going to be out of town the night of the party. Your friend tells you that her older brother will be the chaperone. He is 17. Your parents will not allow you to stay at a friend's house without parents present You really want to go because all of your friends will be there. *What do you do?*

Your friend brought a pack cigarettes to school. Anyone caught with cigarettes is suspended from your school. She asks you to give them to another student who will be in your next class. *What do you do?*

Workshop Outline

Introduction: What makes a person a respected member of the group? Think of someone in your class who is not only liked but respected. What is it about that person that causes others to think so highly of him or her? Can you name specific actions and behaviors?

Table Activity: Meet the people at your table.

Group Activity: **Peer pressure**

Show excerpts of *The Lion King, The Simpsons* and *Back to the Future* (on video) which demonstrate examples of ethical situations where characters are influenced by their peers. Leaders guide discussion with these questions:

- How are each of the scenes in these videos the same?
- What kind of dilemmas do the characters face?
- How is peer pressure used to try to get people to do something?
- In what other situations might students be persuaded to do something they are not sure is the best thing to do?
- Have you ever been in a situation where someone tried to talk you into doing something? How did he do it?

Table Activity: **Characteristics of a respected person**

- Brainstorm characteristics of people you know and feel are respected in your community, neighborhood, school.
- Think of a particular person. Write down two important characteristics of the individual you have in mind.
- Compare your lists and, on chart paper, notice how many of the people have similar characteristics. Check a characteristic each time a team member mentions it. Which characteristics are noted the most?
- Discuss specific examples of the way you have seen this person act toward others, behaviors that helped form your opinion of this person.
- Discuss specific examples of things you have heard this person say to you or others that have helped form your opinion.

Table Activity: **Being respected and personal success**

- Discuss how these characteristics help people reach daily and long-range goals. What would some middle school and high school goals be? Discussion starters: doing well in school, making friends, doing well in sports, being voted to Student Council, becoming a cheerleader, getting a job. Long-range goals: get a good education, go to college, get a good job, etc.
- How do the characteristics discussed on the chart influence how successful a person is in life?

Workshop Outline (continued)

Group Activity: **Presenting characteristics**

Chart paper is posted around the room. A student from each table volunteers to present the characteristics discussed at their table. The lists of each group are then analyzed and combined into a master list.

Group Activity: **Relevance of respect to personal success**

Discuss how people demonstrating these characteristics are more successful than other people in reaching their goals. How do these characteristics influence success?

Table Activity: **What's Important to Me? (Worksheet)**

Each table is given a list of values and definitions. All participants work on their own value questionnaire.

Group Activity: **The importance of values when making decisions**

Discuss how our values affect every decision we make in life. If we have a strong character and positive values, we will make ethical decisions—even if we have to stand alone—because we will have confidence in our ability to make the right decision based on our values.

Table Activity: **Dilemmas**

Examples of dilemmas (see samples on page 118) are developed and distributed in this way: Two tables receive a copy of the same dilemma, two other tables receive a different dilemma and so on. Time is allowed to discuss and reach consensus. Presenters from each table share how the group resolved the dilemma.

Closure: Thank table leaders. Distribute evaluations.

Sample Lesson

Activity: Choices and Values

Objective: Students will decide what they value and how values affect their choices and leadership in everyday living.

Time: 30 minutes

Equipment: Overhead projector, blank transparencies, chalkboard or flip chart Handouts: "What's Important To Me?" "Value Characteristics" and "Key Terms Defined." Copy these for all participants.

Process:

Ask students what choices they have made today (getting up, what to eat, what to wear, whether to go to school). How do they know they made a "good" or "right" choice in each of these situations? (Learned from parents, teachers, friends, church, etc.) As they get older and become more a part of society and less dependent on their family, how will they know what is a "good" or "right" choice in high school, the workplace, etc.?

For the next several weeks, they will be looking at values, both personal and societal, and how to apply them to everyday living to help make good choices.

Have students fill out the checklist "What's Important To Me?" (Note: before copying, review list for any that may not be appropriate for your community and delete or change.)

Ask students to go back through the list and pick the four to five values that are the most important to them and write the numbers in the blanks at the bottom. Then have them refer to the "Value Characteristics" handout, find the numbers they have chosen on the left side of the page and write the corresponding words on the lines at the bottom of the page.

Refer students to "Key Terms Defined." Discuss the definition of values. Do the students think the four or five they have selected are the qualities that motivate them to act as they do? Have students share their values with a friend. Did they have any the same? (It is natural for people to associate with people who share the same values.)

Discuss "Criteria for a Core Value." For example, ask students who are concerned about the environment to raise their hands. For those who raised their hands, ask them if they would be willing to share with the class what that concern is (air, water, noise pollution; ozone breaking down; global warming; landfills; etc.). If they are willing to state their concern, ask them to stand up. For those who are standing, ask those who are *not* recycling at least three items (cans, bottles, paper, etc.) to sit down. Tell the class that for those who are still standing, concern for the environment is a "core" value. (Actions speak louder than words!) This is how you know if something is a core value. Ask the students if they would like to share how they are "acting" on one of their values. If they can't, these values may not be their core values.

What's Important to Me?

Take a few minutes to think about the meaning of the items listed below. Indicate with a check mark the items that are important to you.

1. A physical appearance to be proud of
2. To graduate with honors
3. Being an honest person
4. To have political power
5. Being known as a "real" person
6. A meaningful relationship
7. Self-confidence and personal growth
8. Enjoyment of nature and beauty
9. A life with meaning, purpose, fulfillment
10. Continuing to learn and gain knowledge
11. A chance to help the sick and disadvantaged
12. To be attractive to others
13. Some honest and close friendships
14. A long and healthy life
15. A meaningful relationship with God
16. A good marriage
17. Satisfaction/success in the career of your choice
18. An equal opportunity for all people
19. Freedom to live life as you want
20. A financially comfortable life
21. Accomplishment of something worthwhile
22. A secure and positive family life
23. An enjoyable, leisurely life
24. Unlimited travel, fine foods, entertainment, recreational and cultural opportunity
25. Getting things changed for the better
26. A beautiful home in the setting of your choice
27. A chance to develop creativity/potential in any area
28. Owning a possession of great value
29. To speak up for my personal beliefs
30. To have better feelings about myself
31. To be needed and to be important to others
32. To be a good parent
33. To have a better relationship with my parents
34. To be sexy
35. To persevere in what I am doing
36. Time for prayer
37. To give of myself freely in helping others
38. A safe and secure environment
39. To be loved by a special few
40. To be trusted by others

List below the number of the 4 to 5 items that are most important to you.

1. _____   2. _____   3. _____   4. _____   5. _____

When you have listed the 4 to 5 items that are most important to you, refer to the "Value Characteristics" sheet and write the appropriate characteristics related to these numbers.

Value Characterstics

Number	Characteristic
5	Sincerity
3, 40	Honesty, integrity
7, 30	Emotional well-being, stability
8	Artistic appreciation
2, 10	Education, intelligence, wisdom
11, 37, 18	(Altruism) Compassion, fairness, justice
1, 12, 34	Appearance, beauty, approval
6, 13, 31, 39	Love, friendship, personal closeness
14, 38	Health, personal safety, security
15, 36	Religion, spirituality
16, 22, 32, 33	Family, love, emotional security
9, 17, 21, 27	Fulfillment, intellectual and vocational achievement
19	Personal freedom, independence
20, 26, 28	Financial security, money, status
23, 24	Pleasure, travel, material satisfaction
4, 25	Power, achievement
29	Courage
35	Perseverance

Write the characteristic that corresponds to the numbers you selected on the checklist.

1._____

2._____

3._____

4._____

5._____

Key Terms Defined

VALUES:
Those inner standards from which you receive the motivation to act as you do and by which you judge behavior (both yours and others').

MORAL VALUES:
Those inner standards of right and wrong from which you receive the motivation to act as you do and by which you judge behavior (both yours and others').

ETHICS:
A set of beliefs about conduct based on moral values.

VALUES/MORAL VALUES

I. Going to the movies or the mall.

2. Borrowing a friend's report or plagiarizing one from a textbook.

3. Eating with friends at Pizza Hut or McDonalds.

4. Skipping school to go to the mall, arcade or a friend's house whose parents are not home.

CRITERIA FOR A CORE VALUE

CHOSEN:
Something that you selected freely from alternatives after careful examination and clearly understand the consequences of your selection.

PRIZED:
Being happy with your choice and willing to stand up and tell others what you believe/ selected.

ACTS:
You act on your choice repeatedly in your daily life.

HISTORICAL FICTION
LIT SETS WITH CHARACTER

Students explore traits through literature sets that integrate social studies, language arts and character education.

OBJECTIVES

1. Reinforce the character traits of **caring, commitment, cooperation, goal-setting, honesty, perseverance, respect, responsibility, self-discipline** and **service.**

2. Teach communication skills in a meaningful context.

3. Integrate social studies and language arts.

DESCRIPTION

We suggest a team of teachers and curriculum specialists join forces as they did in the Hazelwood School District to develop a literature series that extends throughout the year. Short of such a labor pool, a committed teacher can design lessons for one book the first year, test it, then add a book a year until there is a full complement of literature sets related to character traits.
- Read the book first.
- Note idea, subject and concepts that connect to the curriculum.
- Design lessons, reading assignments, questions for discussion and performance tasks.

The lessons and activities on the following pages are designed for the novel *Letters from Rifka* and offered as a springboard for teachers as they develop their own plans.

GRADES
6 - 8

FORMAT
Classroom

DISCIPLINES
Language arts
Social studies

TIME
Several sessions

MATERIALS NEEDED
Copies of books
Nystrom desk maps

SUGGESTED HISTORICAL FICTION
Immigrant Kids by Russell Freedman
Journey to Jo'burg by Beverly Naidoo
The Land I Lost by Huynh Zuang Nhuong
Letters from Rifka by Karen Hesse

LANGUAGE ARTS LESSONS

- Discuss ways we know things about the past. Brainstorm students' ideas, being sure to include *word of mouth* and *personal diaries*. Give examples of famous diaries such as those of Lewis and Clark, Anne Frank and Abraham Lincoln as examples. Have students share about friends or family members they know who keep diaries or journals. Discuss why diaries are often more interesting to read than history in textbooks.

- Use Nystrom desk maps to locate Russia. Have students find the city of Berdichev, where Rifka's journey begins. Ask them to trace a possible route from Berdichev to Poland. Discuss what geographic obstacles might make this a difficult journey.

- Discuss the questions: Why do you think a family might leave their homeland to travel to some place far away? (List ideas on chart paper and save for future discussion after the book is read.) What character traits would they have to have? Perseverance? Commitment? Self-Discipline?

- Ask the students to pretend that they are leaving their home to live permanently in a foreign country. Have them write a sample diary entry that tells where they are headed and how they feel about the move. Have them include descriptions about the preparations their families made for the move, thoughts about the people they will miss, etc. Ask them to review the character traits and write about the ones that they will need to practice through this ordeal. (Diary entries can be saved for the culminating activity.)

SOCIAL STUDIES LESSONS

- Discuss intolerance. Ask the students to give examples of intolerance in modern life. Discuss pogroms. Help the students understand the background of the Jewish people in Russia at the time of the story (1919).

- Have students read the first 15 pages of the book. Then have them compare their diary entries with Rifka's experiences. How are they alike? How are they different?

- Research and prepare a presentation (either a written or oral report, or a skit) about the life and works of Pushkin, the Russian poet.

- Illustrate the Polish town.

- Compare modes of transportation used by Rifka's family to the modes of transportation families might use today.

- Research information about the diseases of ringworm and typhus. Explore such questions as: Do people still get these diseases today? Why? Why not? What character traits are evident in people who strive to cure diseases?

- Review what was learned from the story about the Russian and American economies of 1919.

- Explore Russian pogroms. Can examples of other state police attacks on specific ethnic or racial groups be found in history? Where? When? Discuss pogroms in relation to such character traits as respect and caring.

- Examine each of the characters in the book to identify the traits they display. The Character Analysis handout included with *Lessons in Honesty* on pages 61-66 adapts beautifully to this exercise.

- Integrate science and health subject material while reading about the diseases and plagues of the times.

- Use cardinal and intermediate directions to plot a course Rifka may have taken from Europe to America.

- Locate Belgium on desk maps. Identify Antwerp using longitude and latitude. Trace time differences between Belgium and New York using time zones.

- Display products of this unit in the halls or in the library for other students and visitors to see.

HOME

Have students interview family members or friends who have come to America from a foreign country. Learn about their feelings, the values and character traits they needed to leave, survive the journey and live successfully in their new surroundings.

COMMUNITY

Invite speakers who have come into the community from other countries. Have the students explain the character traits they have been studying and ask the visitors to relate their experiences to those traits.

SOURCE OF INSPIRATION

A team of curriculum specialists from Hazelwood School District

DOLLARS & SENSE-ABILITY

This ingenious math and language arts unit simulates the experience of interviewing for a job and earning a paycheck as it teaches basic financial skills.

OBJECTIVES

1. Promote the character traits of **goal-setting, initiative, reliability** and **responsibility.**

2. Acquire life skills in managing a checking account, calculating payroll slips, filing a federal tax form, preparing a resume, completing an application, interviewing for a position and writing business letters.

3. Complete individual profiles which indicate interests and strengths that may be matched to job opportunities.

DESCRIPTION

For one week, math class becomes a place of work. Students earn wages for attending class, bonuses for special efforts, tips for extra service. Earnings are docked for late arrival and substandard performance. Time records are tallied at the end of the week. Paychecks, issued the following week, are cashed at the Team Bank into currency that features teachers' faces in place of familiar U.S. Presidents. This "money" is good at the Team Store, stocked by PTA or parent contributions of candy, chips, soda, pens, erasers, magazines, etc. A celebratory auction at the end of the unit offers another option for spending earned income.

LANGUAGE ARTS COMPONENT

- Students complete a personality profile, which indicates their strengths and interests and is used to select a potential job.

- They research jobs available in the area. As a class, students brainstorm the type of information they need to make their decisions: wages, shifts, average part-time hours, location, requirements—age, experience, driver's licence, vehicle, completion of tests (drug, typing, clerical, literacy, other). In self-chosen

GRADES
6 - 8

FORMAT
Classroom
Team teaching

DISCIPLINES
Math
Computer
Language arts

TIME
Several class sessions

**MATERIALS
INCLUDED**
Lesson Plan
Ways to Pay for Work
Payroll Exercise
Answer key
Payroll Check & Stub
A Working Interview

teams, students research a particular job category, such as fast food, retail, service, mechanical, lawn maintenance, clerical, delivery. They search the Yellow Pages, business guides, classified ads and teen employment services to compile a list of prospective jobs.

- Students obtain job application forms from various businesses. They write business letters to companies advertising jobs in the classified section which explain the school project and ask for one copy of their standard application form.

- Students enter their findings in a database during computer lab time. They learn how to input information and search the database.

- As individuals, students match jobs to their personality profiles. They choose a vocation from the many available, complete the application and assemble a resume.

- Speakers from local businesses and employment agencies augment classroom learning, They explain what employers are looking for at the interview stage, outline basic rights of the employee and employer, and describe attributes of a good employee, such as honesty, initiative, reliability and responsibility.

- Volunteers from corporate personnel departments come to the school to conduct interviews. They evaluate the communication skills, application, resume and conduct of each applicant. Their evaluations are reviewed by the teacher and a "hire" or "no hire" determination is made. Students receive letters the following day indicating their status (hire or no hire) and a copy of the evaluation.

Dear Parents,

Team 3-D is currently involved in their Career Unit. We are teaching important skills to prepare our students for their futures. We could use your help in this endeavor.

Language Arts:
Students will be involved in a mock interview with (name of company) personnel employees on (date).
1. Review your young adult's resume.
2. Role play a job interview.
3. Help plan an appropriate outfit to wear.

Mathematics:
Students will be "paid" for one week of work. They will receive a paycheck and "cash" it to spend at the team auction. The following "overtime" activities are options:
1. Interview an individual who has a formal job and fill out the interview sheet.
2. Discuss a paycheck with deductions, balancing a checking account, paying monthly bills, and/or filing income tax returns with you and return the attached form.

Your young adult is receiving instruction from us but hearing true-to-life experiences from you will make this unit much more meaningful.

Gloria Fairchild & Nancy Kuhlmann

- Students evaluate their own performance in the job interview and reflect on what they learned through the experience. These thoughts become part of a business letter they write and send to the interviewer.

MATHEMATICS COMPONENT
- Students explore ways employees are paid: hourly wages, salary, commissions.

- They assume the role of payroll clerk, calculating the gross and net pay due to 10 fictional characters. To complete the payroll chart they must compute time-and-a-half and double-time, determine Social Security deductions, withdraw taxes and subtract voluntary options such as savings plans or United Way contributions. See pages 133-136 for lesson plan, worksheets and answer keys.

- Students receive a checkbook, donated by a local bank, and practice writing checks, entering the amounts and calculating balances. They also receive paychecks, endorse them and cash them at the Team Bank.

- In preparation for their first job, they fill out a W-4 form. They use sample W-2 forms to complete the 1040 EZ federal income tax form.

- They are hired for work for one week, receiving wages for the time they spend in math class. Job expectations are explained, accented with work-world anecdotes and in-school penalties. For instance, hourly workers are docked a portion of their pay if they punch in late. Tardy students find they are similarly docked.

- Team teachers have a cache of phony money for tips. They tip for errands they request of students, for kindnesses and pleasantries they observe, for tasks done beyond the call of duty. Tips are not given on demand but at the discretion of the teacher.

- Overtime pay is available for the following optional assignment: Completion of *A Working Interview* form shown on page 138.

- Paychecks, with itemized stubs, are completed by the teacher and distributed as soon after the end of the work week as possible. See page 137.

- Paychecks are cashed at the Team Bank during particular hours by trained student-tellers or fellow teachers.

- Cash is spent at the Team Store or at an auction, which wraps up the unit and invites students to bid for candy, soda and school supplies.

HOME

Job histories: Adult family members can share their employment history, explaining when they started working, how they moved from their first job to their present position and what character traits helped them to handle more responsibilities and advance in their careers.

Money management: Parents provide meaningful and practical knowledge as they share their budgeting and check-balancing procedures. They can explain the less visible expenses each month, such as utilities, insurance, mortgage, state and federal taxes, pension plans, college funds and home maintenance.

SCHOOL & DISTRICT

Schoolwide Career Festivals are a natural tie-in with this unit. Often spearheaded by parent volunteers, the prototype Career Day invites professionals from many different fields as guest lecturers. Students select the careers they are most interested in exploring, moving from one workshop to another throughout the day. The individual sessions focus on responsibilities, day-in-the-life details, average salary, career path and academic preparation. The guest presenters reinforce character strengths by associating particular traits with the job. A scientist is exactingly honest in her research. A social worker cooperates with agencies.

District: The business office of the Pattonville School District sponsors a Class Act Day in cooperation with a nearby mall. Workshops offer insights into attributes and abilities employers look for in applicants, common job responsibilities in retail positions and a behind-the-scenes look at store management.

COMMUNITY

In addition to staging interviews and speaking to students, professionals offer short-term, innovative introductions to the real world of work through "mentor for a day" or mini-internships. Consider Chambers of Commerce and Rotary and Lion's clubs as possible sources.

Community-wide career expositions or business fairs provide further resources. Bank representatives and tellers visit the class to explain various accounts. Tellers explain what their jobs involve, including education, training, people skills and character traits (kindness, respect and patience in dealing with customers, honesty and responsiblity for accurate balances).

SOURCE OF INSPIRATION

Gloria Fairchild and Nancy Kuhlmann, Holman Middle School, Pattonville School District

LESSON PLAN: THE ROLE OF THE PAYROLL CLERK

DAY 1

General information and some math problems based on various ways individuals are paid for work (see page 134):

by the hour	Problems #1, #2
by salary	Problem #3
by the job	Problem #4
commission	Problems #5, #6

DAY 2

Figuring hourly pay for the employees of Character, Inc., page 135. Answer key, page 136.

DAY 3

Figuring net pay given deductions and allocations specified by employees, page 135; Answer key, page 136. Option: Students can look up deductions given in the employer's tax booklets. These booklets are available from the Internal Revenue Service. Refer to the box below.

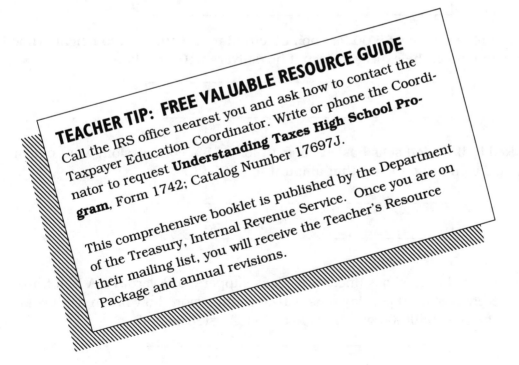

TEACHER TIP: FREE VALUABLE RESOURCE GUIDE

Call the IRS office nearest you and ask how to contact the Taxpayer Education Coordinator. Write or phone the Coordinator to request **Understanding Taxes High School Program,** Form 1742; Catalog Number 17697J.

This comprehensive booklet is published by the Department of the Treasury, Internal Revenue Service. Once you are on their mailing list, you will receive the Teacher's Resource Package and annual revisions.

Student's Name _____

WAYS TO PAY FOR WORK

Use the back of this page or a sheet of paper to calculate your answers and write them in the box below each question.

1. If Frank F. Urder works 40 hours at $8.25 per hour, what is his pay before deductions?

2. If Mary Q. Contrary works 28 hours at $10.55 per hour, what is her pay before deductions?

3. If the new teacher's salary is $24,000.00 per year and she receives a paycheck twice a month, what is the amount of gross pay for one pay period?

4. If Jack B. Nimble receives $5.00 for each 60 circulars he attaches to neighborhood doors, how much can he expect to earn if he delivers 210 circulars?

5. If Ms. L. Red Ridinghood sells baskets of fruit for a 15% commission, what can she expect to make on basket sales that amount to $205.00.

6. If Mr. Prince sells ladies shoes (including glass slippers) at Everday's A Ball Shoe Shop and receives $25.00 per day plus a 10% commission, how much will his pay be on a day he sells $500.00 worth of shoes to ugly stepsisters?

Character, Inc.   Payroll Clerk _____

Character, Inc. pays time-and-a-half for overtime (over 40 hours per week) and double time for all work on Sunday.

Problem #1: Figure the payroll for Character, Inc. for the following week.

NAME	M T W T F S S	TOTAL HRS	OVER TIME	SUN.	HOURLY WAGE ($)	TIME-and-a-HALF ($)	DOUBLE TIME ($)	TOTAL SALARY ($)
Mr. C	8 8 8 8 8 8 5							
Ms. H	8 8 8 8 8							
Mr. A	8 8 8 8 4 4							
Mr. R	8 8 8 8 8							
Mr. A	8 8							
Ms. C	4 4 5 5 4							
Ms. T	10 10 10 10 10 10 10							
Mr. E	10 8 8 6 8 10							
Ms. R	8 8 8							
Dr. S	5 6 5 7 6 4							

Problem #2: Now, figure the take-home pay for each employee.

EMPLOYEE	GROSS PAY ($)	WITHOLDING ALLOWANCES	FEDERAl ($) INCOME TAX	STATE ($) INCOME TAX	FICA ($) Social Security	OTHER DEDUCTIONS ($)	NET PAY ($)
Mr. C		single 1				30% to United Way	
Ms. H		single 1				10% to stock	
Mr. A		single 0				$50 car payment	
Mr. R		single 1				$25 voice lessons	
Mr. A		single 1				3% to savings	
Ms. C		single 1				5% to medical	
Ms. T		singe 1				15% to stock	
Mr. E		single 1				$20 weight loss center	
Ms. R		single 1				0	
Dr. S		single 1				8% to stock	

Character, Inc.   Payroll Clerk _____

Character, Inc. pays time-and-a-half for overtime (over 40 hours per week) and double time for all work on Sunday.

Problem # 1: Figure the pay for Character, Inc. for the following week.

NAME	M T W T F S	TOTAL HRS	OVER TIME	SUN.	HOURLY WAGE ($)	TIME-and-a-HALF ($)	DOUBLE TIME ($)	TOTAL SALARY ($)
Mr. C	8 8 8 8 8 5	40	8	5	4.50	6.75	9.00	180 + 54 + 45 = 279
Ms. H	8 8 8 8	40	0	0	5.00	7.50	10.00	200 + 0 + 0 = 200
Mr.	8 8 8 8 4 4	40	0	0	5.00	7.50	10.00	200 + 0 + 0 = 200
Mr. R	8 8 8 8 8	32	0	8	4.50	6.75	9.00	144 + 0 + 72 = 216
Mr. A	8 8 8	8	0	8	7.50	11.25	15.00	60 + 0 + 120= 180
Ms. C	4 4 5 5 4	22	0	0	7.50	11.25	15.00	165 + 0 + 0 = 165
Ms. T	10 10 10 10 10 10 10	40	20	10	8.00	12.00	16.00	320+ 240 +160= 720
Mr. E	10 8 8 6 8 10	40	10	0	10.00	15.00	20.00	400 + 150 + 0 = 550
Ms. R	8 8 8	24	0	0	6.00	9.00	12.00	144 + 0 + 0 = 144
Dr. S	5 6 5 7 6 4	29	0	4	7.00	10.50	14.00	203 + 0 + 56 = 259

Problem #2: Now, figure the take-home pay for each employee.

EMPLOYEE	GROSS PAY ($)	WITHOLDING ALLOWANCES	FEDERAl ($) INCOME TAX	STATE ($) INCOME TAX	FICA ($) Social Security	OTHER DEDUCTIONS ($)	NET PAY ($)
Mr. C	279	single 1	27	5	21.34	30% to United Way 83.70	141.96
Ms. H	200	single 1	16	2	15.30	10% to stock $20.00	146.70
Mr. A	200	single 0	23	3	15.30	$50 car payment	108.70
Mr. R	216	single 1	18	2	16.52	$25 voice lessons	154.48
Mr. A	180	single 1	13	1	13.77	3% to savings 5.40	146.83
Ms. C	165	single 1	11	1	12.62	5% to medical 8.25	132.13
Ms. T	720	single 1	130	80	55.08	15% to stock 108.00	346.92
Mr. E	650	single 1	110	69	49.73	$20 weight loss center	401..27
Ms. R	144	single 1	7	1	11.02	0	124.98
Dr. S	259	single 1	24	4	19.81	8% to stock 20.72	190.47

These templates are developed to simulate the experience of earning wages. The payroll stub is used to record student "earnings" based on the terms developed for the unit. Refer to the "Mathmatics Component" on page 131.

SENSE-ABILITY, INC.
2243 EQUATION DRIVE
MATH, MS 78201

_____ 19___

No._____
80-361
810

PAY TO THE
ORDER OF _____ $ _____

_____ DOLLARS

SO SAFE BANK & TRUST

⑆06 1003 615⑆   1

PAYROLL CHECK

DAY	DATE	PAY	OVERTIME	FINES
TOTALS				
Gross Pay	**FICA**	**State Tax**	**Federal Tax**	**Net Pay**

PAYROLL STUB

Student's Name _____

A WORKING INTERVIEW

Interview any individual (a parent, sister, brother, neighbor, etc.) who has a job. You will receive extra credit on your grade and overtime on your paycheck for completion of this form. Answer questions 1, 2 and 3 on a separate sheet of paper.

Name of Person Interviewed: _____

Job: _____ Company: _____

How many hours per week does this person work? _____

How often does this person get a paycheck? _____

What deductions are taken out of the paycheck? _____

How is this person paid? If the interviewee is not comfortable with sharing the actual dollar figures, simply check the appopriate boxes.

☐ **By the hour**   pay per hour $_____

☐ **By the job**   give an example of a job_____

     approximate pay for job $_____

☐ **Salaried**   annual salary $_____

☐ **Commission**   salary before commission $_____

     commission percentage _____%

     number of expected sales per (week, month, year) _____

1. What does this person like about his/her job?
2. What does this person dislike about his/her job?
3. What advice does this person have for you as an individual preparing for the job market?

Signature of person interviewed: _____

Date:_____

CREATING MEANING
WITH AN INTERACTIVE DICTIONARY

Students learn to work with HyperStudio® as they define and explore a particular character trait. They also become instructors, teaching elementary students how to access the information from the computer. They model many of the traits they have defined as they work one-on-one with a younger partner.

OBJECTIVES

1. Promote the character traits of **caring, commitment, compassion, confidence, cooperation, goal-setting, honesty, initiative, kindness, patience, perseverance, reliability, respect, responsibility, self-discipline, service** and **sharing.**

2. Teach computer skills associated with HyperStudio®.

3. Relate character traits to personal actions and decisions.

4. Strengthen writing skills.

5. Cast students as instructors and models as they teach younger students to look up character definitions through the computer.

DESCRIPTION

Students individually complete the following tasks and their entries are combined with others to create an interactive dictionary. They
- define a particular trait
- use computer drawing tools to illustrate it
- write a 3-paragraph essay about the trait
- include an experience that demonstrates the trait in action
- write a brief biography "About the Author"
- import a photograph of themselves if Apple Quick Take camera equipment is available

GRADES
6 - 8

FORMAT
Computer lab

DISCIPLINES
Art
Computer
Language arts

TIME
Ten 45-minute sessions

MATERIALS NEEDED
HyperStudio®

Working with HyperStudio® they learn how to:
- design pages, called *cards,* which appear sequentially in *stacks*
- add *buttons* to move forward and backward among the cards
- create transitions or *dissolves* from one card to the next
- link their stack to other stacks
- record their voice and add sound
- input text, select fonts and type size
- import clip art
- use drawing tools to create illustrations

TEACHING OTHERS

They also learn how to teach younger students to operate HyperStudio® and access the dictionary. As a class, students focus on skills that create effective learning environments:
- setting the stage
- communicating expectations
- creating a sense of safety
- providing unspoken and spoken permission to risk, to make mistakes

A guest speaker, perhaps an early elementary teacher, offers insight into the developmental learning abilities of younger children, an overview of curriculum standards for their age, the level of vocabulary that they understand, the approaches that work well. The speaker addresses the importance of careful listening, encouragement, kindness, positive feedback, patience, perseverance, reliability (being there when you say you will), strengthening self-esteem and respect for different learning styles and abilities. Refer to *S.T.A.R.S.* starting on page183 for more background on student mentor roles and teaching skills.

JUST LIKE PLAYING "FISH"
Have you played the card game "Go Fish?" When your partner doesn't have the card you ask for, he says, "Go Fish." Do you remember drawing a card from the deck to add to your hand? That's what we're doing here when we click on a *button.* The computer picks up the next card in the deck and puts it on the screen.

A guest speaker or classroom teacher talks about the importance of keeping the goal of the lesson in mind, and the willingness to try different approaches if one method does not succeed. The student-teachers, as a class or in small groups, brainstorm methods they can use: explanation, demonstration, example (they do it and ask student to follow their example), practice (allowing student to try a procedure several times), questions and answers, analogies, props and memory aids. In these one-on-one relationships, students often experience and express the traits they've defined: cooperation, discretion, honesty, patience and reliability.

The younger students, when fully trained, are able to perform the following tasks:
- open the HyperStudio® program
- select the appropriate "stack" for the Character Education Dictionary
- select a character trait from the directory
- read the definition of the character trait
- activate sound to hear the definition
- identify and activate the button to move to the next card in stack

HOME

A "Character Card Party" brings parents together with their student in the computer lab for an evening. Students instruct their parents in how to access the program, drawing on the abilities they refined in teaching younger students.

SCHOOL & DISTRICT

If the computers in the school building or district are networked, the dictionary can be used by students and teachers in other classrooms or sites within their district. As younger students learn to use HyperStudio® they can add anecdotal stories about a specific character trait they have experienced on new cards as an appendix to the dictionary.

COMMUNITY

As students become skilled at working with HyperStudio®, they explore possibilities of sharing their dictionary on the World Wide Web or in libraries and other schools where students and teachers beyond their district might access their work. A letter or telephone call to Roger Wagner Publishing, Inc. describing the use of HyperStudio® for this character education project might well get a response.

Roger Wagner Publishing, Inc.
1-800-497-3778
Web site: www.HyperStudio.com

COOPERATION
BEING ABLE TO WORK AND SOCIALIZE WITH OTHERS

SOURCE OF INSPIRATION

Barbara Hummel, Gotsch Intermediate School, Affton School District

MOVIE MATINEE

Movies project qualities, both positive and negative, onto the big screen. This unit strengthens students' ability to reflect upon and critique what they watch.

OBJECTIVES

1. Promote the character traits of **caring, cooperation, goal-setting, honesty, humanity, perseverance, respect, responsibility, self-esteem** and **service.**

2. Compare and contrast traits in the movie's primary characters.

3. Write a movie review.

DESCRIPTION

The Matinee, designed as part of a day of activities devoted to Character Education, can be adapted to a block-schedule or divided into segments for three class sessions.

STEP 1: IDENTIFYING TRAITS

Movies selected for their character education content are shown on video. Students work with the Movie Matinee handout on page 145 that includes a list of traits reinforced by the school. They identify traits exhibited by characters within the film and describe the actions involved. The Character Analysis grid on page 64 encourages a more in-depth evaluation of the traits. It can be used to compare and contrast several characters within one film or the protagonists from several similar films. This tool is a helpful exercise in preparing critiques or reviews.

STEP 2: WHAT GOES INTO A PROFESSIONAL REVIEW

Ask students to collect movie reviews from newspapers and magazines. Divide the class into teams. Ask each team to analyze two reviews, comparing and contrasting use of literary devices: sensory words, action verbs, analogies, metaphors, contrasts, quotes. Pay particular attention to how reviewers support their opinions. As a class, list the elements each group has discovered on the chalkboard. Develop a list of common features for reviews.

GRADES
6 - 8

FORMAT
Classroom
Special activity

DISCIPLINES
Language arts

TIME
Variable 3 to 6
class sessions

**MATERIALS
INCLUDED**
Movie Matinee

**MATERIALS
NEEDED**
VCR/TV unit
Video of choice

STEP 3: WRITE A MOVIE REVIEW

Help students decide the movie and the intent of their review. Do they want to encourage others to see the movie or are they telling the readers that this movie is not worth watching? Once they focus on the message they want to convey, the following points offer elements students should consider as they write:

- Provide a brief description of the story line, the setting and the plot. It is important, however, that not too much of the story is revealed, especially if the intent is to stimulate the reader's desire to see the movie.

- Identify key characters and their traits. How are the characters developed? Suggest both their physical appearance and their actions. Again, do not give away any surprises in the story.

- Access the movie's credibility. If the plot is meant to be believable, does it meet that criteria? If, on the other hand, it is fantasy, does it engage the viewers' imaginations?

- Communicate the reviewer's opinion of the movie. How effective is the movie as a vehicle for understanding characters, their traits and their behaviors?

- Support the reviewer's opinion using examples from scenes in the film, quotes and comparisons to similar films or characters.

HOME

Television dramas, situation comedies and movies can launch conversations about specific character traits, decision-making, consequences, values, ethical dilemmas and resolutions. Parents can turn television viewing into something other than a passive experience by asking questions that get their children to think about what they are seeing. What would you feel like if someone did that to you? Do you agree with what he did? Did she have any other options? Who was the responsible one in that situation? How did his daughter know that he cared for her? What would you say to that guy if you could talk to him face to face?

COMMUNITY

Invite a professional reviewer to speak to the class about the nature of the job: its benefits and disadvantages; the skills, educational background, interests and talents needed; the informal "code of ethics" followed; and ethical dilemmas the reviewer has faced and resolved.

SOURCE OF INSPIRATION

Connie Sullivan, Cross Keys Middle School, Ferguson-Florissant School District

Movie Matinee

While watching the movie, name the characters who exhibited the following character traits and a word or phrase that suggests how they did this.

RESPECT _____

_____

RESPONSIBILITY _____

_____

GOAL-SETTING _____

_____

SERVICE & CARING _____

_____

COOPERATION _____

_____

HUMANITY _____

_____

PERSEVERANCE _____

_____

HONESTY _____

_____

SELF-ESTEEM _____

_____

OTHER _____

CHARACTER EDUCATION
COMMERCIALS

Radio commercials, written and produced by students, air over the school P.A. system throughout the school year.

OBJECTIVES

1. Promote an awareness and understanding of all the character traits emphasized by the school or district.

2. Demonstrate **commitment, cooperation** and **goal-setting** in developing the commercials.

3. Strengthen critical and reflective thinking.

4. Involve students in scripting and producing a radio commercial.

DESCRIPTION

Lesson 1: As a class, listen to a series of current radio commercials that have been recorded by the teacher. Students note the message of the commercials and then categorize them by motive (those that provide information; increase interest or desire; or urge a purchase, a change in behavior or other specific action). In a discussion led by the teacher, they identify underlying messages. (i.e., this product will impress your peers, make your life easy, make you look good, feel confident, get better grades or earn more money.)

Students analyze the ads both for what they say and what they do not say. They look for correlations between the character traits reinforced by the school and the attitudes or promises reflected in commercials. For instance, an advertisement may claim to improve student's grades because of the attention of qualified learning specialists, without mentioning the contribution of students' determination, commitment and perseverance. A sports car commercial may boast an affordable price—only $400 per month—without explaining how many months one will have to pay or how much interest is added to the cost of the car because of partial payments. Responsible individuals commit to such a plan only if they know they can follow through with all payments.

GRADES
6 - 8

FORMAT
Classroom and extracurricular

DISCIPLINES
Language arts

TIME
4 to 5 class sessions
1 day for recording

MATERIALS NEEDED
Tapes
Music or sound effects
4-track tape recorder
Access to recording studio or equipment

TEACHER TIP
Invite advertising, radio or communications professionals as guest speakers during this phase.

Lesson 2: Explain the making of a good radio commercial: market research, audience definition, creative copy, talent, execution, sound production, placement and air time. Focus on the considerations for copy development: audience awareness, a clearly defined message, time limits.

Lesson 3: Review the character traits reinforced by the school community. Divide students into cooperative groups of four or five and ask each group to select a trait to advertise, such as caring, commitment, cooperation, goal-setting, honesty, initiative, perseverance, respect, responsibility or service. Encourage variety in their selections so that many different traits are represented in the resulting commercials.

Lesson 4: Review key aspects of a good radio commercial. Return students to their small groups to brainstorm ideas for a short commercial, focus on one concept, compose copy and plan for additional effects they may want, such as music and sound effects.

Lesson 5: Each group practices the delivery of the commercial and performs it before the class. Given some advanced guidelines, the audience makes suggestions or comments that might enhance each group's efforts. Respect for others is expressed in feedback that is presented constructively.

Production: This aspect depends upon the availability of experienced sound and production technicians. They might be found among members of the school or district staff, parents or area professionals willing to serve as partners in this educational project. Optimally, all groups are able to record their commercials. If time does not allow such inclusion, consider a class vote on the top three commercials or select eligible groups by drawing straws. The groups are scheduled for specific recording appointments which may take place over several days.

Airing: The commercials are reproduced on tape cassettes and played over the school P.A. system on a regular basis.

It is wise to start small with this unit, testing it with a language arts class or a group of interested students as an after-school activity. With enough production help and careful organization, it can expand to a team project or involve the entire school. Students representing different grade levels can be combined in creative groups to script and produce commercials. A schoolwide contest can focus attention and stimulate participation in the project. Students can vote to determine the most popular commercials. Faculty members or representatives of the community can serve as judges, selecting the most creative script, most dramatic use of sound, best voice quality and best all-around commercial.

SCHOOL & DISTRICT

The commercials can be duplicated and shared with other schools in the district. They can also be shared with the district administrative staff and members of the school board. Students who create the commercials can speak to the influence of character education as they explain the meaning of their creative work and learning experience.

HOME

The commercials can be recorded on a single audio tape and made available or sold as a fund-raiser to parents for home listening and discussion. Students can also demonstrate how to critique radio and TV commercials, categorizing them by their motive (those that urge a purchase, a change in behavior, action for the good of others), and recognizing underlying messages (this will impress your peers, make your life easy, make you look good). They can discuss with family members the pluses and minuses of the commercial based on the students' learning from this unit.

COMMUNITY

Students can visit a professional sound studio and watch the process involved in mixing tracks and developing tapes. They can work with the studio personnel to produce their tapes. A local radio station might use the commercials on occasion and feature some of the students talking about the traits and their work on this project.

SOURCE OF INSPIRATION

Karen Jansen, Gotsch Intermediate School, Affton School District

Character in Motion

Total physical response (TPR) activities involve action and imagination, catalysts in the mastery of new material. They energize a class by interrupting long periods of seat-work with physical movement. They also elicit cooperation and communication between students.

OBJECTIVES

1. Reinforce the character traits of **cooperation, initiative, self-control** and **self-discipline.**

2. Review simple machines and potential and kinetic energy.

DESCRIPTION

The principle of using body movement to reinforce learning can be applied to any academic subject. The following activities complement lessons in physical science.

PREPARATION
Create a prop box, collecting poster board, paper, rope, tennis balls, marbles and streamers (paper, cloth or plastic strips). Cut slips of paper, enough to equal half the number of students in the class. Write the name of a simple machine on each slip, rotating through the six simple machines and repeating them as necessary to fill all the slips of paper. Fold the slips and place them in a container.

ACTIVITY: SIMPLE MACHINES
This activity is introduced after simple machines have been defined and identified as part of students' science curriculum.
- Pair students with partners. Ask one person from each pair to select a slip of paper from the container. Explain that they are to represent the simple machine noted on the paper by using part or all of their body. For instance, an inclined plane can be represented by extending one leg at an angle to the floor and locking the knee to create a straight line. One student forms the posture while the partner rolls a tennis ball down the leg. They switch positions and repeat the exercise.

tennis ball
leg
floor

GRADES
6 - 8

FORMAT
Classroom

DISCIPLINES
Physical science

TIME
30 minutes
for each exercise

MATERIALS INCLUDED
Reflections

MATERIALS NEEDED
Streamers
Markers, paper
Poster board
Marbles, balls

- Give students 10 to 15 minutes to brainstorm possible responses. Invite them to check out the prop box and to find space within the room that allows them to experiment with different movements and postures. Encourage them to combine imagination and critical thinking and, at the same time, use self-discipline in controlling the volume as they brainstorm with their partner.

- Rotate the pairs to "center stage," an area easily visible to the class. As the pair demonstrates a simple machine, class members call out the name of it.

- Following are three of many examples for simulating simple machines:

  Screw: Stand straight, place both hands on top of head and extend elbows out to each side to create top of the screw. Turn slowly in place or wrap streamers around body to represent the turns of the screw.

  Lever: Place a book on the floor. Slip toes underneath the edge of the book. Lift foot slowly, keeping heel on the ground and raising the edge of the book.

  Pulley: One person stands facing the audience with hands formed into fists, extending them in front at different heights. The partner anchors one end of the rope to an object next to the individual and threads the rope under one fist and over the other to simulate this design.

LEVER
INCLINED PLANE
WHEEL & AXLE
WEDGE
SCREW
PULLEY

ACTIVITY: POTENTIAL AND KINETIC ENERGY

Swing: Students work with a partner to identify four points of a baseball swing:
- bat over the shoulder ready to swing
- bat extended and parallel with plate
- bat at moment of impact with the ball
- bat in full follow-through position

They determine signals or movements that will symbolize the following:
- greater kinetic energy (hop, move a flag),
- greater potential energy (lie down, stand still), and
- equilibrium (hands raised over head).

One student swings a plastic bat in slow motion, stopping at each of the four points. The partner defines the energy by using one of the three signals above.

$$K.E. = \frac{MASS \times VELOCITY^2}{2}$$

The Formula: Form groups of eight. Give students a reasonable time to determine how they will represent the formula for kinetic energy, using body posture, movement and supplies from the prop box. For example, students might form the letters "K" and "E" in body postures, use a label to indicate mass and move streamers to represent velocity. Ask the students to enact or represent what happens to the level of kinetic energy when velocity is increased. What happens when the mass is doubled?

HOME

The principle of total physical response (TPR) can be used as a memory aide. It is especially helpful for students who favor what author Howard Gardner describes in *Frames of Mind* as a body/kinesthetic intelligence. Formulas in math, physics and chemistry can be "embodied," similar to the example for kinetic energy. The Periodic Table can be memorized by forming the letters of the chemical symbols associated with each element in the sequence in which they appear. Vocabulary reviews can be enlivened with an adaptation of the game of Simon Says. The parent generates a movement or posture and calls out one of the vocabulary words. The student imitates the physical movement and spells the word. If spelled correctly, the parent progresses to the next word. If not, the parent reviews the correct spelling, repeats the same motion and calls out the word so the child can repeat the exercise.

COMMUNITY

Invite gymnastic or acrobatic instructors to give a demonstration of difficult moves. Ask students to identify the kinetic and potential energy states during certain phases of these moves. Explore other physical laws that affect gymnastics, such as gravity and inertia.

SOURCE OF INSPIRATION

Amy Richards, Kennerly Elementary School, Lindbergh School District

Reflections
ON THE WAY IT WAS

Your group was given a task and very few instructions on how to do it. Think about how your group came up with a plan of action. Identify people who contributed in the following ways and be sure to include yourself.

Idea-generator

_____

Organizer

_____

Detail Person (one who thinks about the details)

_____

Big Picture Person (one who sees how the pieces fit together)

_____

"Devil's Advocate" (one who tests the idea by asking challenging questions or raising negative consequences)

_____

Bias for Action (someone who wants to get things moving)

_____

Commander (someone who gives out assignments or orders to the others)

_____

Facilitator (one who makes things happen cooperatively, without orders)

_____

How was the experience? Enjoyable? Rushed? Confusing? Satisfying?

_____

HEALTHY EATING CREATES
HEALTHY SELF-ESTEEM

This unit spans several class periods. It requires an invitation to guest speakers, physicians or dietitians, and food intake journals for the students.

OBJECTIVES

1. Promote the character traits of **goal-setting, perseverance, responsibility, self-discipline** and **self-esteem**.

2. Promote an understanding of the connection between healthy eating and healthy self-esteem.

3. Learn the guidelines of healthy eating and develop new eating habits accordingly.

DESCRIPTION

Review the food groups and the essentials for a healthy diet. Invite a dietician to speak to students about nutritional needs, caloric awareness, questionable or dangerous diet plans, exercise and body image. Ask stuents to clip articles from fashion, family, medical, health or news magazines on bulimia and anorexia. Have them highlight or underline definitions, symptoms, suspected causes and treatments. As a class, develop a fact sheet on chart paper for each disorder, noting information as students provide it from their articles. Review the list of causes, identifying those that are related to low self-esteem and negative body image.

Arrange for a physician or therapist who has worked with victims of eating disorders to speak to students about the nature of the disease and how to identify risk factors and early signs. Following the presentation, divide students into cooperative groups. Ask them to review the information on eating disorders and discuss how it relates to them and their lives. Discussion should explore respect for their own health and responsibility to peers who may need help and support.

While still in groups, ask students to review their notes on good eating habits and daily food requirements. Provide them with journal sheets designed to monitor their daily food intake for three days.

GRADES
6 - 8

FORMAT
Classroom

DISCIPLINES
Family and consumer sciences
Health

TIME
Several class sessions

MATERIALS NEEDED
Food intake journals

Encourage students to write down *everything* they eat and the amounts. When completed, ask students to reflect on their records and set one or two goals that would improve their diet nutritionally. Again, provide each student with worksheets. This time they are to record what they eat and what they feel. After a specified time (two or three days), review the journals within a small-group context. Talk about the relationship of mood to self-discipline and self-control. Was it easier to stick to your goal when you felt excited? Accepted? Satisfied? Full? Angry? Tense? Anxious? Rested? Stressed? Ask students to share in groups their successes and their challenges. Help guide their discussion with such questions as: What did a day of success do for your self-esteem? What kind of "self talk" or character traits did you use when you wanted to quit and eat whatever you pleased? What did you do when you weren't able to reach your goal or stick to your plan? How did you persevere? Finally, ask students to talk about the difficulties of changing behavior and the connections between effort, success and self-esteem.

SCHOOL & DISTRICT

Students of the middle school can plan ways to reach younger students concerning healthy eating for healthy self-esteem and implement their plans with class visits, presentations, skits, posters and videos.

HOME

Students can share their food journals and reflections about their eating habits with their parents. Parents can also set personal goals to improve or enhance their eating habits and share their efforts. Family meal planning, shopping and cooking can become a joint effort. Students can assume responsibility for one meal during the week.

COMMUNITY

Students can visit fast-food restaurants and interview the managers about their companies' efforts to make their food healthier. They can research the agencies available to assist with an eating disorder and provide a list of contacts and phone numbers.

SOURCE OF INSPIRATION

Nancy Little, A.B. Green Middle School, Maplewood-Richmond Heights District

ADOPT-A-STUDENT

Marian Wright Edelman's book *The Measure of Our Success* provides guidance and inspiration for a school staff that reaches out to students in one-on-one relationships.

OBJECTIVES

1. Promote the character traits of **caring, commitment, cooperation, goal-setting, honesty, perseverance, respect, responsibility, service, self-discipline** and **self-esteem.**

2. Increase the leadership role of students, defuse inappropriate behavior and address academic problems.

3. Build self-esteem and a sense of belonging in students.

DESCRIPTION

School staff members, including administrators, teachers, aides, secretaries and others, volunteer to "adopt" two students throughout the year. The students, selected by the "adoptive parents," include all races, ethnic groups, and genders; they represent a wide range of grade point averages and involvement levels. Some students express their desire to make a difference in the school, some seek to change the negative image of young teenagers. Still others want to serve as role models. Some students are chosen because their choices or leadership styles are interfering with their school performance. They may feel distanced or disconnected from other students and the school as a whole.

The "adoptive parents" use *The Measure of Our Success* as a source of guidance as they develop their own plan of action to build a caring relationship with their students. Many meet their students for lunch, check in with them during the day or plan occasional activities outside of school, such as bowling, in-line skating or park visits. They talk over successes, goals, problems, disappointments and concerns. Often they bring their adopted students together to share their feelings with one another. They might set up tutoring, discuss lifestyles, share likes and dislikes or compare reactions to an event, TV show or film.

GRADES
6 - 8

FORMATS
Schoolwide

SKILL
Listening
Trust-building

TIME
Intervals
throughout
school year

MATERIALS NEEDED
The Measure of Our Success
by Marian Wright Edelman, Beacon Press, 1992

The program includes a few formal activities throughout the year. An initial kickoff meeting involves parents and friends. The concepts and the goals of the program are explained. Character traits are introduced and defined. A group lunch brings "adoptive parents" together with their students before each upcoming quarter to focus on grades, goals and how to meet the challenges of the quarter ahead. A year-end event—a picnic, dinner or special field trip—provides closure and an opportunity to express appreciation.

The program at Brittany Woods, now more than five years old, has been so successful that incoming seventh graders ask how they can be adopted. Because the demand to be involved is greater than logistics allow, the program keeps a low profile. There are no identifying T-shirts, no extravagant activities for the entire group. The program has had positive effects in the following ways:
- building self-esteem and creating a strong sense of connectedness
- sensitizing students to the feelings and perspectives of others
- improving academic performance
- resolving conflict
- building healthy relationships between peers
- improving interpersonal relationships
- strengthening the parent/school connection
- understanding individual differences
- defusing behavior problems
- communicating and practicing the character traits

HOME

Parents are involved early in this program and are asked to communicate with the "adoptive parents" about any special activities, accomplishments, difficulties or challenges in the student's life. The character traits are explained and defined at the kickoff event and parents are encouraged to reinforce them in home situations throughout the year.

COMMUNITY

Develop an advisory board, including members of the community who can contribute insights, support, effective problem-solving and resources. For example, invite social workers, counselors, attorneys or youth advocates familiar with the court system. Consider representatives from the Y.M.C.A., AmeriCorps (National Service Corp), Boys Scouts of America, Girl Scouts of America, Chamber of Commerce and Rotary and Kiwanis clubs.

SOURCE OF INSPIRATION

Brenda Pierce, Brittany Woods Middle School, University City School District, adapted a program originally developed by National Education Association.

P.R.I.D.E.

PEOPLE RESPONSIBLY INVOLVED, DEVELOPING EXCELLENCE

This reward program affirms students who usually are unrecognized by traditional award systems.

OBJECTIVES

1. Promote the character traits of **caring, commitment, cooperation, goal-setting, honesty, perseverance, respect, responsibility, self-discipline** and **service.**

2. Create a school climate of good citizenship and the recognition of students' efforts to be responsibly involved in the life of the school.

3. Expand the eligibility for awards beyond such traditional categories as high academic achievement, sports participation and student council.

DESCRIPTION

P.R.I.D.E. is a schoolwide program, offering opportunities for *all* students to be recognized award winners. Sponsored by the school staff and the PTA, it awards points for a broad range of student activities and behaviors that exhibit character traits. These points become the basis for earning tangible awards given at a reception held every spring. Students must apply to participate in the program. The enrollment application and subsequent P.R.I.D.E. record sheets become the student's responsibility. They must obtain a teacher's signature for each qualifying activity, record the points, and meet the program's deadlines for completing the paper work. Points can be earned for such actions or behaviors as:

- Acquiring no office referrals during the quarter (50 points)
- Achieving perfect attendance during the quarter (50 points)
- Participation in school-sponsored activities and groups, e.g., student council, clubs, sports, gym games, spectator at sport events and pep rallies, dressing up for spirit day (10-15 points for each action)
- Points for grades: A: 10 points   B: 10 points   C: 5 points

Awards are based on the total points accumulated. There are four levels:

Member	400 points	Magna Cum Laude	1200 points
Member Cum Laude	800 points	Summa Cum Laude	1600 points

GRADES
6 - 8

FORMAT
Schoolwide

SKILLS
Goal-setting
Leadership

TIME
2-hour assembly

MATERIALS NEEDED
Application forms
Record sheets
Award ribbons or certificates

Certain awards are given at each level. Certificates and P.R.I.D.E. buttons indicate the level each student achieves and the traits that contributed to that achievement. Such items as notebooks, bookmarks, pencils and bumper stickers are available to all students. Each student who has qualified is recognized at the annual spring reception. Guest speakers include community leaders.

This program attracts more than 40% of the 800-member student body at Hoech Middle School in the Ritenour School District. The spring reception has drawn as many as 900 family members and friends. One father noted after the award reception that his son, a sixth-grader who was reading at the fourth-grade level, had received the highest award. It was the first time he had ever been publicly recognized for his positive contributions.

SCHOOL & DISTRICT

The program is designed to involve the classroom as part of the total school climate. It is in the classroom that students learn about and discuss the character traits. Teachers create point-earning opportunities, assigning points for activities that exhibit the use of a particular trait. For instance, timely response to a specific project deadline earns 20 points and recognizes the students' goal-setting abilities and commitment. Districtwide recognition of these P.R.I.D.E.-winning students and of the character education program itself can occur in the district newsletter or at a school board meeting.

HOME

Family members can be a part of the program and help their child earn points by becoming involved in school activities. Attending sports events, joining PTA, attending PTA meetings and volunteering to help with schoolwide projects earn points for the student and create a closer partnership between the school and the home.

COMMUNITY

Students can earn points for participation in community service projects designed and coordinated by community groups in partnership with the school. Community leaders can become involved in the presentation of the awards and can be made aware of the traits that support these students' behaviors. The local media can feature the program and the students with an emphasis on the character education efforts.

SOURCE OF INSPIRATION
Connie Burkhardt, Hoech Middle School, Ritenour School District

HIGH SCHOOL LEVEL
GRADES 9-12

Evaluating Character Education in Grades 9 - 12

Do your lessons help students understand the meaning and importance of good character? Can students go beyond basic understanding and apply what they have learned to their own lives? How do you know? Here are a few hints for evaluating the effects of your character education lessons on student learning and behavior. (Also see hints for evaluating middle school lessons on page 98.)

Have students keep a daily or weekly journal on the importance of having good character, character development objectives and ways in which behaving with good character (or not) has affected their daily lives. (Understanding)

Have students discuss ethical dilemmas and identify alternative courses of action and their potential consequences. (Understanding)

Have students develop and share essays, poems, short stories or dramatic presentations on character-related themes. (Understanding)

Have students make presentations to local community service clubs on the role of character in being a good citizen. (Understanding)

Have students debrief a video or movie illustrating positive and/or negative character traits. (Understanding)

Have students dramatize historical events illustrating conflict and show how the outcome might have been different if the parties involved had shown more respect for one another. (Understanding)

Have students conduct a schoolwide survey of students regarding their perceptions of the school climate, and use the results to plan action strategies for addressing negative findings. (Understanding/Application)

Have students conduct formal debates on the pros and cons of a controversial character-related issue, such as drug use. (Understanding/Application)

Divide the class into several teams and have students engage in team problem- solving to develop a solution to a school or community problem. (Understanding/Application)

Have students plan and teach character-related lessons to younger children. (Understanding/Application)

Have students write letters to the editor of a local newspaper in response to character-related articles that have appeared in the paper. (Understanding/Application)

Have students organize a schoolwide conference on the importance of good character, bringing in speakers who reflect a variety of positive character traits. (Understanding/Application)

BUILDING DECISION SKILLS

Your friend pulls a prank and damages school property. The principal asks you what happened. What will you say? This dilemma pits truth against loyalty, bringing two positive values into conflict. An interactive curriculum created by the Institute for Global Ethics equips students with a decision-making process that helps them resolve "right versus right" dilemmas.

OBJECTIVES

1. Promote the identification of character traits through a values-definition process and strengthen **decision-making** skills.

2. Develop an awareness and language for discussing ethical issues.

3. Strengthen reasoning, verbal and written skills.

DESCRIPTION

Sandy Jacoby piloted the Institute's series as a unit in her elective Community Service class. She modified the curriculum's lesson plans to structure a week of class sessions and a foundation for brief, once-a-week discussions of ethical dilemmas. She presents the material to her students as *one way* to approach ethical decisions.

CLASS 1: VIDEO & DISCUSSION
A 28-minute video, *Personal Ethics and the Future of the World,* introduces ethical dilemmas that surface in public disasters—the Exxon Valdez oil spill and the Chernobyl nuclear plant—and personal choices. The message that ethical dilemmas are the "stuff of life" becomes the springboard for discussion as a class and in small groups.

CLASS 2: THE ETHICAL BAROMETER
Use the materials included on pages 167-170 to support the following tasks:
- Share examples of statistics concerning ethical behaviors.
- Introduce the concept of an ethical barometer.
- Divide students into teams. Ask them to discuss the questions on page 170. A recorder summarizes the group's responses on the worksheet.
- As a class, identify similarities, tangents and contrasts between the group reports.

GRADES
9 - 12

FORMAT
Classroom
Extracurricular

DISCIPLINES
Language arts
Social studies

TIME
Five to 10
class periods

**MATERIALS
INCLUDED**
Synopsis of Lessons
Survey Statistics
Ethical Barometer
Exercise & Worksheet

Homework: Scan media reports (TV news, magazines, papers) for examples of ethical dilemmas. Where are people, companies and organizations making the right decisions? Identify those with a clear right and wrong dimension. Identify those with right versus right issues.

CLASS 3: VALUES AND ATTRIBUTES OF AN ETHICAL PERSON

- What are moral and ethical values? (Define and discuss)
- Are there shared values upon which we can all agree? Explain the ground rules of brainstorming and consensus-building. Recognize the respect for others inherent in these processes.
- Ask each individual to develop a list of eight attributes that they associate with an ethical person. Create a class list by recording each person's list on the chalkboard, removing duplicates. Expect a list of 50 to 60 attributes.
- Break into teams and develop consensus on the top eight traits. Report these back to the class.
- Use consensus as a class to establish a final list of four to five traits.
- Compare this list with the handout of global values based on the book, *Shared Values for a Troubled World.*

CLASS 4: IDENTIFYING A RIGHT VERSUS RIGHT CONFLICTS

- What distinguishes a right versus wrong dilemma from a right versus right one?
- Read Robert Frost's poem, "The Road Not Taken." Is this a case of right versus right? Why is each choice right?
- Provide other common examples of right versus right conflicts. Introduce the four right versus right paradigms: truth versus loyalty, justice versus mercy, short-term versus long-term, self versus community.
- In teams, generate two right versus right dilemmas. Discuss these as a class. Identify what makes them right versus right and which of the four paradigms they represent.

CLASS 5: MORE THAN ONE RIGHT ANSWER

- Define ends-based, rules-based and care-based approaches.
- As a class, work through a suggested dilemma, applying each approach.
- Divide into teams. Assign each team a particular approach: Team A will apply the ends-based approach, Team B the rules-based approach.
- Report back to the class. Ask each team to report its approach and the resolution it developed. Compare the differences in resolutions to the same dilemma.
- A quiz reinforces the material and provides closure to the week.

SCHOOL & DISTRICT

Class members can script and role play the resolution of an ethical dilemma for presentation to another class or as part of a school assembly or rally. The curriculum includes an exercise in developing a code of ethics. Class members could facilitate this process with the student body or a representative group, such as Student Council or the *Character Councils* described on pages 235-238. Such a code could be posted prominently within the school.

HOME

Two or three parent volunteers, working with the teacher and the curriculum guide in advance, can develop an evening workshop for parents that introduces the concepts their students will be studying. This may alleviate anxiety and suspicion that the teacher advocates one set of values over another or is grading students on the moral "rightness" of their answers. It equips parents with *one way* to initiate and continue a dialogue with their child about ethical values and decisions. The workshop should present a condensed version of the lessons, including definitions, discussion questions, take-home packets of reading material and experience (individually or in small groups) in identifying dilemmas and applying the three approaches.

COMMUNITY

Volunteers from local businesses can reinforce student learning by sharing a specific right vs. right dilemma from their field of work. They can serve as table leaders and facilitate the discussion of a small group or the entire class. See *Ethical Decision-Making in the Workplace & Society* starting on page 215 for more detailed ways to involve the professional, entrepreneurial and industrial community.

BUILDING DECISION SKILLS
The training seminar, 211-page curriculum and support materials are available from:
The Institute for Global Ethics
P.O. Box 563 • Camden, MA 04843
(800) 729-2615 • fax: (207) 236-4014
Web Site: global ethics.org

SOURCE OF INSPIRATION
Sandy Jacoby, Marquette High School, Rockwood School District

SYNOPSIS OF LESSONS

LESSON 1: ETHICS IN AMERICA: HOW ARE WE DOING?
What is our nation's ethical barometer doing? Is it rising or falling? Are things getting better or are they getting worse and why? What do we as citizens need to do about it?

LESSON 2: THERE'S ONLY ETHICS
How will technology in the 21st century magnify the importance of ethical behavior? Why is personal responsibility more important now than ever before? What do we mean by "ethical relativism" and "obedience to the unenforceable"?

LESSON 3: DEFINING SHARED VALUES
Ethical values are different from other kinds of values, such as economic values or artistic values. How are they different? What are codes of ethics and what function do they play in bringing groups of people together?

LESSON 4: BUILDING A CODE OF ETHICS
Is there a core of shared ethical values on which our class can agree? The process described in this lesson will take the class through a series of steps to build the group's own code of ethics.

LESSON 5: ACTING ON THE CODE
In what specific ways can we apply our code of ethics, personally and as a class? What kinds of behavior do people who are ethical (according to our code) exhibit?

LESSON 6: TESTING FOR RIGHT VERSUS WRONG
Sometimes making an ethical decision depends on a person's ability to understand the difference between right and wrong. If we are in touch with our ethical values, can this help us distinguish right from wrong? What other ways can we use to detect wrong?

LESSON 7: ANALYZING ETHICAL DILEMMAS
The most difficult ethical dilemmas occur when two of our core ethical values come into conflict. How do we know when we have a right-versus-right dilemma? What types of right-versus-right dilemmas can we observe?

LESSON 8: RESOLVING ETHICAL DILEMMAS
It is not enough simply to understand what kind of ethical problem we are facing. How can we approach identifying the higher right? What series of steps can lead us to a resolution?

LESSON 9: PRACTICING ETHICAL FITNESS
Ethical fitness is like physical fitness—it needs to be practiced to be learned. What real-life stories can we find to practice the analysis and resolution process we have just learned?

LESSON 10: MORAL COURAGE
It also is not enough simply to identify our ethical values. They need to be acted upon as well. What role does moral courage play in promoting ethical action? Why is moral courage important, even though it may be difficult? Looking at the world around us, what examples of moral courage can we observe?

THE ETHICAL BAROMETER EXERCISE

PURPOSE

- To develop an awareness of the ethical aspects of day-to-day events

- To begin to ask if ethics is any more important today than it was in earlier times

PREPARATION AND MATERIALS

Have available at least one flip chart, several markers and masking tape. Prepare copies of The Ethical Barometer handout and the Ethical Barometer Worksheet and distribute to students. Divide the class into groups of five or six students.

PROCESS

- Open the lesson by referring to some simple statistics on how people view the current state of our society's ethics (see Selected Survey Statistics handout).

- Then follow up on the homework assignment. Divide students into small groups or pairs and ask them to discuss the ethical content of each news story: What does each story have to do with ethics? Circulate among students and listen to their discussions.

- Introduce the concept of an ethical barometer, using The Ethical Barometer handout. Ask: What might we mean by an "ethical barometer"?

- Divide the class into small groups of five or six students, giving each student a copy of the Ethical Barometer Worksheet for their personal use. Advise students to take notes in preparation for completing the worksheet. Assign each group of students the task of coming up with a list of possible answers for each of the three questions. Allow 10 to 15 minutes for each question on the worksheet. Then, *either*:

  — Have each group list their answers, which will be discussed by the whole class, on flip-chart-sized paper taped on the wall, or

  — Solicit ideas from each group and record them on flip charts at the front of the room. Label three flip-chart pages as follows: "Ethical Barometer UP," "Ethical Barometer DOWN," and "What Each of Us Can Do."

- Finally, discuss the overarching question: Is our society's ethical barometer rising or falling? (Are people any different today than in the past? Are we just more aware of things now than we used to be? Is there anything about today that is significantly different from the past?)

- For homework, ask students to complete the Ethical Barometer Worksheet. Tell students these will be collected, but assure them that their responses will not be judged or graded. These papers will provide a valuable look at your students' scope in ethical thinking and may suggest ways to shape how you present the rest of the *Building Decision Skills* curriculum.

SELECTED SURVEY STATISTICS

THE GOOD NEWS

- More than 99 percent of the 7,700 readers surveyed in December 1994 want their children to have a firm set of values ("Teaching Values" in *Parents Magazine*, June *1995).*

- More than 90 percent of respondents to a 1994 Gallup Poll felt that a number of values are acceptable to teach in the classroom, including: respect for others, hard work, persistence, fairness, compassion, and civility (in *The* Christian *Science Monitor,* August 29, 1994).

- Students see the need for a new focus on values as well. In the 1996 annual survey of high achievers by *Who's Who Among American High School Students,* students identified "the decline of social and moral values" as today's greatest national crisis, as well as the biggest problem facing the teen generation (published by Educational Communications Inc., January 18,1996).

THE BAD NEWS

- In the same *Who's Who Among American High School Students* survey, three of four students admitted to having cheated. Ninety-four percent said they were never caught and five of six caught were not punished.

- In Phi Kappa Delta's 1994 "Study of Core Values" conducted by the Gallup Organization, 48 percent of students surveyed agreed that "in today's society, one has to lie or cheat in order to succeed."

- An October 1995 survey by *Reader's Digest* found that 8 out of 10 high-school students admitted to cheating; furthermore, they say that their teachers often make it easy.

THE ETHICAL BAROMETER

ETHICAL: Having to do with standards for right and wrong.

BAROMETER: 1) Instrument for measuring atmospheric pressure to forecast changes in weather. 2) Anything that indicates change.

ETHICAL BAROMETER: Instrument to indicate change in standards of right and wrong.

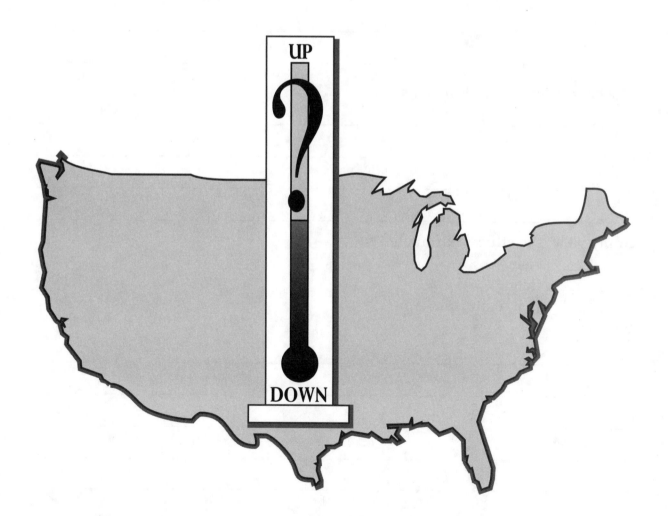

ETHICAL BAROMETER WORKSHEET

Is our society's ethical barometer rising or falling?

1) What evidence do we have that it is rising? (What are our sources of hope?)

_____

_____

_____

2) What evidence do we have that it is falling? (What are our greatest areas of concern?)

_____

_____

_____

_____

3) What can each of us do about it?

_____

_____

_____

_____

In my view, the ethical barometer is:

_____ rising
_____ falling
_____ just about the same

because

_____

_____

_____

_____

THE RIGHT INGREDIENTS

This unit uses a multidimensional approach to build ethical awareness *and* assertiveness. It models a process of contemplation and action, and empowers students with the belief that they can make a difference in the world.

OBJECTIVES

1. Promote the character traits of **compassion, confidence, goal-setting, honesty, respect, responsibility** and **self-discipline**.

2. Identify characteristics of these traits; recognize how they relate to personal meaningfulness and success.

3. Use technological support: video cameras and computers.

4. Research and articulate a well-reasoned response to the issue of teenage violence. Identify positive alternatives to violence. Express these responses in essays, journal entries and discussions.

DESCRIPTION

This project involves (1) a list of traits shown in "Recipe for Success" on the following page, and (2) an editorial on teenage violence on page 175. A news article, TV news clip or documentary that raises similar themes can be substituted. Themes raised in the article might include:

- personal loss
- tragedy
- unpredictability of violence
- assessing blame
- cost of violence at personal and community levels
- the roots of violence
- social conditions that contribute to violence
- connection between character traits, life experiences, feelings, thoughts, need to respond, desire to make a difference
- determining a meaningful personal response
- character traits: responsibility, respect (compassion for and value of the individual), honesty (about feelings), determination (to do something about it)

GRADES
10 - 12

FORMAT
Classroom

DISCIPLINES
Language arts
Social studies

TIME
3 class sessions

MATERIALS INCLUDED
Educators Cannot Ignore Values

EQUIPMENT
Video camera
Computer

Recipe for Success

1 C.   responsibility
1 C.   determination
1 C.   honesty
1 C.   teamwork
1 C.   abstinence
8 oz.   respect
8 oz.

HOW TO USE THESE TWO TOOLS

• *Define traits:* As a class, discuss and define the traits in "Recipe for Success." Brainstorm actions and behaviors that exemplify each trait. When have you expressed such actions or behaviors? How? When have you been affected by someone who chose to [chose *not* to] express one of these traits. What were the consequences of these choices?

• Pass out copies of "*Educators Cannot Ignore Values.*" (An appropriate news article may be substituted.) Read the article together in class. Invite different students to read portions of it aloud.

• *Check for understanding:* Ask students to respond to the article. What happened? How were the five youths involved? How were they affected? How was Myrod involved? What happened to him? What happened to his family? His community? What did his sister decide to do? Why do you think she wrote this editorial?

• *Guided practice:* Discuss the conditions and possible scenarios. What would you imagine the five youths were experiencing? What were they thinking? Do you think they all agreed with what was happening? Do you think they thought through what they were choosing? Did they have any alternatives? What if one of the five had protested before the violence began? What if he tried to leave or threatened to tell? Discuss individual conscience versus group pressure. Offer one alternative. Invite students to brainstorm other options either as a class or in smaller groups. Together, develop a list of realistic, positive alternatives. Write these on the chalkboard or on newsprint. Discuss what students can do in their present role as informed members of the community who recognize the prevalence of random violence.

• *Independent practice:* Assign a one-page essay asking students to reflect and respond individually to the article, focusing on one or more of these aspects:
  • feelings and experiences triggered by the article
  • traits from "Recipe for Success" that they find represented in the article
  • options and alternatives for the five youths
  • options and alternatives from which the author could choose from
  • options or actions students can exercise in their personal lives, among their peers and within their community

• *Cooperative group work:* Identify these four institutions: family, religion, school/education and community. Ask students if their alternatives (developed in the *Guided Practice* session and their essays) involve any of these institutions. Are there things these institutions could do? Brainstorm several ideas collectively and record them where everyone can see them.

- *Develop proposal for community action:* Divide students into self-selected *home groups* of four to six members to research and develop one of the ideas they've brainstormed. Explain the elements of a proposal to the entire class and give specific expectations for their Proposal for Community Action: page length, due date, etc.

  Elements of a proposal
    - purpose
    - reason for purpose
    - recommendations (actions, policies, programs)
    - benefits
    - conclusion

- *Jigsaw groups:* When the proposals are completed, the members of each home group are considered *experts* and are asked to present their research and recommendations to students outside their home group. This is done by creating *expert groups.* Each student in an existing home group counts off: 1, 2, 3, 4, 5. New groups are formed as all the "ones" come together, all the "twos" come together, and so on. Each expert group takes time to listen to and reflect upon each proposal, evaluating it for originality, thoroughness and practicality. The members estimate the time and resources needed to make it happen.

- *Closure*: Ask students to imagine presenting their proposal to the City Council. What would the headline read if it were covered in the newspaper? What would the body of the story report about the goals of the proposal and the time it would take to implement them?

- *Crosstalk closure:* Form students into one large circle to discuss what they have learned and express their feelings about the topic. The teacher acts as a facilitator. In another version of Crosstalk, the teacher starts a discussion by making a statement and repeating it quietly to the student in the first seat of every row. That student adds a comment or sentence and passes it to the next student in the row. That student repeats the first two sentences and adds another, and so on to the completion of the row. The last student repeats the entire sequence for the class.

SCHOOL & DISTRICT

A schoolwide effort to stop violent and angry behavior can be launched, including posters, banners and rallies. Older students can work one-on-one with younger students, modeling self-control, caring and respect, as they explore the issue of anger through age-appropriate stories and through discussions.

HOME

Family members can watch the evening news together or read news articles. How many incidents of violence were reported in one show or edition? What were the circumstances of these acts? Are there some common elements in these stories, such as weapons, age, victims? Talk about the character traits that are noticeably absent in the situations: self-discipline, respect, patience, kindness, cooperation, justice, empathy. During a second family sharing, families watch the evening news or read articles that report efforts to deter violence. What is being done? Who is involved and why? What character traits are evident? Is there evidence of initiative, courage, caring, fairness, respect or responsibility?

COMMUNITY

Ask students to contact the local newspaper, police or crime prevention agencies to gather available data on acts of violence and crime in their community. Enter the data on computer spread sheets and create graphs. Are the incidents of violence increasing or decreasing? What conclusions can be drawn from the data?

Assign groups of students to one of the four institutions: family, religion, school/education and community. Ask them to request an interview with a representative from these institutions. Suggest such questions as:
- What is the institution currently doing about reducing violence and crime in the community?
- What does it hope to do in the future?
- Are there barriers to doing what the institution wants to do?
- What are they?
- What human stories can the institution share to illustrate its work?

The student groups present their findings to the rest of the class using oral and written reports and charts. Each presentation allows time for comments, questions and, specifically, identification of the character traits inherent in the goals and dreams of the institution. Each student group composes and sends a thank you note to the representative who gave the interview, thus expressing their appreciation and respect.

SOURCE OF INSPIRATION

Patricia Johnson, Pattonville Heights Middle School, Pattonville School District

Educators Cannot Ignore Values

Article reprinted with permission of the author. from The Leadership Academy's *Networker*

Dear Editors:

Five black youths should have been enjoying life; instead they stood on the side of a dark strip of highway attempting to rob my brother. The youths ordered my brother to get down on his hands and knees as they calmly debated about whether to kill him. The youngest one, a tall, then 16-year-old with an innocent face, pulled the trigger. A single gunshot ended Myrod's life. He was 22.

When that shot rang out, it signaled the darkest period in the lives of Myrod's devoted family—his mother, father, three sisters and four brothers. It was devastating to us because Myrod's short life defied all of society's stereotypical depictions of young black men; we were so very proud of him. He was a father, provider, a well-liked and well-respected young man in the community. So respected in fact, that 200 of his friends, classmates and teachers eulogized him on the campus of Lincoln University, some 200 miles from the place where he was being laid to rest.

My brother's violent death still haunts me because it made me realize that too many parents are not fulfilling their responsibility to provide children with moral guidance. I feel, therefore, compelled to enter the academic arena in an attempt to make a difference in some child's life.

Children are basically good at heart and grow up to be decent people; however, the realities of their environment harden their hearts. At the root of our children's problems is the inability to distinguish right from wrong and make good decisions. This reflects the failure of parents, the school, the community and the church—the failure to give children moral guidance. That was so clearly evident with Myrod's killers.

Educators cannot ignore these important and necessary values. Children must develop a strong moral sense and the courage to choose right over wrong. Because my brother's killers lacked good moral judgment, Myrod's children are at risk of growing up without anyone to replace him as a good father. Because of their poor judgment, society has lost a productive member who had much to offer. But no other child has to die; no other child has to murder; no other child has to spend time in jail. The schools must lead our children to a new, positive future. This will occur only when respect for human life and dignity is restored in schools and society.

— Patricia Johnson

ROMEO AND JULIET

Imaginative use of resources introduce Shakespeare's timeless themes to students challenged by learning disabilities.

OBJECTIVES

1. Promote the character traits of **caring, courage, kindness, perseverance, respect. self-control** and **self-discipline.**

2. Develop understanding of the themes, motifs, characters, actions and univeral issues presented in William Shakespeare's *Romeo and Juliet.*

3. Demonstrate students' competence with the material equal to that of sophomore-level expectations.

DESCRIPTION

This unit explores the Shakespearian classic with a user-friendly comic book version by Lake Illustrated Classics and the video of Franco Zeffirelli's *Romeo and Juliet.* Students use critical thinking and journal-writing as they encounter such themes as loyalty (to family, friends, team, nation), peer pressure, codes of honor, courage, trust, betrayal, violence, loss, revenge, love and respect for others. They also explore the history of the Globe Theatre and its reconstruction through the Internet.

Background: Introduce 16th century Italy. Review lifestyles, life span, customs, entertainments and culture. Discuss William Shakespeare's importance in literature. Present his biography orally (see page179). Provide information on the Globe Theatre, including copies of "A Story of Perseverance" on page 180. Talk about perseverance and how it is exemplified by Sam Wanamaker.

Introduce the Story: Talk about *Romeo and Juliet* in relation to Shakespeare's other works. Distinguish between tragedy and comedy. Identify members of the Capulets and Montagues.

RESOURCES
Romeo and Juliet in comic book format, available from Lake Publishing Company, 500 Harbor Blvd., Belmont, CA 94002.

Romeo and Juliet (1968) directed by Franco Zeffirelli for Paramount. Length: 2 hrs., 18 mins.

GRADES
9 - 10

FORMAT
Classroom
Resource room

DISCIPLINES
Language arts
English literature

TIME
Several sessions

MATERIALS INCLUDED
William Shakespeare
The Globe Theater
Romeo and Juliet
Questions

MATERIALS NEEDED
TV/VCR unit
Access to Internet

Proceed by alternating between the book and the movie in the following pattern:
> Read Acts I & II. Watch movie through Act I & II.
> Read Acts III and IV. Watch Acts III and IV.
> Read Act V. Watch Act V.

Incorporate these learning experiences as students progress through the play:
Oral reading: After students read Act I, they work in small groups. Each member chooses a character, previews the character's lines, then reads them aloud in a dramatic reading, a cooperative activity with other group members.

Sequencing: Students work with a teacher-designed worksheet that helps them place the events leading up to and following the fight in proper sequence.

Critical thinking: In oral discussion, students identify Romeo's choices and actions, then Juliet's choices and actions. Following Acts II and III, students explain the motivations of Mercutio, Romeo and Tybalt in group discussion, as a journal writing assignment or short essay. They relate the culture represented in *Romeo and Juliet* to today's culture: costume party, party crashing, feuds, gangs, team rivalries, flaring tempers and misunderstandings.

Compare and contrast: Students review the consequences for lawbreakers as represented in *Romeo and Juliet* with the consequences for today's lawbreakers.

Predicting and writing conclusion: After reading and watching Acts II and III, students write a fictional ending to *Romeo and Juliet*. Guide students through writing process if needed.

Reflection: Read book to the end. Show movie to the end. Discuss the elements of tragedy. See questions related to Act IV on page 182.

HOME

Involve parents in the learning experience by asking for specific contributions: family herbal remedies, the code of ethics or conduct from their place of work, post cards and photographs of Italy.

COMMUNITY

Extend the discussion of the feud between the Capulets and Montagues with modern references. Use news reports or refer to the editorial included with *The Right Ingredients* on page 175. Invite a community resource person to speak to students. Consider a parole officer, police officer, social worker who works with juvenile offenders, a court representative or an advocate for youth offenders.

SOURCE OF INSPIRATION
Sherry Webster, Pattonville High School Resource Teacher, Special School District

William Shakespeare

Life History
- Born in England in 1564

- Married Anne Hathaway at age 18 (Anne was 26)

- Children: Susanna (1583) and twins Hamnet and Judith (1585)

Professional History
- Became an actor, then a playwright

- Developed an acting company called "The King's Men"

- The King's Men performed at the Globe Theatre
    - Open-air theatre
    - Rich people sat in balconies (good seats)
    - Poor people sat or stood on the ground: groundlings

- Wrote 37 plays, many sonnets and poems

- His plays included:
    Macbeth
    As You Like It
    A Midsummer Night's Dream
    Romeo and Juliet
    Taming of the Shrew
    Oedipus Rex

THEN AND NOW
THE GLOBE THEATER

Description of theatre: The Globe's original foundation was discovered in 1989, roughly 200 yards from the site of the reconstructed Globe Theatre on the south bank of the River Thames. Archeological evidence suggested a polygonal (20-sided) structure. The interior circular theater is made of 20 wooden bays, each three stories high. The roofs are thatched with Norfolk reed and the walls are made with lime plaster. The stage is roofed and thatched. The back wall is fixed, decorated and carved in early classical style. Oak pillars, painted to look like marble, are on each side of the stage and support a painted canopy over the stage.

A Story of Perseverance

It was in 1970 that Sam Wanamaker first announced his intention of rebuilding the Globe, only to find himself enmeshed in all kinds of legal and theatrical problems: the local council felt that riverside housing should take precedence over a theatre, a tent for some early productions on the site was destroyed in a storm and there were long and bitter economic battles. Wanamaker also had to overcome massive English apathy, not to mention a strong feeling that given the average local summertime weather, a semi-open-air theatre was one thing London could do without.[1] Construction started in 1987 and was targeted for completion in 1992.

"Sure there has been despair along the way, but I never really doubted we'd do it in the end, and I'm still convinced we will have a show on stage for Shakespeare's birthday in April 1992,"[2] Wanamaker predicted. Delays carried completion well beyond that date, but the new Globe Theatre opened to visitors in 1994 and was inaugurated by Queen Elizabeth on Thursday, June 12, 1997.

1. Morely, S. "Magnificent Obsession." p. 108.
2. Morely, p. 107.

The Original Theatre

Opened:	1599
Burned:	1613
Rebuilt:	1613
Closed:	1642

Reconstructed Theatre

Conceptualized:	1970
Construction:	1987
Target date:	1992
Inauguration:	1997
Est. Cost:	$38 million

INTERNET TRAVEL
If using a search engine, type in "The Globe Theatre" or "Shakespeare's Globe." Or try these direct addresses:
www.theatreticket.co.uk/sglo.html
www.rmplc.co.uk/eduweb/sites/citylond/globe.html

The Privileged and the Groundlings
To match the original Globe, the three-tiered circular seating area, which will accommodate 1,031 people, will be covered by a thatched roof. The large floor area where the stage will jut out will not be covered. About 500 theater-goers, called "groundlings" in Shakespeare's day, will be able to stand on the floor nose-to-feet with the performers.
— *St. Louis Post-Dispatch*, Dec. 18, 1994

Questions

Act I & II: Quiz

1. Juliet's last name is _Capulet._

2. She is _13_ years old

3. Her parents are called _Lord and Lady Capulet._

4. Tybalt is _Juliet's_ cousin.

5. The Capulet servants are _Gregory and Samson._

6. The Nurse is a _nanny_ for Juliet.

7. Romeo's last name is _Montague._

8. His cousin is _Benvolio._ His best friend is _Mercutio._

9. An apothecary is a _druggist._

10. Romeo and Juliet live in the city of _Verona._

11. This city is ruled by Prince _Escalus._

12. An herbalist can _make medicines and treatments from herbs._

13. The name of the herabalist is _Friar Lawrence._

14. What do we have in our society today that is similar to an apothecary? _Pharmacy_

15. What profession is similar to the herbalist's work? _Doctor writes perscriptions;_
    pharmacist fills them; homeopathic medicine explores the use of herbs in medicine.

Act I & II: Discussion Questions

1. How does Romeo find out about the Capulet's party?
2. Who is the man Juliet's parents want her to marry?
3. Who told Lord and Lady Capulet that Romeo was at their party?
4. Who told Romeo that Juliet is a Capulet?
5. Who said, "My only love sprung from my only hate?"
6. Who will marry Romeo & Juliet?
7. Why is he willing to marry them? What is his reason?

Themes and patterns that can be developed in discussion: Party crashing, the invited and the uninvited, breaking unspoken rules or codes. Was Romeo daring, foolhardy or courageous when he "crashed" the Capulet's ball? Love and hate are opposites, yet Romeo finds them closely connected. Who does he love and who does he hate? How are they connected? What happens when two "good" forces are pulling in opposite directions? For instance, Romeo wants to remain loyal to his family and friends by hating the Capulets and he wants to express kindness, care and respect for Juliet, who is one of the Capulets. How does he decide what to do? Refer to _Building Decision Skills_ starting on page 163 for background on "right versus right" ethical decision-making.

Act III & IV: Discussion Questions

1. Why did Tybalt want to fight with Romeo?

2. Who did Tybalt fight?

3. Who killed Tybalt?

4. What did Prince Escalus do to Romeo?

5. Why did Lord Capulet decide to let Paris marry Juliet right away?

    What was his reason?

6. Why did Juliet refuse to marry Paris?

7. Who did Juliet ask for help?

8. Who was supposed to be at the tomb when Juliet awoke?

9. Who found Juliet after she drank from the vial?

What is a code of behavior? How do you figure out a code of behavior? Do you follow different codes depending upon who you are with and what you are doing? What is a code of ethics or code of honor? Compare some published codes of ethics: West Point, Boy Scouts, Girl Scouts, YMCA, a community service organization. Does your school have a code of ethics?

Act V: Discussion Questions

1. Who told Romeo that Juliet was dead?

2. Did Romeo get the letter from Friar Lawrence?

3. Who was at the tomb when Romeo got there?

4. How did Romeo kill himself?

5. Why did Romeo kill himself?

6. How did Juliet kill herself?

7. Why did Juliet kill herself?

8. What proved that Friar Lawrence told the truth?

9. What happened to the Capulet-Montague feud?

What makes this story a tragedy? Define a "tragedy." Give some current examples of tragic deaths (Princess Diana, Arthur Ashe). Refer to the editorial that accompanies *The Right Ingredients* on page 175. What is the tragedy in this situation?

S.T.A.R.S.
STUDENTS TAKING ACTION REACHING STUDENTS

This program recognizes the silent "R" in the educational formula: Relationship. Selected high-school students are paired with elementary students in one-on-one mentoring sessions that continue weekly throughout the school year.

OBJECTIVES

1. Promote the character traits of **confidence, cooperation, goal-setting, respect, responsibility, decision-making** and **service.**

2. Create a positive connection to the school environment for at-risk elementary students; build their self-concept as successful learners and members of the school community.

3. Instill personal ownership in learning by becoming an integral part of the education process for someone younger.

DESCRIPTION

High-school students (mentors) are paired with students from four elementary schools. They meet once a week in a cooperative venture. The program, which involves 50 secondary students and an equal number of elementary students, includes these facets:

★   A focus on human connectedness. The mentor's goal is to develop a comfortable relationship with the elementary student.

★   Selection of high-school students through an application and approval process. S.T.A.R.S. requirements do not restrict lower academic achievers. The learning process is stimulated as one teaches.

★   Referral of elementary students by teachers, counselors and principals based on need. This need does not have to be dramatic or entirely academic. Appropriate candidates might include students struggling with vocabulary, shyness, organization, math, the logistics of a research paper, science project or multi-step assignment.

★   Training in roughly eight sessions (1.5 to 2 hours) held after school or on early dismissal days.

GRADES
9 - 12

FORMAT
Extracurricular

SKILLS
Communication
Decision-making
Goal-setting
Leadership
Listening

TIME
8 two-hour training sessions plus
40 minutes/week

MATERIALS INCLUDED
Orientation Meeting
Building Skills

★ Training includes:
  • "ice breakers" and team-building techniques
  • listening skills exercises (see page 188)
  • giving feedback, positive and negative
  • trust-building
  • tutoring techniques
  • lesson-planning
  • review of character traits: what they are, what behaviors one would see while working with students, what it means to model these traits, how you identify and reinforce character actions in your partner, how you initiate discussions about these traits.

★ Contact: Weekly visits between mentor and elementary student at the elementary school. High-school student provides transportation (carpool with older driving students, arrange rides) with help of S.T.A.R.S. coordinator.

★ Lesson-planning: Mentor develops lessons based on the student's identified needs and conversations/interactions with the student during visits.

★ Resources: Ongoing contact with S.T.A.R.S. coordinator and fellow mentors, such techniques as ice breakers and activities experienced during the training sessions and book lists that identify character traits.

★ Journals: Mentors keep a journal of their visits, recording the lesson and its reception (how it worked), comments, feelings and ideas for future lessons.

★ Reflection Sessions: These meetings are held each month with all mentors to generate new lessons and reflect on the experience.
Housekeeping   *10 minutes*
      A time for reminders; remember to sign out, turn in journals, etc.
Positive Exchange   *20 minutes*
      Positive comments *only* are invited at this time. A version of show-and-tell allows the sharing of ideas, lesson plans and approaches.
Reflection Session   *20-30 minutes*

Mentors are divided into small groups. A senior or more experienced student facilitates each group in a discussion of problems, issues or concerns. The temptation to vent steam or complain is cut short by the rules: One problem takes the stage at a time. Every member of the group must participate in exploring it and generating solutions. The second problem cannot be introduced until viable solutions have been developed for the first.

★ Celebration: A year-end picnic brings all mentors and their student charges together in a celebration of meaningful friendships.

★ Credit toward service requirement: All of the time invested in training, meetings, lesson planning, visits and journal-writing may qualifiy as community-service hours, of which many school districts require for graduation.

EXAMPLES OF STUDENT-GENERATED LESSONS

Identified Weakness: Vocabulary Words

Creative Solution: With an advance copy of the vocabulary list, the mentor creates a board game in which a series of squares snake around the board (as in *Candy Land* or *Chutes & Ladders*). Each square contains a vocabulary word from that week's list plus a few from the past. A roll of the dice determines forward movement. When players land on a square, they pronounce the word and spell it without looking at it. If correct, they roll again and continue. If not, the opponent pronounces the word and spells it. The first player checks for accurate spelling. If incorrect, the turn reverts back to the first player.

Identified Weakness: Counting money, making change

Creative Solution: Mentor makes copies of coins and cuts out paper replicas of pennies, nickels, dimes and quarters, then creates collage with labels and actual products, all priced below $1.00: candy bars, pencil, bottle of bubbles, bar of soap. The prices are noted on the collage. The student is asked to (1) choose one dollar's worth of products, (2) decide which one product would provide the most quantity for a dollar, and (3) figure the cost of one pencil and two candy bars, then make the correct change assuming someone had given a dollar for these items.

ASSOCIATED CLASSROOM LEARNING

While attending their regular classes, S.T.A.R.S. mentors analyze the skills needed to do their assigned tasks, both the academic skills (math, spelling, note taking) and the character skills (cooperation, respect, responsibility, perseverance). As part of their journal, they trace how they came to possess these required skills. At what point in their elementary education did they learn the academic skills now being required? How did they learn them? When did they become aware of the character traits needed to be successful in school? How did they discover these traits? Who were their models? Younger students will connect with the true stories their mentors can share with them.

HOME

S.T.A.R.S. mentors interview their parents about the strategies they used to help their children when they were in elementary school. What clues did they use to know when their children could be given more responsibility or trust. How did they convey the importance of these character traits? S.T.A.R.S. mentors may want to interview younger siblings about the things they like to do in school and the ways they like to learn. What are their thoughts about some classmates that are not learning or performing well in school? What do they feel about these students and what ideas do they have about how they might be helped?

COMMUNITY

Educators from nearby universities and schools of education can speak to the mentors as part of their training. What are the characteristics of a "good" teacher? Why do teachers need special training to work with children? What kinds of university classes are required to become a teacher?

SOURCE OF INSPIRATION

Fran DeMaster, Pattonville High School, Judy Rice & Mary Jo Beaulieu, Rose Acres Elementary, Pattonville School District

CONGRATULATIONS!!! You are invited to become a member of Pattonville Senior High's S.T.A.R.S.! This is a special honor and a true privilege which requires a genuine commitment on your part. Your teachers, guidance counselor, and grade level principal have approved your membership, which means they agree that you will be a shining representative of PSH during your work in the elementary school this year. I'm so pleased to have you in S.T.A.R.S.!

Community service credit will be given for each training session and each visit to the elementary school. It is very important that you do your best to attend each training session and commit to regular 40-minute visits with your elementary student on early dismissal days. Parents will receive permission and health forms later in January.

Our 1st training session/meeting will be Oct. 6, at 1:00 p.m.—don't miss it! I'll have snacks.

I'm excited about sharing in your adventure in service learning!

— *Fran DeMaster*

Orientation Meeting

What is S.T.A.R.S.?
Students Taking Action Reaching Students

In this program, qualified 9-12th grade students are selected to work with elementary students on a one-to-one basis. The student-to-student relationship will reflect the philosophy of the character education curriculum. The high school student acts as:
- an encourager
- a positive role model
- a coach/tutor/mentor

The S.T.A.R.S. program takes place on early dismissal days and perhaps several times after school when the activity bus runs.

S.T.A.R.S. mentors will be expected to complete the eight training sessions before they will be placed with the elementary student. These sessions will usually last one hour, but several may last two hours. (You will _always_ have advance notice if a longer session is planned.) Sessions at the elementary school on Thursdays last approximately 45 minutes.

Transportation will be arranged on an individual basis with parental approval required.

Community service credit will be given for the S.T.A.R.S.' meetings and training sessions as well as for each visit to the elementary school.

A S.T.A.R.S.' RESPONSIBILITY is to...
- attend the 8 training sessions and monthly evaluations
- commit to regular visits to the elementary school on the designated days
- notify the elementary school and S.T.A.R.S. coordinator if absent
- be a good role model for the elementary student
- work cooperatively with the elementary school teacher
- be prepared with appropriate lesson plans for sessions with your student
- keep a journal about each tutoring session

Building Skills

TEN WAYS TO BE A BETTER LISTENER:
1. Put your body into a listening attitude; be alert! sit straight!

2. Look at the other person.

3. Try to really understand what is being said; get the message behind the words.

4. Hear out the speaker before judging the message.

5. Concentrate! Good listening is focused on the speaker.

6. Listen for main ideas.

7. Don't interrupt; let the other person finish his or her thoughts.

8. React to what is being said. Nod, make comments and ask questions to let the speaker know you're really listemng.

9. Ask questions about what is being said if you are not sure.

10. Get rid of things that distract you; shut out noise, close the windows, etc.

INSTRUCTION SHEET A: BUILDING SKILLS
You may pick any subject to talk about: sports, school, your family, etc.

Situation 1: Talk about your subject. Look at the other student and really pay attention to what he or she says.

Situation 2: Talk to the other student, look around the room, act fidgety and don't really look at the other student.

Situation 3: Listen to the other student, but act bored. Move around on your chair. Look around the room.

Situation 4: Listen to the other student for a short time. Then interrupt him or her and start talking about a totally different subject.

INSTRUCTION SHEET B
Situation 1: Listen and look at your partner. Really pay attention.

Situation 2: Listen and look at your partner. Nod your head and look really interested.

Situation 3: Talk to your partner; try to get him or her to pay attention to you.

Situation 4: Talk to your partner about something that made you really unhappy.

GROW A ROW

Grow a Row is a student-driven, service learning project designed by two sophomores as an independent study project within the context of the school's gifted program. The concept lends itself to all sorts of collaboratives: an earth science living laboratory; an interdisciplinary unit involving math, science and language arts; a student council or service club project; or a PTA/PTO-sponsored initiative with student volunteers.

OBJECTIVES

1. Promote the character traits of **assertiveness, caring, commitment, compassion, confidence, cooperation, goal-setting, initiative, patience, perseverance, reliability, respect, responsibility, self-discipline** and **service.**

2. Research community needs for fresh produce at area agencies: food pantries, shelters and soup kitchens.

3. Research grant opportunities and target potential sources of funds. Write and submit proposals according to grant specifcations.

4. Design, plant, maintain and harvest a vegetable garden.

5. Develop an effective collection and distribution system to channel home grown produce to soup kitchens.

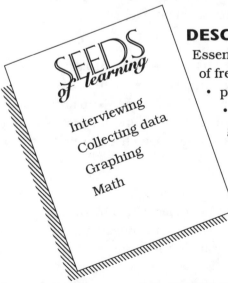

SEEDS of learning

Interviewing
Collecting data
Graphing
Math

DESCRIPTION

Essentially, students provide an ongoing source of fresh produce to local soup kitchens by:
• planting and harvesting a garden
• providing a collection point for home-grown produce from area residents and delivering it to agency sites.

GRADES
9 - 12

FORMAT
Independent study
Club or class project
Science "living lab"

DISCIPLINES
Math
Science
Language arts
Business

TIME
Yearlong project

MATERIALS INCLUDED
Q & A
Final Report

MATERIALS NEEDED
Seeds, fertilizer
Gardening tools

STAGE 1: PLANNING

Research the Need: Students identify and contact local food pantries, shelters and soup kitchens to determine the need for fresh produce: What kind of vegetables? In what condition (washed, trimmed, packaged)? How much? Where and when (optimum delivery)?

Design a Garden: Become familiar with each crop: learn space, light, soil, fertilizer and maintenance requirements. Talk with gardeners or nursery personnel. Develop a list of site requirements based on needs of plants: proximity to water source, adequate sunlight, accessible yet protected from heavy traffic and animals.

Research natural and synthetic methods of insect control. Make recommendations based on research. Estimate yield based on different planting configurations. Chart times for harvesting, indicating when each crop starts to produce and how long it will continue to produce.

SEEDS of learning

Earth Science
Botany
Chemistry
Math
Accounting

Develop a Budget: Determine supplies needed and their cost. Research sources of in-kind contributions. Estimate labor needs. Plan for recruitment. Determine marketplace value of in-kind contributions and volunteer labor. Reflect these costs as part of the total budget.

Develop a Communications Plan: Recruit students to plant, weed, water, harvest and transport produce to the soup kitchens. Enlist donations of garden-grown produce from local residents. Create community support and recognition of the project.

STAGE 2: ANSWER THE QUESTIONS

The grantor for this particular project, the Teens Care Community Service Program administered by the Saint Louis Community Foundation, asked questions that helped students clarify their aims and reflect on their experience. These questions are incorporated in a worksheet on page 193.

STAGE 3: SEEK FUNDING & CONTRIBUTIONS

Research grant opportunities. Select one or two highly probable sources. Develop proposals in accordance with grant stipulations. Write letters explaining goals and requesting material contributions—mulch, seeds, plants—from local nurseries, hardware and gardening supply stores. Present proposal to the school board and local service or civic organizations such as Junior League, Rotary Club and Lion's Club.

STAGE 4: EXECUTION

Write and submit grant proposals. If funding is to be underwritten by the PTA or a source that does not require a grant application, use the questions provided by Teens Care Community Service Program as an initial exercise.

Locate, design and plant garden.

Organize collection and distribution of home-grown produce.

Communicate with student body, school district and general public.
Obtain, in writing, permissions and approvals needed for use of land. Inform key people (principal, superintendent, school board president). Create posters and fliers for school, groceries, stores, nurseries, libraries, city government buildings. Write public service announcements to submit to radio stations or as use for schoolwide P.A. announcements. Draft a news release inviting public contributions of home-grown vegetables and send it to area newspapers, other schools within the district, gardening and service organizations, churches, synagogues, etc. Develop a print ad. Define the target market. Research optimum placement to reach this market. Place the ad.

Schedule garden care throughout duration of the project.

Schedule collection dates: Identify collection point with signs, assign people to receive contributions, assign drivers to transport produce to agencies. Develop a system of tracking mileage and volunteer hours.

Comply with all grant requirements.

At close of project, meet to reflect on the experience. In small groups, identify the character traits you experienced or saw in others as the project evolved. Examples: the compassion of shelter employees and volunteers; the commitment required to make the collection days successful; the initiative of a fellow student; the perseverance involved in maintaining the garden, etc. Discuss Question 7 on the "Final Report" form. (See page 194.)

CLASSROOM CONNECTION
The problem-solving challenges convert to math and science. Teachers pose these questions as real-world problems such as: When will the first crop be ready to harvest? What will it be? How much will a garden of this size produce?

HOME
Plant a garden together as a family or dedicate part of an existing garden to the project. Young children can grow a few vegetables in pots or planters. Relate the word responsibility to the task of watering plants. Mention the rewards of patience as the vegetables are picked and taken to the collection site. Recognize the cooperation involved as one family's contribution is combined with hundreds of others.

COMMUNITY

Individuals respond to the collection drive, reinforcing their own sense of caring and community responsiblity. Area nurseries, botanical gardens, arboretums, garden clubs and gardeners provide counsel, support, material contributions and promotion (posting fliers). The participating food pantries, shelters and soup kitchens increase student awareness of the needs of others and what it takes to mobilize community action. They can invite students to sample a "day in the life" of the agency by accompanying them for an entire day.

To whom it may concern:

My name is Cindy Marlin and my friend, Katie Mullins, and I have recently begun a community service project through an enrichment class at our high school. We have been granted $500 from the Teens Care Fund in order to start our project, entitled "Grow a Row." Our main focus is to obtain fresh produce from local gardeners to donate to food kitchens and homeless shelters. We plan to grow vegetables in our own school's garden, in addition to advertising at local nurseries and produce stores for their donations. In order for our goal to be achieved, we would like to ask for any seed, plant or tree donations so that we can conserve our money for garden bed preparation and advertising, a significant factor in obtaining other donations. We would extremely appreciate any help you could offer us in this project.

Thanks,
Cindy Marlin & Katie Mullins

SOURCE OF INSPIRATION

Katie Mullins and Cindy Marlin, students participating in the Quest enrichment program with advisor Mickey Newyear, Parkway West High School, Parkway School District

Please answer the following questions on separate sheets of paper.
Number your answers, be complete and give details where appropriate.

1. What do you want to do?

2. Why do you want to do it?

3. How will you know you've made a difference?

4. When and where will the project occur?

5. Who will work with you?

6. What will your program cost?

7. For which parts do you need funding?

AGREEMENT

BY SIGNING THIS PROPOSAL, YOU AGREE TO:

√ submit a final report within two weeks of completion of the project
√ keep accurate financial records
√ reflect on the difference this project made in your life

_____
Student signature

_____
Parent or Guardian signature   Date

QUESTIONS REPRINTED WITH PERMISSION FROM THE TEENS CARE COMMUNITY SERVICE PROGRAM.

FIELD-TESTED RESOURCES IN CHARACTER EDUCATION • COOPERATING SCHOOL DISTRICTS OF GREATER ST. LOUIS • PAGE 193

FINAL REPORT

Name of Project: _____

Dates of Project: _____

Your Name: _____

Names of others who participated: _____

_____

1. What did you do?

2. What did you learn?

3. What would you have done differently?

4. How did you present the project to the community?
   (Please include copies of photos, articles, fliers, announcements.)

5. What did the project cost? (Please list expenses.)

6. Approximately how many people were affected by the project?

7. How has your involvement made a difference in your life?

FRENCH CUISINE

French (vocabulary) follows function as students access recipes through the Internet; plan a complete dinner menu; purchase, prepare and present the meal to their family; learn aspects of the language, culture, customs and cuisine in the process; and reflect on the character traits experienced.

OBJECTIVES

1. Promote the character traits of **assertiveness, commitment, cooperation, goal-setting, initiative, patience, perseverance, reliability, respect, responsibility** and **self-discipline.**

2. Access information from the Internet.

3. Master vocabulary related to cooking, dining, table etiquette and qualities of character.

4. Plan, shop, cook, prepare and present a three- to five-course "le déjeuner" for one's family. Use the occasion to introduce French words and customs to family members.

DESCRIPTION

Actual meal preparation and presentation becomes the centerpiece of a learning series built around the objectives above. A scrapbook, complete with photographs or associated video, documents the process.

Access Information from the Internet: Authentic French recipes, written in French, are available through the Internet. If Internet access is not easily available to students, the teacher can simulate the Internet environment with Web Whacker or similar software. Web sites, buttons and associated materials are selected and cut from the activated Internet, then pasted into the software program. The program allows access to the information while offline. It simulates the same sequence of moves, but eliminates time spent chasing down "blind alleys" and prevents students from straying into unrelated areas.

GRADES
9 - 12

FORMAT
Classroom

DISCIPLINES
French; adapts to other languages
Computers

TIME
4 class sessions

MATERIALS INCLUDED
La Cuisine de Famille Vocabulary
Le Projet la Cuisine en France

FRENCH RECIPES ON THE WORLD WIDE WEB

"Le Cordon Bleu" and "Lyon Life Gastronomy with Paul Bocuse" are two sites that offer recipes on the World Wide Web. Use a search engine and the key words "French cuisine" or "French recipes" to see what you can find.

Master the Vocabulary: "La Cuisine de Famille" on page 198 introduces the elements of home cooking and dining. The vocabulary provides additional food-related nouns, action verbs, cooking tools, measures and processes, as well as specific character traits. As students browse the Internet and supplement their search with French gourmet magazines and cookbooks, they acquire new words and record them.

Creating a Scrapbook of the Experience: These personalized vocabulary lists become part of a scrapbook that includes the five-course menu, copies of recipes, cultural background, the shopping list, grocery receipts with price notations converting dollars to francs, printout of home page of culinary web site, photographs of student in action—surfing the net, shopping, setting the table, preparing the meal, displaying the finished dish, serving the meal and cleaning up. The scrapbook might also feature:

- captions that identify action and character trait represented in photograph, e.g., "A lesson in perseverance: Calling all over town to find Tomme and Emmental for the Fondue Savoyarde recipe."
- list of words and phrases student introduced to family members
- evaluation and comments from family members
- personal reflections on the experience

Character Lessons: This experience places students in a leadership role. They persevere through a multi-step process, taking responsibility for all aspects of the meal. If they pair up with another student to create the meal, the importance of initiative and reliability become meaningful. Students introduce French customs, the order of the courses and French phrases that allow the diners to respectfully and politely express themselves; for example:

Enjoy the meal (usually said before people begin to eat): *Bon appétit!*
Please: *S'il te plaît.* Thank you: *Merci.*
Pass the butter: *Passe-moi le beurre.*
This is good: *Que c'est bon! Que c'est délicieux!*

Reflect on the Process: Students share their scrapbooks in brief presentations before the class. They meet in pairs or small groups to answer these questions: What was most enjoyable, detestable, educational, surprising about the experience? What would you do differently next time? What have you gained in terms of understanding and speaking French? Their answers to these questions become the last page of their scrapbook.

HOME

Character education is as pervasive as ambience in this dining experi-ence. Family members cooperate by reviewing meal-oriented French phrases in advance; asking questions of the student; expressing appre-ciation for the effort that went into the task. They risk trying unfamiliar foods and foreign phrases during the natural course of the meal. Together they reflect on the qualities of character that the student has shown in the context of the project, including, perhaps, assertiveness, decision-making, commitment, goal-setting, healthy risk-taking, initiative, patience, perseverance, reliability and responsibility.

SCHOOL & DISTRICT

Students can host "An Evening in France," inviting their parents and members of the community. The evening might include music, art, dramatic readings and, of course, a taste of French cuisine. The ambi-ance is festive and students, who communicate in French, have an opportunity to use much of what they have learned about the country and customs. They also demonstrate cooperation, initiative, responsibility and perseverance in the planning and production of the evening.

COMMUNITY

Students can take the initiative to locate and arrange for a visit with chefs of nearby French restaurants. Questions are planned ahead of time. Notes and photographs taken during the visit can later be tran-scribed into a page for their personalized scrapbook. A video filming can also be used to document their visit. As the students plan their questions, they are mindful of the tone of their queries, being sure they reflect respect for the work-ing knowledge of the chef.

SOURCE OF INSPIRATION

Rosie Altadonna, Parkway West High School, Parkway School District

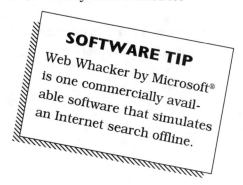

SOFTWARE TIP
Web Whacker by Microsoft® is one commercially avail-able software that simulates an Internet search offline.

La Cuisine de Famille

La femme fait son marché

au supermarché, à l'hypermarché
aux petits magazins du quartier
à l'épicerie
à la boulangerie/pâtisserie
à la boucherie
à la crémerie
à la charcuterie
à la poissonerie
au marché

Les repas

le petit déjeuner: café au lait, chocolat chaud, pain, beurre, confiture, croissant
le déjeuner ou le dîner
le dîner
le déjeuner ou le dîner (repas principal): plusieurs plats, mais les portions sont petites

Entrées typiques

terrine (paté)   jambon
oeufs durs   melon
saucissons   crudités
carottes   râpées
salades (tomates, concombres, pomme de terre- sauce viniagrette)

Soupes/potages typiques (Dîner- remplace l'entrée)

soupe aux légumes
soupe à l'oignon
potage saint-germain

Plats principaux typiques

viande et légume -- accompagnés de pain, vin, eau)
boeuf: rôti (saignant, à point, bien cuit), steak, pot-au-feu
volaille: poulet rôti, poulet sauté, coq au vin, magret de canard, rôti de dindonneau

Poissons et fruits de mer

harengs à la moutard
bouillabaisse   truite
saumon   coquilles St. Jacques

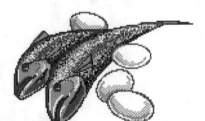

D'autres viandes

lapin (au vin blanc, à la moutarde)   cheval (haché)

veau (escalopes, côtelettes, rôti)   agneau (gigot, côtelettes)

porc (côtelettes, rôti)

Les abats, etc.

coeur   rognons

pieds   langue

tripes   cervelle

Légumes typiques

petits pois   frites

carottes   épinards

haricots verts   asperges

haricots blancs   fenouil

pommes de terre

Salade

salade verte à la vinaigrette

vinaigrette: 2-3 parts huile, 1 part vinaigre, moutarde, sel, poivre

Fromages typiques (accompagnés de pain)

camembert   chèvre

roquefort   port Salut

gruyère   fromage blanc

Desserts typiques

fruits assortis

      pâtisserie

        tarte (aux fruits)

        crème caramel

        yaourt

Pour les parents: un café (petit, noir, fort)

Vocabulary

LES ALIMENTS

la tripe

la côtelette

le roux

le champignon

les escargots

l'ail

l'huile

les huitres

le rognon

la farine

la crème

les oeufs

LES VERBES

couper

mélanger (mêler)

sauter

chauffer

bouillir

mijoter

fondre

assaisonner

cuire

ajouter

battre

verser

cuisiner

laver

hacher

écraser

couvrer

égoutter

évider

LA BATTERIE DE CUISINE

la cocotte

la casserole

le four

la poêle

le plat

le couvert

le four à micro-ondes

LA MANIÈRE DE SERVIR

au grain (gratiné)

à la parisiène

au jus

à la provençale

farci

LES MESURES

une cuillerée à café

une cuillerée à soupe

une pincée

une bouteille

une tasse

THE LANGUAGE OF CHARACTER

assertiveness — l'assertion (f)

commitment — l'engagement (m)

cooperation — la coopération

goal-setting — l'établissement d'objectifs

initiative — l'initiative (f)

patience — la patience

perseverance — la persévérance

reliability — le sérieux

respect — le respect

responsibility — la responsabilité

self-discipline — la discipline personnelle

Le Projet la Cuisine en France

20 points   *Le Repas Familial*

Choisissez le menu pour un dîner familial—votre famille. Préparez ce dîner pour votre famille. Montrez votre menu au prof avant de commencer. Vous rendrez au prof un petit rapport avec les commentaires de toute la famille et la note que votre famille vous aura accordé. Votre menu doit comporter une entrée, un plat principal, un légume, une salade, un choix de fromages, et un dessert. Le professeur vous aidera à choisir un menu qui vous plaise.

Date limite _____

Dear Parents,

We are to about to embark on a journey to a foreign land—your kitchen! We are studying a unit on French cuisine and your student has chosen to create an authentic French meal for the family.

Your role is to sit down and enjoy the meal, write an evaluation of it and give a grade when it is over. The grade should assess the shopping, preparation, presentation and clean up involved in "le diner."

I hope you enjoy the meal. I'll be looking forward to your comments.

Bon appétit!

SENIOR (CITIZEN) PROM

This extracurricular activity began with an idea from the 1988 National Teacher of the Year who described the efforts of a Minnesota high school. Decorations, refreshments and a live DJ are the necessary ingredients to make the night a success.

OBJECTIVES

1. Provide positive interaction between senior citizens and students.

2. Develop a caring community.

3. Promote the character traits of **caring, cooperation, responsibility, respect** and **service.**

DESCRIPTION

The Community Service Committee of the Pattonville High School student council plans and executes the annual Senior (Citizen) Prom. The event, open to all senior citizens in the community, is promoted through newspaper announcements and fliers distributed at community centers. In its five-year history, the prom has attracted from 175 to 300 participants, both couples and singles. A live disc jockey plays selections from the 1940s and '50s. Students decorate the cafeteria, provide refreshments, serve as hosts and hostesses, and are willing dance partners with single seniors or those who want to continue "tripping the light fantastic" while their partners rest. A Prom King and Queen, selected through a drawing, are crowned and prizes are awarded for the best dancers and the "most senior" senior. Stereotypes of "selfish, unruly" students and "sedentary, grouchy" seniors are soon dispelled in a night of fun and music. Feelings of respect and care for one another are felt as well as seen.

The cost of putting on the event, from $700 to $900, is underwritten by profits from the Student Council store, an operation that sells school supplies and other items that students may want or need. The store operates during lunch hours.

GRADES
9 - 12

FORMAT
Extracurricular
Schoolwide

DISCIPLINES
Service learning

TIME
Preparation variable
Two-hour event

**MATERIALS
NEEDED**
Live disc jockey
CD system

RELATED CLASSROOM STUDIES

English: Students write about misconceptions young people have of the elderly, as well as the stereotypes elderly people have of today's youth, in essays, editorials, poetry, anecdotes.

English: Students can write or discuss the meaning of the character traits in light of the Senior (Citizen) Prom project. How does it provide an opportunity to use these character traits in a new way?

Music: Students survey music from the 1940s and '50s: jazz, Big Bands, war songs. They might develop a hypothetical list of the DJ's choices for the night.

Geography: The world map has changed significantly over the past 50 years. Students do a comparative study and trace the origin of the changes they find on today's map.

Social studies: Senior citizens often play a very different role in the culture of other countries. Students can explore and compare how other countries include, honor, respect or care for their elderly.

Science: Students consider scientific breakthroughs in medicine, biotechnology, physics, chemistry and other fields that have occurred over the past 50 years. Each breakthrough can be examined as to the impact it has had on people's lives and the ethical questions and issues it has raised.

HOME

Students interview elderly relatives or friends of the family. What historical events did these senior citizens witness? What major inventions have occurred in their lifetimes? How has everyday living changed between then and now for a high school student? The research can include live interviews, old movies, history books, old newspapers and periodicals, etc.

SOURCE OF INSPIRATION

Ed Robins and Steve Peterson, Pattonville High School, Pattonville School District

S.M.I.L.E.
STORYTELLING MAKING INDIVIDUAL LEARNING EASIER

Stories, drawn from the folklore and fairy tales of many different countries, communicate certain character traits. Students become creative partners in an ageless tradition as they illustrate, narrate and videotape selected stories for use in elementary classes.

OBJECTIVES

1. Promote the character traits of **cooperation, commitment, goal-setting, respect, responsibility** and **service.**

2. Introduce the tradition of storytelling into the curriculum; learn the value and art of storytelling.

3. Research the culture and geography of countries in which the stories originate.

DESCRIPTION

This unit involves collaboration and commitment as well as artistic and technological skills. Referrals by teachers and calls for volunteers combine to attract students from several middle and high schools within the district. The collective efforts of students are focused on stories that illustrate or demonstrate particular character traits and result in two products:
- Live storytelling performances
- Stories produced on videotape

STORYTELLING

In a workshop format, professional storytellers demonstrate the art of storytelling, teach performance skills and coach individual students in developing their own style. Students practice before each other, critiquing and being critiqued. They provide feedback in a caring, respectful manner. The workshop concludes with the students' first public performance before parents and school staff. They meet monthly or quarterly to rehearse, schedule requests for performances, assign and coordinate appearance, and support each other. Because the training is extensive, students are asked to commit two years of availability, responding to occasional requests for storytelling performances during that time.

GRADES
6 - 10

FORMAT
Districtwide

DISCIPLINES
Art
Social studies
Language arts

TIME
40 hours

MATERIALS NEEDED
Art supplies
Canvas
Video equipment
Studio space

TIME MANAGEMENT
The Mehlville School District piloted this unit as a two-week summer workshop for gifted artists, with separate training sessions for storytellers and the video production team offered during the school year. This is one of several scheduling alternatives.

ILLUSTRATING THE STORY

The storytellers also narrate videotaped productions. These video productions create the illusion of a book that turns its own pages. Student-generated illustrations guide the story's progress. The camera slowly pans one scene after another, synchronizing its movement with the storyteller's narration.

Students from several schools are involved in illustrating each story. They are often from honors or accelerated art classes and ask or are invited to participate. The nature and quantity of the work demands their commitment and cooperation. One story may require 20 to 30 separate pieces of art. A group of students are assigned to one tale. Together they perform the following tasks:

- Research the culture and landscapes to accurately reflect the setting.
- Sketch storyboards to indicate the scenes that are to be depicted.
- Create the scenes using watercolors, markers, chalks, oils, acrylics, etc.
- Mount the art in the proper sequence.
- Work with the video production team, selecting appropriate background music and assisting with the staging or set-up.

PRODUCTION TEAM

This team involves students with an interest or experience in video production. Optimally, students work with a professional and have access to a production studio. They work together to:

- Develop a script, keying the story's narration to each visual component.
- Select background music.
- Construct a storyboard that synchronizes the title and credits, narration, background music, camera action (zoom, pan) and transitions.
- Set up illustrations.
- Tape the narration and background music.
- Complete the actual camera work.
- Follow the filming on a monitor. Reshoot footage if necessary or "log" the video, noting portions intended for use. A log entry might read, "Segment starts 5 minutes into filming and continues for 20 minutes."
- Dub in narration and music in the control room.
- Preview and edit.
- Make duplicate copies of final production for video library.

STORYTELLING VIDEO LIBRARY

The video library becomes a resource for teachers and parents at the elementary level. An accompanying guide can be developed by the storytellers to correlate each tape to the trait that it emphasizes.

CLASSROOM CONNECTIONS

The video story or live performance which plays before an elementary classroom audience becomes the foundation for a lesson. The following example demonstrates how the storyteller could explore the trait of honesty with the class.

- Run the storytelling presentation of "The Emperor's New Clothes."
- Ask questions that encourage students to reflect on the story: What do you think the townspeople were feeling and thinking? Why did they say they saw something they couldn't have seen? Have you ever experienced or witnessed a similar situation?
- Introduce the trait of honesty. Define it and place a written version of the definition in a visible site.
- Who was honest in the story of "The Emperor's New Clothes"? What happened as a result?
- Relate other examples of honesty and dishonesty, using situations and terms the students can relate to and understand.
- Ask students to demonstrate their understanding of the trait of honesty by drawing a picture (K-2), writing power paragraphs (3-4) or giving an oral report about the most honest person they know (5-6).

HOME

The availability of the videos can be advertised in fliers sent home with elementary students. Parents should be encouraged to check out the videos and show them at home. A guide can define the traits highlighted in the story and suggest discussion questions appropriate for students at different grade levels. Family trips to libraries, cultural centers and storytelling presentations encourage students to learn more about the stories and the cultures from which they emerge.

COMMUNITY

Community involvement is inherent in the project. Professionals from the fields of communication and production are sought to work with students in creating the videotapes. Storytellers are enlisted to train students in narration. In addition, guest speakers can explore the folklore and culture of the countries in which the stories originate. The local library, shopping mall or community center can display the student-produced storyboards with an explanation of how the artwork is part of the school district's approach to character education.

SOURCE OF INSPIRATION

Sue Hinkel, Mehlville School District

CHARACTER EDUCATION
ASSEMBLY TEAM

A team of students from several grade levels support character education by producing monthly assemblies that focus on the trait of the month.

OBJECTIVES

1. Promote the character traits of **assertiveness, confidence, cooperation, initiative, perseverance, responsibility** and **risk-taking.**

2. Participate as a committed team member.

3. Gain confidence in performing before an audience.

DESCRIPTION

An educator in charge of monthly character education assemblies shares this responsibility with a team of eight to 10 students. The students perform solos, ensemble arrangements and dramatic readings. They also emcee and work backstage to make sure things proceed smoothly throughout the assembly. The team operates as a cohesive, highly motivated group. Members cooperate and support each other. They express assertiveness, initiative, reliability, respect for each other's abilities and talents, healthy risk-taking and perseverance in meeting the demands of the assembly performances.

Students audition to become part of the Assembly Team, and those who join in their freshmen or sophomore years often continue until they are seniors. They are selected for their talent and their interest in character education.

The assemblies usually focus the students on a single trait, such as respect, service or perseverance. The advisor plans the program, inviting a guest speaker and selecting poetry, dramatic readings and songs that reinforce the theme. These pieces are presented by members of the Assembly Team. Other of the school's performing groups—show and concert choirs; string ensembles; jazz, symphonic and concert bands; acting and dance troupes—become part of the program at the advisor's invitation. The following program which focused on respect for self and others, illustrates the contributions of the Assembly Team and the quality of the program selections.

GRADES
9 - 12

FORMAT
Extracurricular

DISCIPLINES
Music
Speech
Performing arts

TIME
45-minute
assemblies,
10+ hours in
preparation
for each assembly

MATERIALS NEEDED
Assorted props

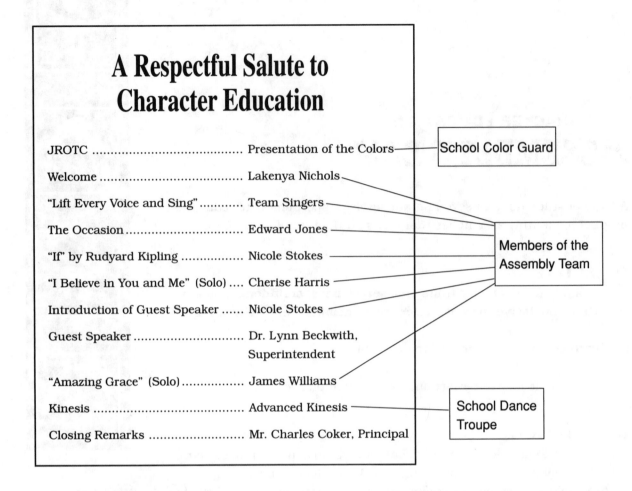

A Respectful Salute to Character Education

JROTC .... Presentation of the Colors —— School Color Guard

Welcome .... Lakenya Nichols

"Lift Every Voice and Sing" .... Team Singers

The Occasion .... Edward Jones

"If" by Rudyard Kipling .... Nicole Stokes

"I Believe in You and Me" (Solo) .... Cherise Harris

Introduction of Guest Speaker ...... Nicole Stokes

Guest Speaker .... Dr. Lynn Beckwith, Superintendent

"Amazing Grace" (Solo) .... James Williams

Kinesis .... Advanced Kinesis

Closing Remarks .... Mr. Charles Coker, Principal

Members of the Assembly Team

School Dance Troupe

HOME

The role of the family and the community in modeling character traits is celebrated in a "service" assembly. The school staff, parents and students respond to a simple questionnaire about their volunteer efforts with community organizations. Parents are selected, based on the results of the questionnaire, to present a brief description of the organizations to which they have committed time and effort.

COMMUNITY

These organizations—Boy Scouts, Girl Scouts, American Red Cross, United Way, Salvation Army and many, many more—become the focal point of the program. As each is introduced, a candle is lit. After these presentations, certificates are awarded by the Assemby Team to members of the staff and student body who have committed a substantial number of hours to volunteer services in the past year.

SOURCE OF INSPIRATION

Vernon Beard, University City High School, University City School District

Credit Union Practicum

Juniors and seniors operate a branch office of a credit union on the high school campus, learning practical financial background, customer service skills and the essential role of positive character traits and ethics in conducting business.

OBJECTIVES

1. Promote the character traits of **cooperation, honesty, respect, responsibility, self-discipline, self-esteem** and **service.**

2. Learn salesmanship, financial management skills, banking procedures and regulations and ethical decision-making.

DESCRIPTION

The Credit Union Practicum is a cooperative effort between a credit union, the high school business department and students. The particular format developed by Pattonville High School and the Educational Employees Credit Union involves several facets:

- Students enroll as juniors in the Credit Union Practicum, a business course with a two-year commitment.

- They invest three weeks during the summer prior to their junior year in training conducted by credit union personnel, including two weeks of on-the-job experience at a branch office.

- The Educational Employees Credit Union provides the school with a computer terminal which is linked to all the branch offices, a safe and a daily courier service to deliver deposits to the nearest branch office.

- On a rotating schedule, students staff the school credit union from 11:00 a.m. to 12:30 p.m. every school day. As a fully functioning branch, the school site is equipped by the credit union and connected by computers to the credit union's central office.

- Four students work each shift: two as tellers and two as account representatives. They are able to process deposits and withdrawals; reconcile their transactions; open checking, savings, holiday and money market accounts; take credit histories; order checks; issue ATM cards, traveller's checks and money orders; and accept Visa payments.

GRADES
11, 12

FORMAT
Classroom
Extracurricular

DISCIPLINES
Math
Business

TIME
Yearlong class plus
3 weeks of training

MATERIALS INCLUDED
Types of Credit
Situational Dilemmas

MATERIALS NEEDED
Computers, safe
Direct link to a
Credit Union

- Students attend the Credit Union Practicum class which meets daily, providing time to manage the operations of the credit union, including:
  - the preparation of daily deposits
  - the preparation of end-of-the-month reports
  - completion of paperwork
  - resolution of problems and ethical dilemmas

- The Credit Union Practicum curriculum includes units on customer relations, income taxes, stocks and bonds, payroll, loans, interest rates, compliance regulations and ethics. They recognize the character traits that ensure success in their operations: patience in dealing with customers, initiative in learning new skills, honesty in handling money and respect for others expressed in confidentiality. Students focus on responsibility in several contexts, including credit management. See page 213 for a related handout. They also discuss and resolve dilemmas that occur in the process of doing business. See "Situational Dilemmas" on page 214.

SCHOOL & DISTRICT

Administrators or school board members can speak to the class about financial management on a large scale, explaining the district's financial goals, its annual budget, loans and investments. Credit Union Practicum students can also speak to classes in schools throughout the district. They explain balance sheets to fellow business students, the risks and responsibilities of credit to Family and Consumer Science students and the computations of compounded interest to math students. They introduce middle-school students to the services of a credit union, including checking and savings options, and they reinforce the role of personal responsibility in financial decisions.

HOME

Parents can ground their student's understanding in reality by reviewing their financial goals, their responsible use of credit cards and the income they devote to savings, retirement and investments.

COMMUNITY

Credit unions express their responsibility as corporate citizens through charitable outreach programs. The members of the class join them. In this particular case, they contributed to canned food drives, an "adopt-a-family" holiday program and a toy drive for an area children's home.

SOURCE OF INSPIRATION

Sandy Recor, Pattonville High School, Pattonville School District
Jodi Harris and Cathy Meeh, Educational Employees Credit Union

Types of Credit

Consumer loans come in two basic types: secured and unsecured. If your loan is **secured,** you'll have to offer the lender collateral or security. Collateral is the property the financial institution has a right to take if you don't repay the loan. For example, if you borrow money to buy a car, the car will serve as collateral for the loan. If you don't make your loan payments, the lender can repossess the car.

If your loan is **unsecured,** you don't have to offer the lender collateral; Your promise to repay is enough if the lender thinks you're a good risk. These loans are also known as "signature" loans since your signature on the loan application is all you need. If you don't make your payments, the lender can start legal action to get the money, which can harm your credit rating. Credit cards are one type of unsecured loan.

General purpose credit cards such as MasterCard and Visa are issued by many credit unions, other financial institutions and companies. These revolving accounts, which may charge an annual fee, allow you to charge up to a preset amount—your credit limit—and either pay the balance in full each month or extend payments over time. The quicker you pay off the balance, the less interest you're charged. Surveys show you're likely to find the best deal on these credit cards at a credit union. Many credit unions offer lower interest rates, lower annual fees and better grace period options than elsewhere.

Retail store credit cards are revolving accounts that can only be used at the stores or companies that issue them. Although they generally charge no annual fee and may be easier to get than general purpose credit cards, they usually charge a higher rate of interest.

Oil company credit cards generally require you to pay your bill in full each month. However, for more expensive purchases, such as tires and car repairs, some issuers let you make monthly payments and charge you interest.

The Costs of Credit

Loan rates and terms from finance companies, retail stores and financial institutions can vary greatly. Compare these things when shopping for credit:

Annual percentage rate (APR): This is the standardized interest rate you must pay the lender each year for the use of borrowed money.

Finance charge: This is the total dollar amount the loan will cost you. It includes fees and interest, plus any other charges.

Loan maturity: A longer repayment period lowers your monthly payments but increases the total amount of interest you pay.

Grace period: This is the length of time you have before interest gets charged. For example, on credit cards the grace period for new purchases is typically 20 to 30 days. If the card doesn't have a grace period, or if you carry over a balance or take a cash advance, you're usually charged interest right away.

Situational Dilemmas

Ethics are the principles of morality or rules of conduct Ethical behavior conforms to these rules; unethical behavior violates them. We seek to learn what makes actions right or wrong. Deciding the difference can be a more complex process than it might seem at first. Below are some situations that can be analyzed involving ethics in the credit union and the workplace. People base ethical decisions on their personal values and principles, which are developed through individual life experiences. Therefore, since everyone has different experiences, decisions about each case will vary.

1. A sign was placed over the ATM machine at a bank: "ATM Machine is out of order." The customers were asked to drop their deposits in the box next to the ATM and their deposits would be processed at a later date. The perpetrator walked off with the contents. How would you have felt if this happened to you? Could this theft have been prevented?

2. You walk by a day-and-night teller machine in a mall. You see a bank credit card that was left there by a previous user. You look around and see that there is no one nearby to claim the card. If you leave it there, someone else may find it. What will you do?

3. You make a payment on your credit account at a customer service center. The worker, who is new and in training, accidentally credits your account for more than you paid. For example, you gave her $25 and she credited your account for $50. What will you do?

4. A friend comes into the credit union needing money for lunch. She asks you, as a teller, to slip her money from your teller drawer. She states, "You can put the money back tomorrow." What will you do?

5. A member at the credit union brings in a deposit to you As a teller, you deposit the money into the person's account. After the customer leaves the counter, you realize he gave you $20 more than was stated on his deposit slip. What will you do?

6. Sally Smith came into the credit union to make a rather large deposit. After she left, a worker in the student credit union started discussing her balance with others around him. "I cannot believe how much money Sally has in her account. I think I will ask her out on a date." What do you think?

ETHICAL DECISION-MAKING
IN THE WORKPLACE & SOCIETY

This one-day, interactive workshop introduces an ethical decision-making process to seniors, using realistic dilemmas from the workplace and society. Professionals from diverse career fields voluntarily serve as table leaders and facilitate the discussion and learning among small groups of students.

OBJECTIVES

1. Promote the character traits of **caring, commitment, cooperation, goal-setting, honesty, perseverance, self-discipline** and **service.**

2. Develop an understanding of how values are acquired and the relationship between values and ethics.

3. Learn and apply an ethical decision-making process.

4. Explore the application of ethical values to career fields and real-life dilemmas.

DESCRIPTION

The format for this workshop builds progressively on information and understanding developed throughout the day. In early sessions, students identify qualities that are important to them (e.g., being an honest person, graduating with honors, gaining self-confidence and personal growth, finding a way to serve or care for others). They recognize individual values, how these values might differ from person to person, and how values influence personal choices. Students also identify group and community values using worksheets similar to those included with *License to Lead* (pages 117-124). Through case studies, students realize what happens when values are taken into a setting where hard decisions must be made. Here they learn a five-step decision-making model that applies to the dilemmas shown on video or described through worksheets. In this process, students (1) identify the problem, (2) discuss the possible causes of the problem, (3) brainstorm possible solutions, (4) determine what

GRADES
12

FORMAT
One-day workshop

TIME
Preparation time
Workshop: 6 hours

MATERIALS NEEDED
Curriculum guide

ETHICAL DECISION-MAKING IN THE WORKPLACE & SOCIETY
A curriculum guide and supporting materials are available from NASSP:
National Association of
Secondary School Principals
1904 Association Drive
Reston, Virginia 20191-1537
(703) 860-0200
Product No. 6619101

values support each of the proposed solutions and (5) use a grid to weigh values with solutions in order to finally decide what action to take. In the afternoon, the students apply what they have learned to an ethical dilemma developed by their table leader as a realistic example of a situation that could occur on the job.

This workshop is used in high schools throughout the country. The following ideas suggest variations that a few educators developed.

- Chris Holmes has introduced the subject with a series of movie clips that dramatize ethical dilemmas from such films as *The Fugitive* and *Indecent Proposal*. Discussion helps students connect the choice-making they see on the screen to values and ethics.

- Clint Blandford extends the afternoon discussions with professionals to include other aspects of the job and increase students' career awareness.

- Ginny Schenck maximizes the workshop's potential for bringing different communities together. She coordinates three workshops. One involves students from two schools in the same district. Another combines students from several schools in two districts. A third draws students from 10 area high schools.

CLASSROOM CONNECTIONS

Class sessions designed to prepare students for the workshop can include an historical review of ethics, a comparison of moral and legal codes in different cultures and an examination of current ethical issues that appear in the news. See *Ethics in Science and Technology* starting on page 223 for ideas.

HOME

Students can be encouraged to share the workshop experience with their families and to continue the conversation about values, ethics and workplace dilemmas. Each member of the family may have opinions and stories to share that will add an even deeper understanding of the origins of values, work place challenges and ethical decisions.

COMMUNITY

Professional table leaders can be encouraged to provide follow-up contact with students, one-on-one, at the work site. They can enhance career awareness as they talk about aspects of the position: educational requirements, experience, day-to-day activity and opportunities for growth.

SOURCE OF INSPIRATION

Chris Holmes, School District of Clayton • Clint Blandford, Lindbergh School District • Ginny Schenck, Rockwood School District

CHARACTER STUDIES

This advanced placement English course is built on the notion that literature challenges us to take an informed moral stand, to examine lives well-lived and lives squandered and to examine our values in light of others. Students hone their reading and analytical skills while exploring timeless questions of identity, moral choices and what gives life dignity and purpose.

OBJECTIVES

1. Promote the character traits of **commitment, honesty, perseverance, respect, responsibility, self-discipline** and **service.**

2. Practice for the advanced placement exams in language and literature, concentrating on style analysis and written responses to literature.

3. Learn how to obtain, organize and synthesize information.

4. Enhance the development and refinement of a value system through reading, writing and discussing.

DESCRIPTION

The course is organized into quarter-length units. Each unit explores a broad theme through an extensive reading list.

UNIT 1: WHO AM I?

The search for identity is a universal human endeavor that encompasses values, interests, dreams, goals and perceptions. Literature facilitates this search as it explores the lives of fictional characters and experiments with various points of view, style and tone. Amid the more structured assignments are quick-write questions, described in "Teacher's Notes" on page 220. Students write a response to a question in 10 minutes. For example, "Does Oedipus get what he deserves?" *(Oedipus Rex)*, "When have you felt invisible?" *(Invisible Man)*. In the first quarter, students complete the following required readings and select one book from the Unit 1 list on page 221.

Aristotle. From *The Poetics*
Sophocles. *Oedipus Rex*
Flannery O'Connor. *Wise Blood*
Ralph Ellison. *Invisible Man*

Leslie Silko. *Ceremony*
James Joyce. *A Portrait of the Artist as a Young Man*
Franz Kafka. *Metamorphosis*

GRADES
12

FORMAT
Classroom

DISCIPLINES
English literature
Language arts

TIME
Yearlong course

MATERIALS INCLUDED
Teacher's Notes
Course Bibliography
Some Approaches
to Morality

UNIT 2: WHAT IS TRUTH?

This unit is focused on truth in both its metaphysical and narrative dimensions. Students examine the nature of "fact" and "truth" as presented through various media. They study works that merge past, present and future, that retell the same event from different perspectives and use language to confuse as well as to illuminate. They meet literary characters who examine the truths by which they live and grapple with what is a meaningful life. They, in turn, reflect on the facts, truths and nature of their own lives.

Students select one book from the Unit 2 bibliography shown on page 221 and complete the following required readings:

George Orwell. "Politics and the English Language"
Margaret Atwood. *The Handmaid's Tale*
Edward Albee. *Who's Afraid of Virginia Woolf?*
Annie Dillard. "Teaching a Stone to Talk"
William Shakespeare. *Hamlet*
Plato. "Allegory of the Cave"
William Faulkner, *As I Lay Dying*
T. S. Eliot, *Four Quartets*
George Orwell. *1984*

UNIT 3: HOW DO WE MAKE MORAL CHOICES?

This unit examines situations involving moral choices. Historically, cultures have determined what is good and what is evil, codifying some of these decisions into laws and precepts. In our current culture, good and evil are increasingly arbitrary, contextually based or ambiguous. "Some Approaches to Morality" on page 222 recognizes the latitude among definitions of what is good, moral or right. The content of the *Building Decision Skills* curriculum (pages 163-170) helps to work with this latitude. Based on Rushworth Kidder's concepts, it identifies dilemmas that bring two positive values into conflict and offers a way to look at resolution from more than one perspective. For instance, in *Antigone*, Creon must choose between justice and mercy, two positive values. In considering the state as a whole, Creon chooses justice and an "ends-based approach" to resolve the issue. Students select one book from the bibliography for Unit 3 on page 221 and complete the following required readings:

Annie Dillard. "The Deer at Providentia"
Dante Aligheri. *The Inferno* (trans. Ciardi)
Fyodor Dostoevsky. *Crime and Punishment*
George Orwell. "Shooting an Elephant"
Robert Penn Warren. *All the King's Men*

Sophocles. *Antigone*
Joseph Conrad. *Heart of Darkness*
Henrik Ibsen. *An Enemy of the People*
William Shakespeare. *Macbeth*

UNIT 4: WHAT IS THE NATURE OF A GOOD LIFE? FINDING PURPOSE

For some, "the good life" means being financially secure; for some, it means adhering to family traditions and values; and for some, it means daring to challenge the status quo or persevering to bring about needed change within the system. From an existentialist viewpoint, individuals are responsible for creating their own meaning apart from meanings prescribed by community, family or country. This unit examines various definitions of "a life well lived." Students select one book from the Unit 4 bibliography shown on page 221 and complete the following required readings:

Annie Dillard. "Living Like Weasels"   Joseph Heller. *Catch-22*
Albert Camus. *The Plague*   Herman Hesse. *Siddhartha*
Samuel Beckett. *Waiting for Godot*

SCHOOL

The National Forensic League sponsors competitive events in dramatic readings as well as debate. The literary works studied in this course— T. S. Eliot's poetry, for instance, or scenes from *The Glass Menagerie*— provide excellent material for students to present in these competitions. Dramatic readings also enrich character education assemblies. See *Assembly Team* on pages 209-210 for an effective program design.

HOME

In a note accompanying the class syllabus, parents are asked to look at the bibliography and identify books they have read for pleasure or past school assignments. They reflect on the question, "Who are the heroes you remember and why are they heroes?" Students write a brief synopsis of the conversation with their parents.

COMMUNITY

Area libraries and book stores can be enlisted to support students' efforts. They can post a copy of the course bibliography or develop a series of posters that challenge adult readers to read some of the selections in each unit and address such questions as "Justice or mercy? Would I respond as Creon did in *Antigone*?" or "What is a well-lived life?" A book discussion led by students from the class and sponsored by the library or book store becomes a natural extension of the poster campaign.

SOURCE OF INSPIRATION

Kathleen Puhr, Clayton High School, School District of Clayton

Teacher's Notes

Invisible Man by Ralph Ellison

This novel is the first one I teach in Unit I on Identity (Who am I). I distribute the novel early in the quarter and give students about two weeks in which to read it outside of class. At the same time, I give students several 4" x 6" cards. These are divided into four sections so they can jot down words they don't know and passages from the text that they find puzzling, interesting or beautiful.

On the first day of discussion, I have students write for 10 minutes about the question, "When have you felt invisible?" I ask volunteers to read their comments and I collect the students' papers. We talk about factors that contribute to invisibility. By the end of our study of the novel we have talked about who and what gives us our identity, who and what makes us "visible."

Thematically, we work with the notion of sight versus blindness, a carryover from our discussion of *Oedipus Rex*, the first work of the course. I particularly promote the burial and resurrection theme. We read aloud several sections from the Epilogue, note the echoes from Emerson and talk about the importance of recognizing that our identity is linked to our society and culture. We can and do make a difference to the world. This theme is central to the unit and to the course. In conjunction with our discussion of the novel, we listen to blues recordings by Robert Johnson and Billie Holiday and examine poems about identity and invisibility, including Paul Lawrence Dunbar's "We Wear the Mask."

Ceremony by Leslie Silko

We begin the study by discussing Diane Burns' poem, "Sure You Can Ask Me a Personal Question" and the notion of stereotyping as a convenient way of assigning identity. We trace the history of Native American involvement in wars since many of the novel's characters are World War II veterans, and we read a Navajo creation story. We discuss the role of myth in the novel's narrative and thematic design.

In a broad sense, Silko challenges us to study the story of our lives. We spend time discussing the ceremonies in students' lives and whether or how ceremonies should change.

Thematically, one of the key notions of the novel is that we all belong to the web of existence and that our actions do, in fact, cause the web to change. This theme, too, becomes central to our discussions throughout the year. It reemerges in an obvious way in Robert Penn Warren's *All the King's Men*, a novel we study third quarter.

Independent Reading List

UNIT I: WHO AM I?

Thomas Pynchon. *The Crying of Lot 49*
Toni Morrison. *Sula*
Amy Tan. *The Joy Luck Club*
John Okada. *No No Boy*
Joyce Carol Oates. *Wonderland*
Nellie Larsen. *Quicksand*
Virginia Woolf. *Orlando*
Henri-Beyle Stendahl. *The Red and the Black*
William Faulker. *Light in August*
Jane Austen. *Pride and Prejudice*
Lewis Carroll. *Alice's Adventures in Wonderland*
Willa Cather. *My Antonia*
Annie Proulx. *The Shipping News*
Gloria Naylor. *The Women of Brewster Place*
Francis Sherwood. *Vindication*
Gish Jen. *Typical American*
Michael Dorris. *A Yellow Raft in Blue Water*
Henry James. *The Portrait of a Lady*
Kazuo Ishiguro. *The Remains of the Day*
Henry Ibsen. *A Doll's House*
Edmund Rostand. *Cyrano de Bergerac*
Tennesee Williams. *A Streetcar Named Desire*
Kenzaburo Oe. *The Silent Cry.*

UNIT 2: WHAT IS TRUTH?

Kurt Vonnegut. *Slaughterhouse Five*
Don Delillo. *Libra*
D.M. Thomas. *The White Hotel*
Joyce Carol Oates. *Expensive People*
Virginia Woolf. *To the Lighthouse*
G. Garcia-Marquez. *One Hundred Years of Solitude*
Jean Toomer. *Cane*
John Fowles. *The French Lieutenant's Woman*
D.H. Lawrence. *The Fox*
Truman Capote. *In Cold Blood*
Bobbie Ann Mason. *In Country*
Jayne Ann Phillips. *Machine Dreams*
Martin Amis. *Time's Arrow*
Toni Morrison. *Jazz; Beloved*
Italo Calvino. *Invisible Cities*
Richard Powers. *The Gold Bug Variations*
E.L. Doctorow. *Ragtime*
Joseph Heller. *God Knows*
William Faulkner. *As I Lay Dying*
Henrik Ibsen. *The Wild Duck*
Erich Maria Remarque. *All Quiet on the Western Front*
William Shakespeare. *A Midsummer Night's Dream*
Tim O'Brien. *In the Lake of the Woods*
Tom Stoppard. *Rosencrantz and Guildenstern are Dead*

UNIT 3: HOW DO WE MAKE MORAL CHOICES?

Mary Wollstonecraft Shelley. *Frankenstein*
Alan Paton. *Cry, the Beloved Country*
Gustav Flaubert. *Madame Bovary*
Herman Melville. *Moby Dick; Billy Budd*
Charlotte Bronte. *Jane Eyre*
Thomas Hardy. *Tess of the D'Urbervilles*
Fyodor Dostoevsky. *Notes from Underground*
Donna Tartt. *The Secret History*
Gloria Naylor. *Linden Hills*
Chinua Achebe. *Things Fall Apart*
Ernest Hemingway. *The Sun Also Rises*
Tom Wolfe. *The Bonfire of the Vanities*
Theodore Dreiser. *Sister Carrie*
Edith Wharton. *The House of Mirth*
Charles Baxter. *Shadow Play*
Jane Smiley. *A Thousand Acres*
Oscar Wilde. *The Picture of Dorian Gray*
Richard Wright. *Native Son*
Upton Sinclair. *The Jungle*
Aldous Huxley. *Brave New World*
E.M. Forster. *A Passage to India*
Voltaire. *Candide*
Christopher Marlowe. *Dr. Faustus*
Robert Bolt. *A Man for All Seasons*
Archibald Macleish. *JB*

UNIT 4: FINDING PURPOSE

Robert Pirsig. *Zen and the Art of Motorcycle Maintenance*
Albert Camus. *The Stranger*
Barbara Kingsolver. *The Bean Trees; Animal Dreams*
Margaret Atwood. *Surfacing*
Graham Greene. *The Power and the Glory*
Fyodor Dostoevsky. *The Brothers Karamazov*
David James Duncan. *The Brothers K*
Jack Kerouac. *On the Road*
Charles Johnson. *Middle Passage*
Leo Tolstoy. *Anna Karenina*
Anne Tyler. *Dinner at the Homesick Restaurant*
Tom Robbins. *Even Cowgirls Get the Blues*
Charles Dickens. *Great Expectations*
Annie Dillard. *The Living*
Sylvia Plath. *The Bell Jar*
Marilynne Robinson. *Housekeeping*
Agnes Smedley. *Daughter of Earth*
Ayn Rand. *The Fountainhead*
Bernard Malamud. *The Fixer*
Reynolds Price. *Kate Vaiden*
John Irving. *A Prayer for Owen Meany*
James Baldwin. *Go Tell It on the Mountain*
Boris Pasternak. *Doctor Zhivago*

Some Approaches to Morality

Socrates-Plato Evil is due only to ignorance or madness. Therefore, no person voluntarily does evil. Wrong action is always due to intellectual error. Philosophers are uniquely able to look past the sensory world and to discern that which is "good." [See *Plato's Republic,* Book VI]

Aristotle The goal of human existence is the well-being of the rational soul. Virtue is a means to this end. Virtue is always identified as a means between two extreme possibilities. For instance, too much or too little exercise destroys health. [See *Nicomachean Ethics*]

Epicureanism Pleasure is the standard of "good." "Pleasure" is best achieved by moderate indulgence of the appetites and cultivation of the intellect.

Religious Many religions require that one follow the dictates of a Supreme Being, otherwise risking eternal punishment of one's eternal Self (soul). On the other hand, some religions, such as Buddhism, presuppose neither a Supreme Being nor a Self.

The Law of the Jungle
Every person lives for himself or herself; no holds barred.

Immanuel Kant
Kant believes we should act in accord with fixed rules.

The Golden Rule
"Treat others as you would like them to treat you." Although most world religions offer a moral principle similar to the Golden Rule, the New Testament provides two clear defintions in Matthew 7:12 and Luke 6:31. This principle is care-based, putting love for others first.

Utilitarianism "Actions are right as they tend to promote happiness and wrong as they tend to produce the reverse of happiness. Happiness is considered pleasure and the absence of pain. This system is ends-based, requiring speculation on possible futures (cost-benefit analysis) and is the basis for much legislation.

Friedrich Nietzsche
Nietzsche's "revaluation of all values" requires the testing and hypercritical scrutiny of all of society's most treasured values. [See *The Gay Science, On Genealogy of Morals* and *Beyond Good and Evil*]

Rushworth Kidder
One of the many contemporary voices in the discussion of morals and ethics, Rushworth Kidder argues that the toughest ethical choices occur when two positive values are brought into conflict with each other. Kidder suggests that although the particulars of ethical dilemmas vary greatly, they can be distilled to one of these four patterns: Loyalty versus Truth, Justice versus Mercy, Short-Term Goals versus Long-Term Goals and Individual versus Community.

ETHICS
IN SCIENCE AND TECHNOLOGY

This yearlong course is designed to equip seniors with the knowledge, confidence and skills to respond to ethical dilemmas they might meet in their future careers.

OBJECTIVES

1. Promote the character traits of **caring, cooperation, commitment, honesty, perseverance, respect, responsibility** and **self-discipline.**

2. Equip students with historical background and ethical decision-making skills. Strengthen written and oral articulation skills.

3. Apply these skills to current ethical dilemmas that occur in the fields of health care, biotechnology, chemistry, computer technology and environmental science.

DESCRIPTION

This unit sketches aspects of a comprehensive, two-semester senior class curriculum. An outline on page 227 provides a skeletel overview and text resources for educators interested in designing an ethics course. On a smaller scale, the course uses such teaching strategies as a personal inventory, journal-writing, role-play and video viewing to enhance character education in existing classes. The subject matter adapts to the disciplines shown on the right and the strategies apply to nearly all classes.

PERSONAL INVENTORY
At the start of the course, all students complete a six-page Personal Inventory, registering their responses to issues that arise in daily and professional life. A sampling of the questions appears on pages 228-229. The exercise enhances self-awareness and reinforces a classroom ethos that validates personal views and different perspectives. The same survey is taken again near the end of the course. Students compare their answers and explore changes in their perceptions and opinions in an essay that becomes part of their final exam.

LECTURES
Lectures at the beginning of the course define ethics, law and religion. They introduce the basic tenets of world philosophies dating from 1800 B.C. to

GRADES
12

FORMAT
Classroom

DISCIPLINES
Social studies
Life sciences
Chemistry
Biology
Health
Technology
Business

TIME
Yearlong class

MATERIALS INCLUDED
Course Outline
Personal Inventory
Hammurabi's Code
Journal Assignment
Ethics at the movies

modern moral theories. Students survey, compare and contrast ideas expressed by Hammurabi, Hippocrates, Plato, Aristotle, Pythagoras, Zeno, Epicurus, Lao Tse, Confucius, Muhammad, Immanuel Kant, Thomas Aquinas and Thomas Jefferson among others. They recognize many perspectives rather than a single value system or ethical code. An early assignment, for instance, asks students to compare the Code of Hammurabi to Mosaic Law. The understanding of different value systems, ethical positions and legal standards serves the students throughout the class. They learn to identify resolution strategies with the principles of particular philosophies.

JOURNAL WRITING

Journal-writing assignments are structured around articles from newspapers and news magazines that raise ethical questions or dilemmas. The topics may correlate with the unit of study or current events. For instance, students have wrestled with the ethics of genetic testing, the death of a student who was denied medical treatment because of the parents' religious beliefs, the right to stage a gay parade. They follow a four-part outline:

- Background: summarize what is happening in the situation
- Determine the ethical issue and state it or present it as a question.
- Give your personal evaluation, recommendation for resolution or judgment
- Support your response with reasoning and reference to specific ethical theories or principles

The student sample on page 232 follows these guidelines. Journal responses are assigned weekly and become the basis of a Friday discussion. Students orally present the question they formulated and their response to it. Other students question them, counter their assertions and offer their own perspectives during these discussions.

ROLE-PLAY

Role-play allows students to "travel a mile in the moccasins of another person." Two approaches are used in the class. The first one provides the most structure and predictability. The teacher chooses a situation that correlates to the unit of study. For instance, a script that raises the issues of surrogate parenting from the multiple perspectives of the surrogate mother, the doctor and the expectant parents reinforces the biomedical unit. The teacher assigns the parts to students to enact and concludes the activity with a discussion of the ethical dilemmas presented. The advantage of this approach is that a specific case can be used as a real-life example and a predetermined value judgment can be illustrated. Because the teacher conducts the research and provides the facts in the script, the integrity of the story is preserved. The disadvantage is that it rarely taps students' creative energies. The second approach is riskier in terms of its effectiveness in reaching a desired outcome. The teacher poses a fictional situation that presents an ethical dilemma. Rules or norms for the role-play must be established and characters created. Students assume the roles, consider the position of their character and create their own lines. The teacher stays involved during this creative work to make sure the students understand the task and are dealing with the dilemma realistically. Once interaction between the characters begins, the activity takes on the air of improvisational theater. Different groups of students working with the same sitatuion may well arrive at different conclusions, but this can make good discussion material. Both formats engage the imaginative dimension of learning and complement the reading and analytical work that is done. They allow students to pinpoint traits that helped or prevented the characters they portray from arriving at responsible decisions.

VIDEOS: VIEWING AND ANALYSIS
Ethical issues are frequently the subject of talk shows or prime-time investigative news programs. "60 Minutes," "48 Hours," "20/20," and "Prime Time" are recommended sources. A viewer's guide can be developed to focus the students on character traits that are present or noticeably lacking in these situations.

Ethical dilemmas are often projected onto the big screen in full-length films. Discussion questions, similar to those developed for *The Elephant Man* on page 233, involve students in identifying the issues, applying various philosophical approaches and models and determining where they stand.

DISCUSSION
Discussion is the cornerstone of this course. Each Friday is dedicated to discussion based on the week's journal entries. Discussion also follows video viewings, role-plays and many textbook assignments. In each case, students are encouraged to:

- formulate their own opinions through critical thinking and reflection,
- support them with sound reasoning,
- articulate them orally, and
- respond to questions and challenges from other students.

Students strengthen their ability to articulate and "think on their feet." They express several character traits as they assert their thoughts, perceptions and opinions; initiate challenges; and respect points of view that differ from theirs.

SCHOOL
The dilemmas explored in *Ethics in Science and Technology* are often relevant to other classes. Students research and articulate conflicting perspectives on issues as part of their ongoing journal and class assignments. With a little polish and teamwork, these can be presented as Point-Counterpoint sessions in social studies, biochemistry, health management, patient care and other classes. "Where does one draw the line between the media's right to free speech and the individual's right to privacy?" (social

studies), "Should individuals have the right to sell their organs?" (health, premedical courses), "Are the advances in invitro reproduction toying dangerously with creation?" (biochemistry).

HOME

Parents are invited to an evening meeting which introduces the course content, the methods of comparative study and the way students are evaluated. The emphasis on exploration, critical thinking, sound reasoning and articulation rather than "right" or "wrong" answers to issues is made clear. Parents receive a copy of the Personal Inventory that students take at the beginning of the course. They are encouraged to complete as much of it as time permits, compare their responses with those of their student and to use the inventory as a tool for meaningful and continuing conversations at home.

COMMUNITY

The interests and passions of people from the community—activists, advocates, ethicists, concerned citizens and professionals in medicine, media, law, research, business, technology and ecology—are matched to course topics. For instance, managers of the Mid-America Transplant Association present the complexity of issues that surround allocation of scarce organ supplies. Representatives from abortion rights and pro-life organizations present their positions. These guest speakers not only inform students, they model the qualities of personal responsibility, sound reasoning and effective articulation of one's ideas.

SOURCE OF INSPIRATION

Michael Pfefferkorn and Richard Rosenow, Gateway Institute of Technology, St. Louis Public Schools

Note: The basic scheme of the course was the result of a yearlong cooperative effort involving Cooperating School Districts (CSD), the META group, McDonnell Douglas and the social studies supervisor for the St. Louis Public Schools.

Course Outline

UNIT I: WHAT ARE ETHICS?
Definitions of values, morals/ethics,
law and religion
Survey: Personal Inventory

UNIT II: HISTORY OF ETHICS
From the Code of Hammurabi (1600 B.C.)
to Jeffersonian ideals (18th century A.D.)
Film: *Quiz Show*

UNIT III: MAJOR MORAL PHILOSOPHIES
Utilitarianism
Kant
Non-malfeasance
Beneficence
Autonomy
Distributive justice
Natural law

UNIT IV: BIOMEDICAL ETHICS
Text: *Interventions and Reflections: Basic Issues in Medical Ethics*
Films: *Coma, The Doctor, The Elephant Man*

UNIT V: ETHICS IN THE WORKPLACE
Film: *Bitter Harvest*
Ethical Decision-Making Process
Game: Gray Matters

UNIT VI: ENVIRONMENT, HUMAN ECOLOGY
Human ecology focuses on how cutural groups
treat each other ethically.
Environmental issues involve economic and
social needs of humans versus the quality of
life for all organisms on the planet.
Film: *The Mission*

UNIT VII: PERSONAL ETHICS
Text: *Index of Leading Cultural Indicators*
Retake Survey: Personal Inventory

CURRICULUM GUIDE AVAILABLE
Ethics: A View of Life, a curriculum guide for
Ethics in Science and Technology, is avail-
able by contacting CSD:
Cooperating School Districts
St. Louis Regional Education Park
8225 Florissant Rd.
St. Louis, MO 63121
Toll free: (800) 478-5684 ext. 4523
E-mail: ceconnect@info.csd.org

Course Materials

Bennett, W. J. *Index of Leading
Cultural Indicators*. New York:
Simon and Schuster, 1994.

Munson, R. *Interventions and
Reflections: Basic Issues in
Medical Ethics*. Belmont, CA:
Wadsworth, Inc., 1992.

Personal Inventory, pp. 228, 229

Ethics at the movies, p. 233

Personal Inventory

LOYALTY VERSUS TRUTH

A neighbor, whom you don't like, observed your best friend spraying graffiti on her garage. She reported it to the police. His alibi was that he was with you. If you lie, your friend won't get into any trouble. If you don't, you will lose a friend. You choose to: (A) back your friend or (B) tell the police the truth.

_____ (A) _____ (B) because_____

PEER LOYALTY VERSUS EMPLOYER LOYALTY

Your employer, Burger Heaven, pays 50 cents an hour over the minimum wage. Burger Heaven allows a meal break and food allowance of $3.75 once during each shift, Your (boy/girl) friend drops by almost every day. A fellow worker suggests that you give (him/her) a free hamburger and write it off as spoilage. You (A) follow or (B) refuse his advice.

_____ (A) _____ (B) because_____

RESPECT FOR LIFE VERSUS FREEDOM TO CHOOSE

Mary, an unwed 16-year-old, has plans to go to college to become a teacher. She is eight weeks pregnant, confused and sees her world crashing around her. Her boyfriend offers no help but demands she get an abortion. She should (A) carry the baby to term or (B) get an abortion.

_____ (A) _____ (B) because_____

FAIRNESS VERSUS COMPETITIVENESS

You are sitting behind a partition in the school cafeteria when you overhear a familiar voice. Janis Warren is detailing her team's strategy for an upcoming debate contest. The contest will decide the in-school champions who will compete in the regional tourney. Each member of the area-wide championship team will receive $1,000 in scholarships plus $150 in cash. Janis is unaware that you have joined the opposing debate team. You could remain where you are, listen to the entire planning session and tell your team captain as much as you remember. Or you could move elsewhere out of earshot and forget what you heard. You (A) move elsewhere or (B) divulge your findings.

_____ (A) _____ (B) because_____

INTEGRITY VERSUS INITIATIVE

World-Chem Inc. downsized and laid you off. Top-paying jobs are scarce. Euro-Chemical Corp. has a position open. You know some of World-Chem's trade secrets. Do you (A) refuse to betray your former employer or (B) use this knowledge to get the job.

_____ (A) _____ (B) because_____

Personal Inventory

Indicate whether you agree (A) or disagree (D) with the following statements.

ABORTION

____ A woman should have an exclusive right to control her own reproductive function.

____ Abortion is never a right, with the exception of saving the mother's life.

____ The claim of a fetus as a person must be given weight and respect in deliberating any action that would terminate its life.

____ The fetus is no more than a complicated clump of organic material and its removal involves no serious moral difficulties.

EUTHANASIA

____ If a person has a disease that will ultimately destroy the person's mind and the person wants to take his or her own life, a doctor should be allowed to assist the person in taking his or her own life.

____ A patient is in a coma, the doctors say brain activity has stopped and the patient is nourished through a feeding tube. A close family member should have the right to tell the doctor to remove the feeding tube and let the person die.

EXPERIMENTATION AND INFORMED CONSENT

____ Weller, Enders and Robbins developed the polio vaccine. The initial phase of their clinical testing involved injecting 30,000 children with a substance known to be useless in the prevention of polio—a placebo injection. It was realized, statistically, that some of those children would get the disease and die from it; however, they succeeded in proving the safety and effectiveness of their polio vaccine with this control group. Therefore, they were justified in not providing 30,000 children with a vaccine they believed to be effective.

____ In 1975, legal charges were brought against several Boston physicians who had injected antibiotics into living fetuses that were scheduled to be aborted. The aim of the research was to determine by autopsy, after the death of the fetuses, how much of the drug got into the fetal tissues. Such information is considered to be of prime importance because it increases our knowledge of how to provide medical treatment for a fetus still developing in its mother's womb. This type of research is both necessary and ethical.

____ A traditional medical-school demonstration consists of exsanguinating (bleeding to death) a dog to illustrate the circulation of blood. This instructional method is morally unacceptable.

Code of Hammurabi versus Mosaic Law

HONESTY
Code of Hammurabi

If a seignior accused a(nother) seignior and brought a charge of murder against him, but has not proved it, his accuser shall be put to death.

Old Testament

Exodus 23:1-3—Thou shalt not raise a false report; put not thine hand with the wicked to be an unrighteous witness.

Deuteronomy 5:20—Neither shalt thou bear false witness against thy neighbour.

Deuteronomy 19:16-21—If a false witness rises up against any man to testify against him that which is wrong: Then shall ye do unto him, as he had thought to have done unto his brother: so shall thou put the evil away from among you. And thine eye shall not pity; but life shall go for life, eye for an eye, tooth for tooth, hand for hand, foot for foot.

ENSLAVEMENT
Code of Hammurabi

If a seignior has stolen the son of a(nother) seignior, he shall be put to death.

Old Testament

Exodus 21:16—And he that stealeth a man, and selleth him, or if he be found in his hand, shall be surely put to death.

Deuteronomy 24:7—If a man be found stealing any of his brethern of the children of Israel, and maketh merchandise of him, or selleth him; then that thief shall die; and thou shalt put evil away from among you.

VALUE OF LIFE
Code of Hammurabi

If it was a life that was lost, the city and governor shall pay one mina (about 60 shekels) of silver to his people.

Old Testament

Deuteronomy 21:1ff—If one is found slain in the land which the Lord thy God giveth thee to possess . . . And it shall be, that the city which is next to the slain man, even the elders of that city shall take an heifer, which hath not been wrought with and which hath not drawn in the yoke: . . . and shall strike off the heifer's neck in the valley. And all the elders of that city shall wash their hands over the heifer that is beheaded in the valley. And they shall answer and say, Our hands have not shed his blood, neither have our eyes seen it.

Code of Hammurabi versus Mosaic Law

Compare Hammurabi's Code with Mosaic Law by listing answers for each of the following situations.

What is the penalty for bearing false witness?

*Code of Hammurabi*_____

_____

*Mosaic Law*_____

_____

What is the penalty for the forced enslavement of a countryman?

*Code of Hammurabi*_____

_____

*Mosaic Law*_____

_____

What is a city's responsibility for protecting lives?

*Code of Hammurabi*_____

_____

*Mosaic Law*_____

_____

Which of the two legal standards do you view as the harsher one? Check one.
Hammurabi's Code____ Mosaic Law____ Explain your choice.

What underlying principles are common to Hammurabi's Code and Mosaic Law?

How would these principles (which you gave when answering the above question) apply to modern law and ethical behavior?

Journal Assignment

Article Title: "Sexual Offense or Speech? UMSL Judges Must Decide"
Source: *St. Louis Post-Dispatch*

background

BACKGROUND

A sign was put up by fraternity, Sigma Pi, on the campus of the University of Missouri at St. Louis, as to boost up the attendance for a party featuring the "sexy legs" contest open for both male and female. The sign exposes two long-legged figures in high heels and bikinis bending down. One of the students, Linda Hutchinson, found the sign offensive and so she took her case against Sigma Pi to the student court. Hutchinson says that "these so-called men are inviting violence against the women of this campus as well as perpetuating the institutionalized oppression of women in our society." Thomas A. O'Keefe, Jr., a member of the fraternity, argued that they are "fully protected by freedom of speech," and "it's what we use to sell stuff in our society."

stating the ethical issue in the form of a question

ISSUE

Did a fraternity err in displaying on campus a sign showing bikini-clad women?

personal response

support response with sound reasoning

use of analogy to demonstrate point

OPINION

I personally found that sign offensive also. And to think them as colleagues, they would have some higher thinking than that. Even though they may not intend to invite violence upon women, they are in a way encouraging the harassment toward women. It is true that they are protected by the freedom of speech and the freedom of press, however, there are other things that are more decent that they could've put on to feature their party. I mean, what does a "sexy legs" contest have to do with someone's behind and wearing bikinis? If the contest was for both male and female, they could have put up a sign with both genders wearing regular school clothes. Neither of them would have to bend over to show their behinds....Second of all, the way that they're selling their fraternity is wrong. Take this to compare: If you want to sell your socks, would you have an image of someone wearing boots that have covered your socks? Just like how it is for the two females in the sign wearing bikinis and bending down. It shouldn't have been that way!

Major moral principle

Teacher's Note:
Students correlate major moral principles (MMP) to their journal entries after Unit III in the second semester and after this particular assignment. From the issue at hand, the student could apply distributive justice— the concept that everyone has an equal right to basic liberties and if there are inequalities, the least advantaged should receive the greatest benefit. The sign objectifies women without applying the same treatment to men.

Ethics at the movies

The following movies have been used in conjuction with the *Ethics in Science and Technology* course. The brief descriptions are paraphrased from *Leonard Matlin's 1997 Movie & Video Guide*, except when noted otherwise.

Bitter Harvest
A made-for-TV movie concerning a dairy farmer who tries to discover what is killing his herd. The farmer battles bureaucracy to find the truth, as the health of the community comes into conflict with the livelihood of the area's major source of economic activity. (From *Video Hound's Golden Movie Retriever*, 1994)

Coma (1978) PG   125 minutes
Someone is killing and stealing patients from a big-city hospital. A woman doctor bucks her superiors to pursue her suspicions. Starring Genevieve Bujold, Michael Douglas and Richard Widmark. Scripted and directed by Michael Crichton.

The Doctor (1991) PG13   125 minutes
A successful surgeon is diagnosed with throat cancer and learns what it is like to be a patient at the mercy of hospital bureaucracy and cold-blooded doctors. Starring William Hurt and Christine Lahti. Based on Dr. Ed Rosenbaum's experiences described in *A Taste of My Own Medicine*.

The Elephant Man (1980) PG   125 minutes
This is a moving dramatization of the life of John Merrick, a grotesquely deformed man who drew the attention of an eminent doctor in turn-of-the-century London. Starring Anthony Hopkins, David Lynch and Anne Bancroft. Screenplay by Christoper DeVore.

Quiz Show (1994) PG13   130 minutes
The engrossing story of a TV quiz show scandel in the late 1950s exposes the behind-the-scenes manipulation that cast Charles Van Doren, the scion of a socially prominent, intellectual family, as the winner of the game. Starring John Turturro, Rob Morrow and Ralph Fiennes. Directed by Robert Redford.

The Mission (1986) PG 125 minutes
Natives of the jungles of Brazil are lured into a community lifestyle by Jesuit missionaries, which ultimately leaves them vulnerable to political decisions and ruthless slave merchants. Starring Jeremy Irons and Robert DeNiro. Screenplay by Robert Bolt.

DISCUSSION QUESTIONS
The Elephant Man

Why do you think John Merrick chose to end his life?

What do you think is the most important lesson to be learned from this film?

What is the motive behind the carnival master's relationship with John Merrick? What is the motive behind the doctor's relationship with John Merrick? Are there any similarities?

What are the problems that arise in working with a severely deformed patient?

What was the fate of "freaks" in the 19th century?

How are deformed people treated in the 21st century?

CHARACTER COUNCILS
STUDENT TEAMS THAT SERVE
SECONDARY SCHOOLS IN CHARACTER EDUCATION

Councils are representative groups of secondary school students who assume leadership roles and help develop their school's character education process. The key word in the description is "representative." The group is representative of the student body in regard to gender, race, ethnicity, economic levels, grade levels, grade point averages and degrees of social involvement.

OBJECTIVES
1. Promote the character traits of **commitment, cooperation, decision-making, goal-setting, honesty, perseverance, respect, responsibility, self-discipline** and **service.**

2. Develop a group that represents the diversity of the student body.

3. Increase students' ability to identify and reflect the needs, concerns, and reactions of others within the school community.

4. Develop a communication avenue within the student body that can disseminate information and provide feedback.

5. Strengthen skills in conflict resolution, decision-making and problem-solving.

DESCRIPTION
Three programs in three different school districts illustrate the effectiveness of these councils. Each program chooses students who have exhibited interest in the council, either by application or by their behavior. The number of students involved on each council ranges from 28 to 45.

Training is another common feature of the three programs. Training involves an off-site workshop with team experiences that include outdoor challenges, instruction in active listening, defining and discussing character traits, problem-solving and, in one case, conflict resolution.

GRADES
9 - 12

FORMAT
Extracurricular

SKILLS
Conflict resolution
Problem-solving
Decision-making

TIME
Monthly or intermittent meetings

MATERIALS NEEDED
Meeting room
Offsite conference location (optional)

MATERIALS INCLUDED
Corridors of Respect

The **Flight Team,** comprising 45 students at Lindbergh High School, is divided into response groups of nine who meet regularly for two hours each month. These smaller groups respond to issues within the school, airing concerns and applying the problem-solving approaches learned in training. Members provide a sounding board to administrators and teachers on policies. They act as a liaison to other students, reporting back to them on resolutions and changes. The Flight Team, as a whole, was consulted regularly throughout a three-year process that expanded the school day and reorganized class schedules at the high school. One response team determined how to deal with a Ku Klux Klan group that was using the campus to advertise its mission. Another response team discussed school dress codes and made recommendations.

Northwest High School's **Committee of Forty** operates in the same fashion as the Flight Team. The group meets regularly for two hours each month with a faculty sponsor and the school principal. There are no formal structures, officers or dues. The students know they can provide candid and honest input in their sessions without repercussions. Topics discussed during regular sessions include brainstorming strategies to generate pride and spirit within the school; problem-solving such issues as dissatisfaction with school programs; soliciting feedback on a proposed reward system; or providing input on which classes should be weighted. The group is also called together to respond to special issues that arise, e.g., violence, vandalism or such crises as suicides or accidental deaths among their peers.

Brentwood School District's **Respect & Responsibility Student Task Force** involves students from the 6th through 12th grades who meet before or after school. They work in teams as they respond to the following responsibilities:

- *Monitoring the efforts of each grade level*: Each grade level is assigned a time period within the school year when they are responsible for communicating the concepts of respect and responsibility to the entire student body. Suggested activities for the campaigns include banners, posters, P.A. announcements, competitions and contests. Members stay in touch with grade leaders and stay abreast of plans and progress of the group.

- *Assembling The Corridor of Respect:* Each month the task force selects a student and a faculty or staff member who exemplify respect and responsibility. Their photos are posted with "respect and responsibility statements" that define and explain their contributions.

- *Assisting in coordination of special events:* One day is set aside each quarter to promote awareness of respect and responsibility. The organizers may ask staff and students to dress in a way that reflects their cultural heritage; to focus on perfect behavior for the day; or to change roles for the day, allowing students, staff, and administrators to switch roles in order to gain a deeper respect for one another's responsibilities and capabilities. Other examples of special events are motivational assemblies, character education days and appreciation ceremonies.

• *Planning student leadership conferences:* Task Force members plan, organize and facilitate conferences on character education. Every other year they produce a daylong program attended by 200 to 300 students from area high schools. Keynote speakers address issues in respect and responsibility. In break-out sessions, students from different schools present their efforts in character education.

The brief description of these three organizations—the Flight Team, Council of Forty and Respect & Responsibility Student Task Force—provides models for schoolwide councils at the middle and high school levels.

HOME

The handout on page 238 simplifies the concept of the Corridor of Respect and invites family members to quietly honor someone they know who exemplifies the traits of respect and responsibility. The take-home exercise is designed to encourage conversations about the way these people touch the lives of others and make a difference in their community.

COMMUNITY

The council members of the Flight Team and Council of Forty are chosen, in part, for their ability to represent their peers. At times, they are asked to articulate the concerns and interests of fellow students whether they are consistent with their own views or not. Elected officials—aldermen, representatives to the state or federal legislature—can be invited to address the ethical demands of such representation. How do they interpret the mandate to serve and represent their constituents? How do they stay in touch with their constituents? How do they know what their constituents think about certain issues? Who do they represent when their constituents do not agree? How do they vote when the stance of their constituents directly opposes their own view of the issue?

SOURCE OF INSPIRATION

Pam Ford, Brentwood High School, Brentwood School District
David Skillman, Lindbergh High School, Lindbergh School District
Sandy Wynn, Northwest High School, Northwest R-1 School District

CORRIDOR OF RESPECT

Please ask each member of your family to print the name of someone they know—a friend, relative, coach, neighbor, teacher, business associate, leader—who expresses the traits of respect and responsibility. As you circulate the form among your parents and siblings, take time to ask how their nominees communicate respect for others and a sense of responsibility to the greater community.

Name _____

Nominated by _____

Name _____

Nominated by _____

Name _____

Nominated by _____

Name _____

Nominated by _____

Name _____

Nominated by _____

PROJECT H.A.R.T.
HEALTHY ALTERNATIVES FOR RELATIONSHIPS AMONG TEENS

This course introduces valuable interpersonal skills, examines gender stereotypes and explores safe dating expectations and practices. Designed and conducted by representatives from two social agencies, it offers a proactive response to the prevalence of date rape and domestic violence.

OBJECTIVES

1. Promote the character traits of **caring, commitment, cooperation, goal-setting, honesty, perseverance, respect, responsibility, self-control** and **self-discipline.**

2. Teach life skills that increase awareness and help ensure the individual's safety in today's social climate.

3. Increase self-awareness and strengthen interpersonal skills.

DESCRIPTION

This course combines lecture, handouts, discussion and experiential learning activities in thirteen 50-minute sessions. The sessions focus on giving and taking criticism, resolving conflicts with win-win negotiation, managing anger, exploring gender stereotypes and sexism, examining media messages about gender roles, understanding the cycle of domestic violence, recognizing the dangers of date rape, and creating safe dating relationships. The character traits of caring, honesty, self-discipline, respect for self and others, and responsibility for one's feelings are defined and discussed as they relate to the subject matter. For instance, Lesson 3 is entitled "Taking It" and encourages students to:
- describe at least one situation in which they had to listen to someone else's criticism or anger directed at them.
- review suggestions for taking criticism shown on page 240.
- role-play these steps with a partner to practice taking criticism without starting an argument.
- identify the character traits that help to listen and respond effectively to criticism.

GRADES
9 - 12

FORMAT
Classroom

DISCIPLINES
Health, Family & consumer science

TIME
Up to 13 sessions, 50 minutes each

MATERIALS INCLUDED
Lesson: Managing anger
How do you deal with anger?
How do you cope?
Jealousy—the Green-eyed Monster

resolving conflicts

GIVING IT: HOW TO GIVE CRITICISM

- Ask to talk with the other person. *(Assertiveness, Initiative)*
- Say something positive, if you can. *(Respect for others)*
- Tell what you feel and why. *(Honesty)*
- Ask if the other person understands. *(Respect)*
- Ask for a change in behavior.
- Ask if he will agree to change his behavior. *(Commitment, Self-discipline)*
- Thank him for listening. *(Respect)*

TAKING IT: HOW TO TAKE CRITICISM

- Listen. *(Respect for others)*
- Stay calm. *(Self-discipline, Patience)*
- Don't talk back or argue. *(Self-control)*
- Ask them to explain anything you don't understand. *(Assertiveness)*
- Ask, "What can I do to make things better?" *(Respect, Cooperation)*
- Agree and apologize *(Honesty)* **or** tell your side of the story. *(Honesty, Assertiveness)*

WORKING IT OUT

- Say how you feel. *(Honesty)*
- Show that you understand the other person's situation or feelings. *(Caring, Empathy, Respect)*
- Ask for what you want. *(Honesty)*
- Offer a compromise. Brainstorm with someone if you need help with ideas for a compromise. *(Cooperation)*

The ability to recognize and validate one's feelings and use healthy strategies for expressing them is related to several traits, from assertiveness to self-control. These traits are reinforced in Lesson 5 which explores anger and how to manage it. The lesson and related handouts are included on pages 242-248.

The course culminates with a discussion of fair and safe dating expectations. As a final activity, students identify five guidelines that will empower them to create safe, respectful dating environments. They are asked to commit to using these guidelines.

SCHOOL

Students can develop a survey and poll classmates on their perceptions of male and female roles. They can identify peak television viewing times for their age group, then track and analyze the portrayal of men and women in commercials during these times. The results of these efforts can be published in the school newspaper. If the school does not offer peer mediation, class members might initiate plans for a team of students trained in conflict resolution. Refer to the unit on *Peer Mediation* (pages 109-115) for additional information and resources.

HOME

The content and intent of the course is explained to parents in advance, in a meeting or by letter. The unit on gender roles offers a chance to gain perspectives from family history. Students can interview elderly relatives about the options they felt were available to them in terms of domestic responsibility and vocational opportunity. They can review genealogical records, noting trends in masculine and feminine roles. These trends may show dramatic shifts during times of war, immigration and transition from rural to urban lifestyles.

COMMUNITY

Representatives from social and legal agencies can speak to the class on aspects of domestic violence: prevention, litigation, victim advocacy and victim protection measures. Service learning opportunities can be developed that complement the content of the course, i.e., supporting a hot line service, a shelter or related services for battered spouses. Refer to *Community Service* in Variations on a Theme (pages 259-260) for more ideas.

SOURCE OF INSPIRATION

Jill Svejkosky, Horton Watkins High School, Ladue School District
The Women's Self Help Center and the Progressive Youth Center

PROJECT H.A.R.T.

For more information about this program and curriculum, contact Joleene Unnerstall or Gretchen Hull of the Women's Support & Community Services 2838 Olive Street • St. Louis, MO 63103
Phone: (314) 531-9100 ext. 113 or 123
Fax: (314) 531-3449
Web site: www.womensupport.org

Lesson 5
Managing Anger

MATERIALS:

Handouts: How Do You Deal with Anger?
The Good, the Bad, the Ugly
Anger Iceberg
Jealousy (optional)
Quick Release Relaxation Exercises
(optional)
Total Truth/Love Letter Process
(optional)

ACTIVITY:

Briefly introduce Managing Anger as the
topic of today's lesson and ask students to
complete "How Do You Deal with Anger?"
as a discussion starter. (5 min.)

ROUND:

Have the students complete the sentence,
"When I get angry, I usually..."
Facilitator might encourage students to
contribute by asking open-ended
questions:
"How does that work for you?"
"What strategies work better for you?"
"How did you learn to respond to anger
the way you do?"

DISCUSSION:

To facilitate a discussion about anger, ask
the group to define anger.

1. What is anger?

Anger may be defined as a physiological
response to perceived threat; a signal to
fight; energy that needs to be spent.
Threats can be physical, i.e., a hand
raised to strike. More frequently, threats
are psychological, e.g., threats to your
self-esteem, reputation, peace of mind,
sense of well-being, etc.

2. What happens to your body when you get angry? How do you know when you're angry?

Because the body releases adrenaline
when we are angry, we may experience
increased heart rate and respiration, and

Project H.A.R.T. – Healthy Alternatives for Relationships among Teens
Because everyone deserves safe and happy relationships.

increase in muscle tension. Symptoms include: flushed face, gritting teeth, headache, sweating, moist palms, nausea, tapping feet, clenched fists, etc. Since the autonomic nervous system functions outside of our conscious control, symptoms may seem to happen automatically. Whatever our particular physical responses are, they are important indicators that we should put our safety plan into action.

3. Is anger bad?

No, anger is not bad. It is a signal that something is wrong in our lives or our relationships. However, what we do with our angry energy may be constructive or destructive.

4. Does anger help or does it get in the way?

Sometimes it can help; sometimes it can get in the way. Anger can blur our vision, misdirect our attention, deplete our psychic energy, breed other painful emotions, and destroy cooperation in our relationships.

Sometimes anger can help us when it is for a good cause when it is appropriately (assertively) expressed, or when our physical health or well-being is in danger.

Ask the students to identify some examples of situations in which anger could be helpful/hurtful.

The following explanation, comparing anger to an iceberg, may help students recognize their power in resolving anger non-violently.

BRIEF LECTURE: About Anger

1. Anger is a secondary emotion. The energy that expresses as anger builds up from primary emotions that have not been attended to.

In many cases, a situation which might lead to anger can be resolved if one takes responsibility for the primary emotions that arise first.

This is a key element in creating safe and happy relationships because for many people anger is expressed in violent behavior.

Referring to Role-Play #1, ask students to identify how alternative, non-violent behaviors could have been used with happier and healthier results for everyone.

For example, at the end of the role play, Jeff takes Maria out to dinner. This shows that he does have a non-violent way to get his need for food/dinner met.

In order to handle our emotions effectively, we need to understand that anger is a secondary emotion.

Project H.A.R.T. – Healthy Alternatives for Relationships among Teens
Because everyone deserves safe and happy relationships.

The following steps represent how unresolved primary emotions create a fertile environment for anger.

1. Before we feel anger, we experience a need, real or imagined.
2. With the need we develop an expectation, real or imagined, that someone will act to meet the need.
3. A failed expectation results in disappointment that the need is not met.
4. Repeated or severe disappointment develops into one or more of the following emotions: hurt, fear, guilt, frustration, shame, grief or loneliness.

In order to solve a conflict, we need to identify the primary emotions that occurred before the anger. By understanding the primary emotions (hurt, fear, guilt, grief, etc.) we can more easily recognize the needs and expectations we had.

The most important step in solving the conflict is to take responsibility for our own needs while avoiding unrealistic expectations of others. We can only do this by working through the anger to the primary emotions. Trying to resolve a conflict while maintaining or justifying angry energy is futile, like a dog chasing its own tail.

This explanation of anger can be represented by comparing it to an iceberg. The tip of the iceberg, the top 10%, floats above the surface of the deeper emotions, which represent 90% of the issue.

Students can increase the effectiveness of their "I Messages" by identifying a primary emotion with each expression of anger.

For example:
I am angry when you lie..
might be expressed more completely by naming a primary emotion with the anger: *I am hurt and angry when you lie..*

ACTIVITY: Healthy Responses

Have students use the handout: "The Good, the Bad, the Ugly."

1. Each student can circle one positive response to anger under the GOOD column. Encourage students to get curious about experimenting with the choice the next time they are angry. Try it and if it works, add it to their list of what to do. If it doesn't work, try another choice.

2. Looking at the BAD and UGLY lists, encourage students to cross out any behaviors they use that are destructive.

HOW DO YOU DEAL WITH A–N–G–E–R?

(Put a check mark (✔) by all that apply.
Put a star (★) by those you use most often.

WHEN I GET ANGRY I...

_____ Deny

_____ Block

_____ Bottle

_____ Stay nice on the outside, get furious on the inside.

_____ Take it out on someone else.

_____ "Stuff" it (swallow it).

_____ "Collect stamps" (save up a collection of resentments to cash in later).

_____ Stonewall (refuse to give in).

_____ Start hitting someone or something

_____ Release anger through physical activity, etc.

_____ Translate anger into other feelings (hurt, fear, sadness, etc.).

_____ Withdraw.

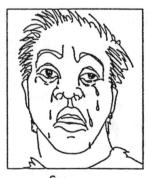

_____ Cry.

_____ Yell a lot.

_____ Pray or meditate.

??? _____ OTHER (describe) _____

Project H.A.R.T. – Healthy Alternatives for Relationships among Teens

THE GOOD

- Ask a friend
- Keep a journal
- Relax head and neck
- Run
- Dance
- Help someone else
- Daydream
- Cry
- Read a book
- Remember your best moments
- Create something
- Play hard with a friend, brother, sister
- Clean your room
- Write a letter
- Say "No"
- Say "Yes"
- Make a list
- Get a massage
- Give a massage
- Go for a walk
- Listen to music
- Sing
- Play an instrument
- Talk to someone
- Pray
- Surprise someone
- Set reachable goals
- Dig in the mud
- Plant something

The Bad

- Eat something
- Have a cigarette
- Put someone down
- Go to sleep
- Keep so busy you don't have time to think
- TV addiction
- Withdraw
- Pout
- Pretend
- Rationalize
- Hurt someone
- Keep it all inside
- Break something
- "Kick the dog"
- Go on a spending spree
- Get pregnant

The Ugly

- Take a drink
- Take a pill
- Steal something
- Try to kill yourself or anyone/anything else
- Lie
- Drive too fast
- Yell at people you care about
- Hit, kick, punch someone

Project H.A.R.T. – Healthy Alternatives for Relationships among Teens

Jealousy - The Green-Eyed Monster?

We cannot say why jealousy is often referred to as a "green-eyed monster." Because jealousy can cause explosive anger and undermine safety in a relationship, it bears special attention.

Have you ever been jealous?
If so, what did you think you would lose?

How do you handle jealous feelings?

How do you respond to jealousy directed toward you?

What have you learned about jealousy from observing relationships around you?

Redefining Jealousy

Jealousy is one of the most destructive emotions that can arise in relationships. Abusers often justify their violence by claiming they experienced jealousy. A victim of abuse may be flattered by her/his friend's jealousy, mistaking it for a sign of love.

Jealousy involves suspecting rivalry or infidelity. Bottomline, jealousy implies ownership of something. The person who is the object of jealousy is regarded as a thing to be possessed and guarded. S/he loses her/his personhood and is reduced to the status of a slave.

 Someone who is jealous fears losing something, of having something taken away. In relationships the expression of jealousy is abusive and about exerting power to control, manipulate or intimidate another. To the extent that the mixture of fear and anger that compound jealousy are expressed the safety and health of the relationship is compromised or may be destroyed.

The reality of relationships is that people grow and change. Someone may decide to end the relationship and choose another significant other. A healthy response is concern about the happiness of the other. We may feel sad when a relationship changes or ends. Life offers few guarantees, it is "like a box of chocolates."

If we are truly concerned for another, we will want him/her to be happy. If someone believes s/he would be happier relating to someone else, s/he deserves that freedom to choose. The person who responds by demanding that a significant other stay in a relationship is also refusing to realize that s/he is denying his/her highest potential.

Jealousy follows a predictable pattern that is based on
destructive self-talk and mistaken beliefs about relationships.

JEALOUSY

1. Ownership - Someone who is jealous may believe "S/he belongs
to me." Human beings are not objects to be owned.
It is irrational to think of another person as a possession.

2. Insecurity/Fear - Because the belief in ownership is
false, it easily gives rise to the fear that the significant other
person may leave or that someone else may try to steal him/her
away. Irrational statements that reveal this stage are "S/he
is looking to meet someone else and will leave me" and "That
person is trying to steal my partner from me."

3. Threat - Because loving a person and loving an object are confused by the jealous person,
s/he attempts to control the partner. S/he may try to protect her/his possession by
restricting where and when the significant other persongoes and whom s/he sees or talks to.

4. Abuse - By maintaining control, the jealous person is abusive. The abusive behavior may be
physical, verbal, psychological and/or sexual. During this phase, the abuser rationalizes her/his
behavior by denying responsibility and blaming the significant other. "S/he must be taught a
lesson" and "I would not do this if I didn't love him/her so much" are common irrational beliefs.

5. Out of Control - Because the abuser is refusing to be accountable for the controlling
behavior, s/he may act as if the jealousy is in control of his/her abuse. The truth is that each
person is responsible for how s/he responds to situations. Jealousy does not cause abuse; the
abuser is using it to justify abusive behavior.

Someone who experiences jealousy can decide to monitor the destructive thoughts that
develop into unhealthy belief systems. We can change destructive emotional patterns by
refusing irrational beliefs.

A healthy response to the fear that someone we might love and want to be with could leave the
relationship is to feel glad about the relationship as it is. We are less likely to take it for
granted. If the relationship changes and the person leaves, we can appreciate the good that
has come to us during the time we spent together.

We can also choose to believe deeply in our own value by recognizing that we can be open to
another and be enriched by sharing in another relationship.

If someone leaves us, it is because someone more "right" for us is coming our way.

SERVICE LEARNING

This unit is organized around the components of service learning.

OBJECTIVES

1. Promote the character traits of **caring, initiative, patience, perseverance, respect, responsibility** and **service.**

2. Gain an understanding of the elderly through respectful, positive interaction.

3. Develop curriculum materials based on solid research techniques.

DESCRIPTION

Service learning is a process that involves several steps:
- brainstorming
- focusing on one area or topic of interest
- investigating the topic
- designing a plan
- implementing a plan
- reflecting on experience
- evaluating the efforts
- celebrating the experience

The following project, originated by students in a freshmen civics class, follows these steps.

BRAINSTORMING
Students tracked the local news and talked to family and friends to identify areas of need within the community. They offered these ideas in a brainstorming session. Brainstorming brings several character traits to the foreground: initiative, assertiveness, healthy risk-taking, cooperation and acceptance of different ideas. Students are encouraged to come up with as many ideas as possible. Their thoughts often generate ideas in others. All suggestions are accepted, recorded on the chalkboard or newsprint and protected from criticism. Critical remarks or attempts to evaluate suggestions stop the creative process at work. They are not allowed during this phase, without exception.

GRADES
9

FORMAT
Classroom
Extracurricular

DISCIPLINES
Civics
Social studies

TIME
20-30 hours

MATERIALS NEEDED
Tape recorders
Audio tape cassettes

FOCUSING ON ONE TOPIC

These questions filter the brainstorming ideas, shortening the list of possibilities.

- Which ideas do we like the best?
- Which ideas might help the most people?
- Which ideas might help us learn the most?
- Which ideas relate to our learning in the class?
- Which ideas are manageable within the time we have to give?
- Which ideas are manageable within the resources we have? Resources may include money, transportation, goods, space, technological aids, etc.

As the members of the civics class worked with these questions, they narrowed and refined their focus. Although students are not expected to arrive at the same conclusion as they brainstorm ideas, this unit will continue to trace the development of one particular project. The members of the civics class wanted to connect with elderly people in their community in a positive way. Their interest gravitated toward oral histories. They took this concept one step further as they envisioned a student-developed curriculum that incorporated the insights, memories and perspectives of their interview subjects. To make the project manageable they concentrated on a particular time period, the decade of the 1940s. They also asked their interview subjects about the character traits that helped to meet the challenges they faced during that period.

INVESTIGATING THE TOPIC

The next step involves investigation. These civics students researched the history of the 1940s. They called area nursing homes, finding staff members at two facilities who were willing to work with them. The teacher enlisted guest speakers who sensitized students to the issues, concerns and limitations that might surface in the interview process.

DESIGNING A PLAN

Students work together as a class to develop a plan of action. They listed all possible tasks, then ordered them, assigned them and set target deadlines. The chart below suggests a small portion of their planning.

ACTIVITY	WHO DOES IT?	WHEN
Develop a list of questions to guide the interviews	All of us	Jan. 15
Order audiocassette tapes	Larry	Jan. 20
Schedule appointments with interview subject	Each student	Jan. 30

IMPLEMENTING A PLAN

Students put their plan into action. They worked individually and cooperatively to complete the tasks involved.

REFLECTING ON EXPERIENCE

Reflection was a continuing part of the process. Students kept journals, recording their intermediate goals, scheduled appointments, questions to be asked of their senior partner, feelings and responses after each contact with their senior partner, self-evaluations of the interview, obstacles that cropped up and character traits that came into play during the experience. In small group sessions, students debriefed after their interviews. They shared their journal entries and discussed their experiences and what they thought their senior partner learned from it. They listened to the recorded histories taken by members of their small group and evaluated the manner of presentation: clarity of voice, use of inflection, choice of questions and conversational techniques. As students drew excerpts from their interviews and researched the history of the times for the written curriculum, they experienced a form of reflection. They saw the individual story against the chronicle of events and movements that defined the era.

A project of this scope lends itself to videotape review, another method of reflection. Each step of the process can be recorded and replayed, much as a coach replays footage from a game. For instance, students can analyze a brainstorming session, recognizing suggestions that stimulate the creative process and identifying comments that slow or derail the process. They can assess their small-group behavior, practice their communication skills in mock interviews and identify character traits that are expressed as the project proceeds.

EVALUATING EFFORTS

Reflection dovetailed into a comprehensive evaluation, including portfolios and traditional grade assessments. The portfolios incorporated the following:
- questions asked during their interview
- historical research
- notes taken during learning sessions
- journal entries
- cassette tape of the interview
- letters or significant comments from their interview subject
- draft of their contribution to the curriculum
- copy of completed curriculum
- self-assessment

Students reviewed their portfolios in a reflective session and wrote a two-page essay describing what they learned from the experience. The essays and their contributions to the curriculum received letter grades.

CELEBRATING EFFORTS

This project prompted more than one celebration. As each oral history was completed, the student and the interviewee celebrated by listening to it together and talking about the experience. When the curriculum was printed, there was a second opportunity to celebrate. A festive ceremony applauded the students' efforts and the contributions of the interview subjects. Copies of the curriculum were given to each senior member involved.

SCHOOL & DISTRICT

A natural extension of the project is to present the curriculum to other classes. Students are divided into teams and each team teaches the curriculum at least once, reinforcing the value of their work and the character traits of initiative, cooperation, healthy risk-taking and shared responsibility. Related classes throughout the district—government, civics or social studies at the middle- and high-school levels—are candidates for the curriculum.

HOME

The project generates connections that invite the family to express care, respect for others and community responsibility. Some students discovered a relationship with their interview subject that they wanted to continue through occasional visits, letters and remembrances on holidays. Families supported this interest by informally "adopting a grandparent." The project also stimulated interest in recording oral histories from elderly relatives.

COMMUNITY

The residential facilities and nursing homes represent part of the greater community involved in this project. News releases developed by students might attract the support and attention of local media. Area businesses might underwrite the printing costs of the curriculum.

SOURCE OF INSPIRATION

Janet Schuster, Kirkwood School District

Variations on a Theme

There is more than one way to accomplish an objective, especially when creative minds are involved. The following pages offer several approaches to the objectives shown below.

COMPREHENSIVE APPROACHES

Many schools combine mission statements, visual communications, programs, strategies, activities and curricular approaches in a comprehensive approach to character education.

INVOLVING THE WHOLE SCHOOL

The mission statement, core curriculums and grade-level expectations at Bristol Elementary School emphasize four central traits— responsibility, respect, cooperation and honesty. A kick-off rally for character education sets the tone for the year, while the "Random Acts of Kindness" program reinforces student behavior continuously. Students who exhibit the traits at home or at school earn commendation on a paper link that becomes part of a chain that encompasses the building. Specific class time is set aside periodically for character education activities developed by the counselor. Schoolwide and classroom service learning projects, peer conflict mediation and peer helpers (students tutoring younger students) are a few of many initiatives that translate students' knowledge of the character traits into action. *Bristol Elementary School, Webster Groves School District*

ALSO INVOLVING THE WHOLE SCHOOL

Wedgwood Elementary School provides a working model of a fully integrated program with an integrated curriculum, schoolwide service projects and activities planned by teacher teams to emphasize and experience a particular trait. Rallies, assemblies, field trips and parades are scheduled throughout the year. A program called PREP Pals brings students of various grade levels together in small groups to increase the sense of belonging and community. More subtle are the language and expectations that permeate the school. Personal responsibility is reflected in how the teachers teach and the staff treats each other. It shows in the response to discipline challenges, in the way expectations are communicated to the students and in the quality of parental involvement. Character education even extends to visitors. Guests receive a brief lesson in the language of character education. As visitors incorporate the terminology in their conversations with students, they reinforce the foundation that parents and teachers have built. These children see over and over again that the adults who touch their lives believe the development of good character traits is important. *Wedgwood Elementary School, Ferguson-Florissant School District*

THE VISUAL IMPACT OF CHARACTER EDUCATION

The commitment to character education at Gotsch Intermediate School begins with a visual response. Members of the Student Senate named the school's corridors. Street signs with names such as "Responsibility Road" and "Self-Control Stairway" hang prominently from the ceiling. Professionally printed posters in the corridors, library and lobby announce the trait of the month. In addition, each class has created a banner for a particular trait and these hang outside classroom doors. Students become walking billboards when they wear T-shirts each class designed to illustrate a particular trait. In an interdisciplinary project, the designs were scanned into a computer, then students silk-screened them onto their T-shirts. A large bulletin board is used to reinforce positive student action. Staff members and parents are involved in detecting the traits in action. They send in brief forms that communicate what the students have done and their names appear on the board for that month. *Gotsch Intermediate School, Affton School District*

HOME COURT

Home Court, named for the sense of belonging that these daily small group meetings generate, provides a specific time to focus on character education. Sixteen to 18 students work with one teacher throughout the year. They meet for 20 minutes before first period. A weekly schedule rotates the groups through character education lessons, enrichment activities, silent recreational reading, service learning and career development. In addition, the teaching staff of Sperreng Middle School uses several different character education curriculums. More than 70 teachers use the Jefferson Center's Responsibility Education Program with 180 lessons focused on the concepts and skills of personal responsibility (see *Lessons for Success* starting on page 79 for more background). Eighteen teachers use the 95 skill-building sessions in Quest Skills for Adolescents and 15 teachers are experienced in Personality Fitness Training which strengthens self-confidence and interpersonal skills. *Sperreng Middle School, Lindbergh School District*

THE BIG R CLUB

"R" stands for responsible and is the backbone of the Big R Club. Each quarter Brennan Woods Elementary focuses on one of these themes: Responsible Listening, Responsible Caring, Responsible Health Choices or Responsible Cooperation. Each week a trait related to the primary theme is emphasized, defined, discussed and creatively integrated into ongoing studies. For instance, such traits as self-esteem, honesty, respect, kindness and friendliness are developed within the theme of responsible caring. Several efforts fit together to create a schoolwide awareness of these qualities, including the Reward Chart, announcements and posters of the "word of the week," classroom activities and student journals. *Brennan Woods Elementary School, Northwest R-1 School District*

RESPECT

Parkway Central Middle School responded to the district's emphasis on 15 character traits with two successful internal steps. They identified and collected what teachers were already doing in character education and documented these ongoing strategies and activities. The second step involved a consensus-building process to determine the unique focus the school wanted to develop. This process effectively engaged all of the teachers. The character education committee that had once included a handful of teachers now involved the entire staff. Faculty members voluntarily organized into numerous committees to explore and develop different aspects of the program from an ambitious "Respect Week" to a revamping of the discipline policy. Respect Week involved a 15-minute discussion of various qualities and traits every morning. Each academic discipline developed a focus for one day of the week. Science classes examined the school environment and adopted hallways (keeping them clear of litter) for the rest of the year; math classes studied the rain forests and environmental concerns; unified subjects (social studies and English) issued a free writing assignment on Respect for Self, and the Fine Arts block promoted "Random Acts of Kindness." The week concluded with an assembly. *Parkway Central Middle School, Parkway School District.*

S.T.A.R. (SUCCESS THROUGH ACCEPTING RESPONSIBILITY) ASSEMBLIES

S.T.A.R. is the vehicle for all character education initiatives within the school. Among the activities are Monday morning assemblies which last 30 minutes and focus attention on the theme of the month (one of 10 character traits). All members of the staff—teachers, counselors, cooks, custodians, administrators—are involved in planning assemblies. They divide into teams; each team is assigned to a particular assembly date. The teachers involve their students in the production. Original material is developed. Music, drama, oratory and poetry are featured. These assemblies set the tone for the week as they define and illustrate the traits. They are reinforced by posters, bulletin boards and banners throughout the school. *Sherman Elementary Community Education Center, St. Louis Public School District*

Positive Reinforcement

When students demonstrate the character traits they've learned, staff members are ready to let them know what they've done. Several methods, approaches and incentive plans are offered in the following selection.

MAGIC CARPET AWARDS
Students who model the character trait of the month are given "Magic Carpet" awards—the opportunity to lunch with the principal on the magic carpet in his office. Parents make the awards while the princpal hosts lunch once a month. *McGrath Elementary, Brentwood School District*

RANDOM ACTS OF KINDNESS
A sample act is described over the P.A.system in the morning. At lunch, the principal asks who can tell about the message and selects among volunteers. The principal passes the microphone to the student who rephrases the morning message and its meaning. A soda and the chance to use the microphone are welcome rewards. *Riverview Gardens Middle School, Riverview Gardens School District*

This theme is introduced with short readings from *Random Acts of Kindness* over the P.A. system. Giant paper hearts line the main hallway. Small, hand-sized hearts are available in every room. Teachers and students record acts of kindness or respect they see happening in the building. These small hearts include the names of those involved and find a place of honor on one of the large hallway hearts. *Point Elementary, Melhville School District*

STUDENTS OF THE WEEK
Each week, teacher teams at each grade level submit the name of one person who exhibits the trait of the month. The names are displayed on an electronic message board in the cafeteria and read over the P.A. system with the Monday morning announcements. The honored students invite one friend to sit with them at the center table in the cafeteria throughout the week. They receive treats (soda, ice cream bars, etc.) every day of the week. *Pattonville Heights Middle School, Pattonville School District*

BUILDING CHARACTER ONE BRICK AT A TIME
Poster board "bricks" (11" x 4" pieces of colored poster board) are awarded to students as they demonstrate respectful behavior. Students decorate their brick, sign it and place it on the Wall of Respect down the central corridor of the school. Teachers, administrators, custodians, cooks and secretaries award the bricks. Students recommend other students for the prize. Close to 400 bricks already line the wall, a visual confirmation of character in action. *Wren Hollow Elementary, Parkway School District*

CHAIN LINKS

Large pre-cut chain links are supplied to each teacher and counselor. When students exhibit the trait of the month, they receive a link with their name and the trait inscribed. They add this to the class chain, which is added to all the other chains throughout the building. An assembly, held quarterly, at the end of each semester or at year-end, demonstrates the strength of character throughout the student body. *Willowbrook Elementary, Pattonville School District*

MEDAL OF HONOR

Decorated boxes, one for each grade, line one shelf in the front office. When staff members see a student displaying a characteristic that expresses the trait of the month, they issue a medal of honor. They write the student's name, room number and grade on the back and slip the paper medal into the appropriate box On Fridays, a name from each grade level is drawn and announced. The winners choose prizes from P.T.A.-donated school supplies. *Keysor Elementary, Kirkwood School District*

H.E.A.R.T. AWARDS

Students set personal goals related to responsibility skills, e.g., be on time, be prepared. They set one goal for home and one for school. These are copied and sent to parents with an explanatory note. When the goal is accomplished or consistently expressed, the teacher or parent signs a form which is turned over to the H.E.A.R.T. Committee. The committee plans an awards assembly held at the end of each quarter. Students who have completed both their home and school goal are recognized and given a rectangular metal pendant with H.E.A.R.T. engraved upon it. *Ridge Meadows Elementary, Rockwood School District*

PEACEMAKERS BALL

Students fill out a form saying they are peacemakers because they see goodness in other people. They "catch" others expressing the character traits the school reinforces and report them on a form by circling the appropriate trait. Their report goes to the counselor who, in turn, finds each nominated student and awards a piece of yarn that is added to the "peacemakers ball." This ball of yarn represents the awards of all previously nominated peacemakers. The forms are also tallied each month to chart the characteristics that are getting the strongest workout. *Townsend Elementary, Hazelwood School District*

THE BIG R CLUB

The reward chart at Brennan Woods coordinates with the school's focus on responsibility. Teachers and staff members award "R-slips" when they see a child exhibiting qualities or actions related to the theme of the week or the quarter. Students who receive three or more "R-slips" in one quarter are added to the reward chart posted by the principal's office. This chart includes their name and picture. *Brennan Woods Elementary, Northwest R-1 School District*

COMMUNITY SERVICE

Character traits that are defined, discussed and modeled become internalized when students put them into practice. Community service is rich with opportunities to practice and experience what it means to respect and care for others. The following selections offer several ideas.

DISTRICTWIDE EMPHASIS

The Kirkwood School District emphasizes service learning at every level, from early childhood to high school. Classroom learning is coordinated to reinforce the students' experience, expand their knowledge base and provide time to reflect. One of the district's high-school efforts is described on pages 249-252. The following is a further sampling of past projects:

- Students stenciled "Do not dump" on storm drain sewers in a two-year project, sixth graders painted park trash cans and high-school members of the Black Achievement Culture Club acted as mentors and role models for elementary students.

- An after-school group organized fund-raising events for a home that takes in infants and children who have been abused, born addicted or born with the HIV virus.

- Everyone at one middle school pitched in to make sandwiches once of month for the homeless.

- Other middle-school students extended a simple service project (raking leaves) into an ongoing relationship with residents of a Home for the Visually Impaired. They learned how to use braille machines to correspond with residents. *Kirkwood School District*

SCHOOL & SERVICE

This semester-long course trains students in problem-solving, communication and helping skills during the first quarter. They identify problems within a community, conduct surveys, write action plans and implement the plans. During the second quadrant, they apply what they have learned to an issue within the school community. (e.g., peer pressure, student attitudes, school-wide services such as hosting a Special Olympics event.) A course called Community and Service, now in the development stage, will continue the program into the second semester and move students into the community. A complete course description is available and correlated with the book *Peer Power*. (See References, page 281.) *Hazelwood East High School, Hazelwood School District*

SKILLS FOR ACTION

The high school is the pilot site for Quest International's *Skills for Action* curriculum. (See Resources, page 284.) This semester course in social responsibility is required for all freshmen. The first half focuses on such skills as empathic listening, decision-making, cooperation, group planning, identifying positive qualities and problem solving. The second half involves the design, plan, and follow through of a service learning project in the community. Past projects have involved beautification efforts, teaching conflict resolution skills to students of the elementary school and "adopting" a family who lost their home in a fire. *Maplewood-Richmond Heights High School, Maplewood-Richmond Heights School District*

COMMUNITY SERVICE CLASS

This semester course in Community Service explores the tradition of philanthropy through outside speakers, articles, history and discussion. The service component is student-driven from the development of project proposals to action, implementation and evaluation of their efforts. The projects have been substantial and varied, including the following:

- A Variety Show was presented to audiences at a Shriners' Hospital, nursing homes and Salvation Army locations. Students developed skits, dance and musical numbers and a baton twirling exhibition. They scripted and choreographed the show and scheduled the times for their appearances.

- A mural of Walt Disney characters was designed and painted on the walls of a Salvation Army homeless shelter.

- Students researched the history of a large county reserve. They developed and recorded a script that is now part of a computer-operated informational guide at the park.

- Students worked during after-school hours, including school holidays, to rehab an inner-city home. A massive cleanup effort involved clearing debris from within and without the home, cutting overgrowth in the yard and cleaning the interior. The home was sold for a profit of $4,000 and the proceeds supported a local shelter for the homeless and needy.

- Fourteen teams of students carried out teaching sessions in the district's elementary schools. They researched, prepared and presented lessons once a week to children in three different elementary schools.

Eureka High School, Rockwood School District

RCONFLICT
RESOLUTION

PEACE TEAMS

This program has several unique facets, including "Recess Clinic." The Clinic operates during recess periods, with age-appropriate programs designed by counselors. First- and second-graders who are disruptive or involved in fights attend sessions in which they learn how to sit, walk in a line, answer politely, raise their hand, listen to one another, talk over a problem and express how they feel with "I" messages.

At the third- and fourth-grade level, a counselor trains a core group in the conflict resolution process. These students form a panel of eight, available on a daily basis to work with students who want to resolve a disagreement or problem.

Fifth- and sixth-grade students are trained and work in pairs as Peace Teams. They rove the playground and halls and intervene in the early stages of conflict. Peace Teams involve more than 40 fifth- and sixth-graders, those who understand fights first-hand. They receive three weeks of training during recess time in anger control and conflict resolution. They work in pairs, act as problem-solvers in the early stages of disputes, mediate conflicts among peers and younger children and reinforce positive action in those recently released from Recess Clinic. *Valley Park Elementary School, Valley Park School District*

FIGHT-FREE PROGRAM

An elementary school uses the Fight-Free program developed by Dr. Peggy Dolan to teach students to resolve conflicts without resorting to fighting. The definition of "fight" includes inappropriate pushing, shoving or hitting. Outside each classroom is a banner that serves as a non-fighting pledge and is signed by students. It remains up on days there are no fights; it comes down when there is a fight. At spirit assemblies, members of classes that have been fight-free for the month carry their banners into the auditorium. *Spoede Elementary School, Ladue School District*

PEER MEDIATION
See pages 109-115

CURRICULUM & CLASSROOM
INTEGRATION

MEGASKILLS

This early childhood center integrates the *MegaSkills* curriculum (see References, page 280) developed for preschool students into its daily teaching plans. The program focuses on one skill each month, including problem-solving, common sense, effort, patience, responsibility, initiative and teamwork. The skill is defined in simple terms and experienced through an activity. Teachers reinforce the understanding as they identify and call attention to students who exhibit the trait. *Normandy Early Childhood Center, Normandy School District*

RESPONSIBILITY THROUGH PET CARE

Fish, hermit crabs, butterflies, lady bugs and a parakeet help transition students (between K and 1st grade) and demonstrate the concepts of responsibility and care. A representative from the Humane Society teaches the class about pet adoption and care. Students use their knowledge to help the teacher select the kinds of animals they acquire, considering self-sufficiency during the weekends, feeding schedules and space requirements. Students are responsible for naming, feeding and watering the animals and cleaning cages. A chart tracks their rotating weekly assignments. *Monroe Elementary School, St. Charles School District*

DREAM CLASSROOM

A third-grade teacher infuses character education into every aspect of the classroom environment. She centers her approach around the theme of a "Dream Classroom." Visual displays throughout the room echo this message, from the definition of 15 character traits to the "Classy Compliment Tree" to a series of paper clouds on the ceiling that boast "dream words" such as empower and envision. She selects one of the 15 character traits or a dream word and spends a few moments each day discussing it with her students.

Early in the year, students write down their dreams for the future, recording such goals as becoming a veterinarian, learning piano, playing baseball, competing in the science fair. The teacher helps them determine intermediate steps toward their goal and finds ways to support them. She might arrange a tour of a veterinarian's clinic or match an aspiring scientist with a mentor.

At the same time she inspires her students, she gives them a high degree of responsibility: they determine the rules of the classroom, check off their name when they've turned in assignments, observe and compliment other students on good behavior, estimate their grades and choose their favorite paper of the week to post on the "Hats Off" wall. They compile their own portfolio by filing the work they want to save. If they receive a warning for misbehavior, their name does not go on the blackboard, but on a more discreet behavior tracking sheet attached to a clipboard. They own their actions as they write their name and circle the warning that applies. *Carman Trails Elementary School, Parkway School District*

THE FOURTH R

A core group of 20 teachers and administrators worked with the texts from each curricular area and at each grade level, kindergarten through sixth grade. They developed activities, discussions, perspectives and projects that correlate character traits to academic textbook material by page number and lesson. *Mehlville School District*

HIGH SCHOOL LESSON PLANNING THAT IS ON TARGET

A bull's-eye graphic organizer suggested in *The Mindful School: How to Integrate the Curriculum* (R. Fogarty, 1991) is adapted to lesson planning in the Brentwood School District. The modified design helps high school teachers integrate character education with learning and critical thinking skills. The bull's-eye consists of three concentric circles: the inner circle identifies the content or concept being taught, the second circle identifies a critical thinking skill associated with the lesson and the third circle addresses character traits that are to be related to the lesson. Rubber stamps are made from the design and available to all teachers. Teachers stamp the top page of their lesson plans and fill in each category. A math lesson on right angles, for example, might be completed as follows:

BULL'S-EYE PLANNER

CHARACTER TRAITS
Honesty, Perseverance, Work ethic

LEVEL OF CRITICAL THINKING
Analysis, Evaluation, Decision-making

CONCEPT
Right Angles

Concept— Define and illustrate right angles.
Skill—Measure series of angles with protractor. Indicate which ones are right angles.
Critical Thinking—How do architects and builders use right angles in their design of homes, buildings or bridges? How important is the knowledge, precision and thoroughness of the architect and the builder? Give examples.

PREP Character Traits—What work ethics help architects and builders achieve optimum results and ensure the safety of those who use their structures? Why is it important that these people care about the end result of their work?

The bull's-eye pattern provides a visible reminder of the character education component and clear documentation of progress toward the goal of infusing character education into all academic areas.

MENTORING

OFFICIAL MENTORS

A mentoring program developed for at-risk students has, in one year, made such significant changes in the students' sense of identity, purpose, and constructive action. A group of fifth-grade students, considered at-risk and posing behavior management challenges, are paired with individual law enforcement officers. These officers are recruited, screened, selected and trained by the school social worker. They act as a friend, advisor and role model. They stop in for short visits at the school roughly once every two weeks, check in by phone after school and initiate some light activities for the two of them, e.g., a trip to McDonald's. They are asked to use "self-talk," revealing the mental process they use in making decisions. Young people see the results of adult decisions, but rarely have access to the thinking and sorting process that leads to the final choice. The officers also assess the communication skills of their student at the start of the relationship and note any progress: if he or she uses complete sentences, asks questions, initiates conversations.

This group of students meets regularly with the social worker to discuss issues of personal responsibility. Group activities involving all the officers and their students are planned every three or four months. In the third quarter, mentors are asked to find and involve their student in an existing group with a strong community structure. This step is designed to lessen the students' dependency on one person and provide a continuing source of involvement. *Washington Elementary School, Normandy School District*

ADOPT-A-STUDENT
See pages 157-158

S.T.A.R.S.
See pages 183-188

Student
PORTFOLIOS

The Ferguson-Florissant School District developed a student portfolio system that incorporates character education. Certain traits are identified in terms of specific behaviors on rubrics that students use in their self-assessments, including:

- taking responsibility for a task (responsibility)
- completing a task on time (responsibility, reliability)
- taking a risk (healthy risk-taking)
- problem-solving (initiative, perseverance)
- following a plan of action (perseverance, self-discipline)
- cooperating with a group (cooperation)
- recognizing and accepting the ideas of others (cooperation, respect)
- accepting constructive criticism (honesty, cooperation, respect)

Students from kindergartners to seniors use rubrics to evaluate not only what they learn but how they learn. The samples on pages 266-274 illustrate how qualities of character are part of the self-assessment process. The completed forms become a part of students' portfolios, along with other content rubrics and artifacts that provide evidence of reflection, awards, leadership involvements and service commitments.

The self-assessments are completed in classrooms or homerooms and are shared with parents at conferences.

PRIMARY SELF-ASSESSMENT

 I was a good listener.

  I followed directions.

 I tried it by myself.

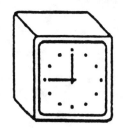 I stopped on time.

 I learned something new.

PRIMARY SELF-ASSESSMENT

 I cooperated.

 I remembered to use kind words.

 I waited for my turn.

 I helped a friend.

 I take care of materials.

SOCIAL STUDIES

Generic Student Self-Assessment Indicators Model on Social Studies Skills
Six outcomes are listed below. Skills are listed below each outcome. Think about the project/ assignment you have just completed. Put a star (*) next to the skills you used. Put a circle (o) next to any skills you didn't use, but which might have helped you complete your assignment more successfully. After each skill you check or circle, elaborate.

For instance, if you starred "interviewed," you might tell a little about the person you interviewed. If you starred "hypothesized," you might tell what you hypothesized and why! If you put a circle next to "sequenced information," you might add, "If I had put my information in the correct order, my paper would have been easier for the class to understand."

Elaborating will help you recall the important details, so when you're conferencing with your teacher, who says, "Tell me how you reached this hypothesis," you won't have to reply, "I'm sorry, but I can't remember!"

Outcome: Data Gathering
____ Made observations
____ Used survey skills (counting and quantifying)
____ Interviewed
____ Experimented
____ Located information
____ Selected
____ Interpreted pictures and cartoons
____ Used a computer to get information or explored ways to solve a problem

Outcome: Data Organizing
____ Classified information
____ Compared information
____ Mapped
____ Modeled (for demonstration purposes)
____ Graphed and charted information
____ Organized information into appropriate statistical format
____ Sequenced information
____ Re-organized information
____ Summarized
____ Distinguished fact from opinion
____ Defended my answers

SOCIAL STUDIES

Outcome: Data Credibility
____ Distinguished fact from opinion
____ Identified cultural differences
____ Identified prejudices
____ Identified motives

Outcome: Using and Evaluating
____ Inferred
____ Deduced
____ Generalized
____ Explained
____ Hypothesized
____ Identified cause/effect relationships
____ Illustrated
____ Implemented ideas
____ Created/participated in simulations

Outcome: Group Processes
____ Listened attentively to the viewpoints of my classmates
____ Contributed relevant ideas
____ Accepted group goals
____ Could have done something to make the group work better

Outcome: Personal Skills
____ Thinking independently
____ Valuing
____ Verbalizing opinions
____ Deciding
____ Self-disciplined
____ Remembering
____ Listening
____ Questioning
____ Recognizing needs of others
____ Self-evaluating
____ Modeling behavior

SCIENCE SELF-ASSESSMENT

Name of Student	**Project Assessment**

A. I investigated these things: (Exploring and Discovering)
- ❏ 1. I made observations and recorded ideas
- ❏ 2. I asked questions about what I observed
- ❏ 3. I organized my observations in tables, charts, graphs and diagrams
- ❏ 4. I used science equipment safely & properly
- ❏ 5. I compared different things

Name of Project

B. I learned these things: (Knowing and Understanding)
- ❏ 1. I understand more science words and can use them in writing and speaking
- ❏ 2. I recognize how science is used in daily life
- ❏ 3. I know about science discoveries that are recent and long ago
- ❏ 4. I was able to defend my answers

Required Resources

C. I used my own ideas: (Using and Applying)
- ❏ 1. I made decisions about taking care of our environment
- ❏ 2. I distinguished science facts from science fiction
- ❏ 3. I made good decisions about my personal health

Required Components

D. I was a good worker: (Feeling and Valuing)
- ❏ 1. I was honest in recording data
- ❏ 2. I cleaned up my work area when I finished
- ❏ 3. I showed respect for creatures, the environment and equipment
- ❏ 4. I worked carefully and safely with materials
- ❏ 5. I evaluated interaction in the group process
- ❏ 6. I have contributed something positive to my classroom, school, environment or community

On the back of this sheet, write a brief paragraph describing your project.

LANGUAGE ARTS SELF-ASSESSMENT

Name of Student

Name of Project

Required Resources

Required Components

On the back of this sheet, write a brief paragraph describing your project.

Project Rubric

A.   I have these skills in reading.
- ❏ 1. I understand what I read
- ❏ 2. I can talk about what I read with others
- ❏ 3. I can tell story events in order
- ❏ 4. I can explain causes/effects of story events and characters
- ❏ 5. I can draw conclusions from facts, events and what characters do or say
- ❏ 6. I enjoy reading

B. I have these skills in writing.
- ❏ 1. I can find a topic for writing
- ❏ 2. I can put my ideas down in a rough draft
- ❏ 3. I can revise my ideas and sentences
- ❏ 4. I can edit my writing to correct spelling, punctuation and grammar
- ❏ 5. I can write about what I read

C. I have these skills in listening and speaking.
- ❏ 1. I speak so others can hear me
- ❏ 2. I speak using correct grammar
- ❏ 3. I speak in complete sentences
- ❏ 4. I join in discussions

D.   I have these research and study skills.
- ❏ 1. I have good study habits
- ❏ 2. I take meaningful notes
- ❏ 3. I have the correct materials and supplies
- ❏ 4. I use study skills to complete my work
- ❏ 5. I know how to identify a research topic
- ❏ 6. I can write a report or give a speech based on the research I collect

E. I have these skills in working by myself and with others
- ❏ 1. I work well alone when necessary
- ❏ 2. I respect others' opinions
- ❏ 3. I respect others' materials
- ❏ 4. I do my share when working in a group

ETHICS COME IN CHILD-SIZED SERVINGS

by Diane Stirling

Ethics is a wizard's word. Raging with a lion's might, its power has dashed presidential ambitions, collapsed the fortresses of entrenched politicians and cleaned house more than once in corporate America. But among children, its magic is friendly. Like Merlin, the wizard who took a liking to young King Arthur, this powerful, morally sophisticated concept transforms itself into a mouse and scurries among children's daily activities and routines.

"Teaching ethics is not like teaching math or reading. There is a time when you are not teaching math or reading, but you cannot not teach values. They are intertwined with everything you do," says Barbara Kohm, an elementary school principal and early childhood educator. "The question is, are you teaching the values you want to teach?"

Answering that question requires self-reflection, the ability to take responsibility, a clarifying of personal and family values, and an awareness of how these values are expressed in attitudes and choices.

WITH THE WISDOM TO CONCENTRATE ON A FEW IMPORTANT VALUES, PARENTS CAN TEACH CONCEPTS THAT WILL SERVE THEIR CHILDREN THROUGHOUT THEIR LIVES.

"None of us are perfect about values, and kids can deal with a certain amount of ambiguity," says Kohm. "But the one skill that is invaluable to a parent or an educator is the ability to stand outside of yourself and watch yourself behaving." With this skill and the wisdom to concentrate on a few important values, parents can teach concepts that will serve their children throughout their lives.

Learning about values begins long before children can spell *ethics*. A three-year-old learns of his capacity for sharing and fairness as he divides the pack of sunflower seeds into one pile for his sister and one pile for himself. Kindergartners learn patience as they wait in line at the drinking fountain. In class, the teacher instructs the children to cut out a string of paper dolls, label the last doll with their name and draw a drinking fountain in front of the first figure. "This project helps them understand that they don't always have to be first in line to get what they want," explains Margaret Dickenson, a kindergarten and first-grade teacher. "They talk about what happens as each person gets a drink and they move forward in the line. The children learn that they will receive what they want. What they want is not wrong. They also learn to put a name, 'patience,' to the experience of waiting."

Patience means waiting with trust—trust that the want or need will be met. The methods Dickenson and other teachers use to explain an abstract concept like patience can be transferred to the home environment. For instance, Dickenson's students learn they can affect the experience of waiting. They watch the clock in their classroom for one minute. Then they spend one minute creating a list of words that the teacher writes on the board. They are asked to compare the two experiences: "Did time move faster when you were watching the clock or when you were making a list of words?" Parents can recreate this experiment at home, in a doctor's office or wherever a child is frustrated by a long wait.

FREEDOM TO WANT

One of the issues Dickenson's class faces is that of a "want" that cannot be immediately satisfied. "Wanting is like feeling. You just want what you want," explains Kohm. "The old ways of parenting and teaching often made children feel guilty about what they wanted. This destroys their dignity," she says.

However, children do not always want something as obtainable as water from a drinking fountain. They want to be taller or prettier. They want to move in with their best friend or to be liked by the popular kids at school. They want a baby sister or to trade their brother away to another family or they want more serious, heartbreaking desires. A problem-solving approach to such 'wants' allows children to acknowledge and accept their feelings. They can answer certain questions as the parent works through the problem with them. "There is a price and a promise to everything we want. Let's look at both of them. If you move in with Amy you will have to give up your room and your hamster."

Rediscover Disney's Wonderful World

by Linda McKay

A wonderful way to impart positive values to your children is by watching many of the classic children's stories Walt Disney Studios has developed into motion pictures. I recently rediscovered this resource as my grandson and I scanned the aisles of video stores. He headed for the latest releases with a three-year-old's awareness of the popular culture. His grandmother, looking for less violent and suggestive alternatives, headed for the children's section.

It was there that we found the story of *Pinocchio*, which explores honesty and loyalty. Jeremiah Kincade and the Wise Old Owl in *So Dear To My Heart* reveal the importance of courage, love and perseverance. Snow White advises us to "Whistle While We Work," cheering and lightening our attitudes about work and responsibility. These are only a few of many classics that illuminate ethical concepts. Others that come to mind are *Bambi*, *Cinderella*, *Sleeping Beauty*, *Wind in the Willows*, *Alice in Wonderland*, *Dumbo* and *The Sword and the Stone*.

I remember once hearing Walt Disney say in an interview that in all of his films he tried to show the important elements or emotions of life and positive ways to deal with them. So as the stories unfold about love-hate, evil-good, joy-sadness, life-death, obstacles-rewards, his films demonstrate that the courage to choose strong values helps individuals succeed.

Linda McKay is director of the Character Plus, a project of Cooperating School Districts.

Children are able to choose between options at an early age, but the ability to develop options takes many years. Even at five and six, children struggle with this process. "So we develop options for them," says Kohm. The toddler who pulls the doll out of Melissa's hands because she wants to play with it learns that she has other options: she can ask Melissa to share the doll, offer a valued toy in trade for the doll, choose another toy or wait until Melissa's attention with the doll wanes. These options are described in simple language words or role-played. The parent, for instance, suggests that she will pretend to be Melissa while her child offers her a toy in trade. As Melissa, she refuses the trade. Resuming the role of parent, the mother can ask her child to talk about how she feels and what she might try next.

UNDERSTANDING CONSEQUENCES

Part and parcel of having *options* is the concept of *consequences*. "Children need to know they are important and that what they do has a bearing on other people," says Connie Lohse, a first-grade teacher. She described the child whose task is to set the silverware and fails to do so. If the parent does not intervene and do the job for her, she will realize that the family can't eat when they sit down to the meal. Someone will say, and perhaps not so politely, "Please go do your job so that we can have dinner." In such a concrete situation, the child learns that what she does affects not only herself but everyone at the table.

Lohse stresses the importance of giving children responsibilities and making them accountable. "Every teacher has a job chart and gives each child in the classroom a responsibility," she says. "The students learn that what they do counts and they know when they've done their jobs right. When parents ask me what they can do to help their children do well in school, I tell them to give them responsibilities they can handle. I started giving my own children more responsibilities and they became much more aware of what others do," she says.

THE WORKING PARTS OF ETHICAL DECISION-MAKING

Thus, the working parts of ethical decision-making include awareness, options, choices and consequences. These are weighty elements that stride through an adult's life with the power of a lion. To apply these elements to the issues that dominate a young child's life is to transform the lion, with Merlin's sorcery, into a mouse.

THIS ARTICLE IS EXCERPTED WITH THE AUTHOR'S PERMISSION, GROWING TIMES, VOL. 7, ISSUE 2 © 1989

ENRICHING CHARACTER EDUCATION

The following information outlines the elements that foster lasting character education efforts.

WHAT IS
CHARACTER EDUCATION?

Good character means understanding, caring about and acting upon core ethical values such as honesty, respect and responsibility. Character education, then, means helping students develop the strength of character they'll need to further our democratic society as ethical adults. While this concept isn't new—teachers have been instilling the "golden rule" in students since before Thomas Jefferson's time—schools across the country are now developing approaches to character education that are much more formal, purposeful and systematic.

Character education recognizes that each student's moral development is as essential to the school mission as academic learning and is a key, but often neglected, element of school reform.

More than just an add-on to the busy school day, character education addresses such critical concerns as student absenteeism, discipline problems, drug abuse, gang violence, teen pregnancy and poor academic performance. At its best, character education integrates positive values into every aspect of the school day.

THE MISSION OF CHARACTER*plus*

CHARACTER*plus* is an initiative designed to weave character education throughout the school day, integrating it into curriculum, discipline policies, after-school activities and reform initiatives.

As an essential part of the initiative, educators secure community consensus regarding their role in teaching and reinforcing such basic values as honesty, respect, responsibility, caring and perseverance.

BUILDING ON
COMMON GROUND

One of the reasons **CHARACTER**plus has been so successful throughout the St. Louis metropolitan area is that it focuses on areas of agreement and uses the community's common ground as the foundation for each school's program. The following is an outline of the consensus-building process used by member districts to help communities identify and define the core values they want to reinforce.

Brainstorm a list. Each individual brainstorms a list of character traits, such as: cooperation, respect, honest and responsibility.

Form small groups. Have each person share his or her list. Each small group makes a list with the top five to seven traits agreed upon. (Consensus is an agreement that all members of a group can live with.) The final list is then written on a large sheet of paper.

Synthesize lists. Post the lists on the wall and assign synthesizer groups to survey all lists. Look for overlaps and produce a synthesized list with all the traits submitted by the small groups.

Discuss. Give people an opportunity to speak out for or against the suggested traits. This is a time to allow discussion and clarify interpretations.

Select top three choices. Issue an index card to everyone. Have each person put three choices from the synthesized list on the card and rate their preference: three points for first choice, two points for second and one point for third.

Tally. Tally all ballots and the top-rated traits become the district's character education components.

Define the traits. A facilitator chooses or asks for volunteers to be part of a group that will define the traits. This group is then divided into smaller units and each unit is assigned the task of drafting a definition for one of the qualities. Encourage people to talk to colleagues, family and friends to gain insights and a sense of the community's comfort level with the suggested traits.

Using this process, each school develops a character education curriculum and program that meets its community's unique needs. No two programs are alike.

COMPONENTS OF
CHARACTER EDUCATION

After more than a decade of experience with diverse communities, we've learned that these components are critical to the lasting success of character education.

Community participation. Have educators, parents, students and members of the community invest themselves in a consensus-building process to discover common ground that is essential for long-term success.

Character education policy. Make character education a part of your philosophy, goal or mission statement by adopting a formal policy. Don't just say it, put it in writing.

Defined traits. Have a meeting of parents, teachers and community representatives and use consensus to get agreement on which character traits to reinforce and what definitions to use. Formally state what your school means by "courage" or "perseverance" before they are discussed with students.

Integrated curriculum. Make character education integral to the curriculum at all grade levels. Take the traits you have chosen and connect them to class-room lessons, so students see how a trait might figure into a story, be part of a science experiment or how it might affect them. Make these traits a part of every class and every subject.

Experiential learning. Allow your students to see the trait in action, experience it and express it. Include community-based, real-world experiences in your curriculum that illustrate character traits, e.g., service learning, cooperative learning and peer mentoring. Allow time for discussion and reflection.

Evaluation. Evaluate character education from two perspectives. Is the program affecting positive changes in student behavior, academic achievement and cognitive understanding of the traits? Is the implementation process providing the tools and support teachers need?

Adult role models. Children "learn what they live" so it is important that adults demonstrate positive character traits at home, school and in the community. If adults do not model the behavior they teach, the entire program will fail.

Staff development. Provide development and training time for your staff so that they can create and implement character education on an ongoing basis. Include time for discussion and understanding of both the process and the programs, as well as for the creation of lesson plans and curriculums.

Student involvement. Involve students in age-appropriate activities and allow them to connect character education to their learning, decision-making and personal goals as you integrate the process into their school.

Sustaining the program. The character education program is sustained and renewed through implementation of the first nine elements, with particular attention to a high level of commitment from the top; adequate funding; support for district coordination staff; high quality and ongoing professional development; and a networking and support system for teachers who are implementing the program.

COMMUNITIES
OF PEACE & RESPECT

The following section provides innovative, creative and collaborative ways to build communities of character. Some involve small groups of students, some the entire school. Some are designed for elementary grades, others for middle and high school. Supplemental handouts and suggested resources accompany these initiatives.

COMMUNITIES OF
PEACE & RESPECT

This section explores ways to create the peaceable communities we want to live in. Sometimes it starts with something very simple. When schools in the St. Louis region wanted to join a community-wide effort to "Increase the Peace," the Peacemakers Ball described on page 256 was suggested. More than 50 schools joined in this exercise, their staffs busy catching students in acts of peace, caring and conflict resolution during a specific 40-day period. They awarded a strand of yarn for each act. These strands were tied to one another and rolled into colorful yarn balls that symbolized the collective magnitude of individual action. The peace ball activity has become an annual tradition, with a community celebration that showcases the balls from each school and brings more than 700 students together. Schools saw the activity as a starting point and enhanced it with:

- peace rallies and assemblies
- peace walks and marches
- peace pledges
- art and essay contests
- human peace symbols created with their entire student bodies
- peace poles with the word inscribed in different languages
- a comprehensive approach to school discipline and culture called "The Peaceable School"

The following reports describe ways of bringing the concepts of peace and respect into the lives of students and the culture of the school.

WHERE TO GO FOR MORE

THE PEACEABLE SCHOOL
Training and manuals from the
National Center for Conflict Resolution Education
Phone: (800) 308-9419
Web site: www.nccre.org
E-mail: info@nccre.org
Also see Resources, page 314

PEACE POLE MAKERS USA
3534 West Lanham Road
Maple City, MI 49664
Phone: (616) 334-4567
Web site: www.peacepoles.com
E-mail: info@peacepoles.com

PEACEJAM:
REALIZING ONE'S PEACEMAKING POTENTIAL

Kirkwood Middle and High School students experienced the transforming power of their own peacemaking efforts as they studied under the tutelage of Nobel Peace Laureate Rigoberta Menchu Tum. They participated in PeaceJam, an international education program involving 11 Nobel Peace Prize winners who are matched with groups of young people throughout the country. The students were involved in a three-part process:

- a six-week, service-learning curriculum developed by PeaceJam
- a two-day conference with Menchu Tum in Kansas City, Missouri, involving 300 students from 20 schools. Similar conferences were held with other Nobel Laureates in Colorado, Washington and New Mexico.
- continuing discussion, reflection and action as an integrated part of the language arts curriculum at the middle school and a service learning class at the high school

GRADES: 6 - 8
9 - 12

PEACEJAM: INSPIRATION THAT GENERATES ACTION

As part of the service-learning curriculum from PeaceJam, students researched Menchu Tum's life story in the context of the socio-political climate of Guatemala. They identified similar obstacles to peace and unity within their own community and developed ways to respond. At the two-day conference, they met and worked with Menchu Tum directly. As one high school junior reflected, "Rigoberta helped me to see that I can be as strong as she is and stand up for what I believe in. She made me realize what a difference that makes."

The PeaceJam experience was integrated into the existing academic structure. At the middle school, one team of 85 students worked with the project as an integral part of their language arts curriculum. At the high school, 30 members of an elective service-learning class participated. From these two sources, 10 students were chosen to attend the two-day conference and share their experiences with their classmates.

In addition, all members of the middle school team and the high school class were involved in planning peace initiatives. The high school students organized a "Peace Week" to focus on local and global issues, co-sponsored a concert with the international and language clubs, and raised awareness about the destructiveness of gossip, racism and sexism in their school life. Middle school students originated projects individually or in small groups. Several designed board games based on peace and mediation strategies. One student developed a video about breast cancer from the perspective of its effect on the family of the patient and organized student participation in an American Cancer Society walk. Two girls raised funds and coordinated efforts that brought a Holocaust survivor to speak to students. Other projects involved mock peace table talks representing Israel and Palestine; a Jeopardy-styled game show based on recent civil rights events; a PeaceJam mural; and a video that recorded adult reflections on historical civil rights movements.

Kirkwood Middle School & Kirkwood High School, Kirkwood School District

WHERE TO GO FOR MORE

PEACEJAM FOUNDATION
2427 West Argyle Place
Denver, CO 80211
Phone: (303) 455-2099
Web site: www.peacejam.org
E-mail: peacejam@aol.com

PEACE POSSE:
EMPOWERING STUDENTS AS PEACE KEEPERS

The Peace Posse at Lexington Elementary discovered a safe, effective way to empower themselves as witnesses and stop disputes before they escalate into fights. Thirty fourth and fifth-graders are selected as members of the posse at the beginning of the year, identified by badges, trained in mediation and expected to "peace out" students who are involved in name calling, arguing, bullying or fighting. The "peace out" signal—the peace sign and the spoken words "peace out"—is recognized and respected by the student body.

The signal provides a way to alert parties of a need to adjust their behavior, without placing posse members at risk. They confront the problem without having to make physical contact or engage in verbal debate. If other posse members are within earshot and hear the words "peace out," they offer reinforcement. The parties in conflict are expected to stop. If they do not, they are reported with the notation that they received the "peace out" warning. The disciplinary response is intensified if students have ignored the warning.

GRADES: 4 - 5

Peace posse members have a natural affinity with the students (see selection process below) and a mobility that makes their presence effective. In the course of the school day, they have access to situations and encounters adults do not see, particularly on the bus, in the hallways, and on the playground. In its first year of operation, the Peace Posse and its use of the "peace out" signal had a positive effect on the school culture. The number of fights declined, membership in the peace posse became a respected and coveted position among students and, most significantly, the role of "enforcer" became a shared responsibility between educators and students.

KEYS TO MAKING IT WORK

Selection Process: Recommendations for posse members come from three sources: students, teachers and counselors. In a counselor-led class session, students learn about conflict resolution and identify the characteristics that mediators need to do their job. Fairness and approachability surface high on the list, and the students are able to vote for people they trust. Teachers also recommend a certain number of students, and the counselor intentionally chooses a few who do not surface in either the teacher or student selections. For instance, a student who uses a wheelchair and others who bordered on difficult behavior have been successful members of the posse. The recognition of their leadership potential increases their positive contributions to the school. In turn, they legitimize the Peace Posse with a sense of inclusiveness, providing a connection for students who feel socially or academically disenfranchised.

Schoolwide Awareness: Peace Posse members are announced over the p.a. system, introduced in each fourth and fifth-grade classroom and identified by a badge they wear daily. Schoolwide awareness is reinforced through the "Right

Attitude" program, a pro-active behavior management program developed by the school and based on the character traits of self-control and responsibility. Peace Posse members are recognized as positive role models of the "Right Attitude."

Parent Communication/Parent Video: Parents of posse candidates receive letters congratulating their children and explaining the program. In addition, all parents are invited to participate in the video aspect of the "Right Attitude" program. They are asked to create a commercial or a rap that expresses what the right attitude involves and why it is important. Their presentations are filmed at the school and edited into a video. The video makes its debut at a PTO meeting designed for the entire family. It is shown throughout the year to students who are asked to reflect on their behaviors and adjust their attitudes.

Training and Team-building: The posse members receive two days of mediation training. In weekly meetings, they reinforce their sense of mission with a pledge that relates character traits to their actions and emphasizes their positive role at school, at home and within the community. They also strengthen their skills in active listening, critical thinking, problem-solving, conducting meetings and leadership. Perhaps most importantly, they recognize how their skills can be used beyond the school setting with their families and as responsible citizens in the community.

SEE THE PEACE POSSE "COUNT DOWN" HANDOUT ON PAGE 284

Reporting and Administrative Support: Peace Posse members report altercations immediately to the counselor. They give a verbal report, naming the parties involved and what happened. Often, they are aware of subtle exchanges or ongoing conditions that aggravate the conflict, and this becomes part of the story. The counselor takes statements from everyone involved, writes up a report, and sets a course of action that is consistent with the nature of the exchange and the policies of the school. The response to the "peace out" signal is part of the report, and the administration reinforces its significance by commending students who heed the warning and by increasing the penalties for students who ignore the warning. *Lexington Elementary, St. Louis Public Schools*

Count Down 6...5...4...3...2...1

6 most important words:
"I made a mistake. I'm sorry."

5 most important words:
"You did a good job!"

4 most important words:
"What is your opinion?"

3 most important words:
"I can help."

2 most important words:
"Thank you."

1 the least important word:
"I"

WORKING IN TANDEM:
COMMUNITY BUILDING AND ACADEMICS

To create a community of learners, students need to feel cared for, listened to and respected; and they need to be able to respond in kind. Too often such community-building is separated from academics, but at Clearview Elementary they work in tandem. The school is in its second year of the Caring School Community Program, a national program from the research-based Developmental Studies Center. This comprehensive approach strengthens the sense of connection between student and student, student and teacher, and home and school with four components:

- **class meetings**
- **buddy activities**
- **schoolwide events**
- **homeside activities**

GRADES: K - 5

In the Caring School Community Program, *class meetings* are held as an integral part of school operations. They provide opportunities to experience and express respect intentionally. Students practice listening skills. Younger ones take turns holding a teddy bear or talking stick, signifying their time to speak. Older students, having experienced the democratic style of class meetings through their years at school, develop facilitation skills that allow the teacher to become a full participant in the meeting. The focus of the meetings is meaningful to students, giving them a voice in the governance of their class, academic activity and relationships. They help set goals and rules at the beginning of the year. They might choose which of four literature sets they will tackle or design the scoring guide for a geography assignment. They problem-solve their way through upsets and disputes and take ownership of their role in the solution.

BUDDY ACTIVITIES: CHANGING THE SOCIAL CONTEXT OF THE SCHOOL

Buddy activities are more than babysitting ventures. Older students are entrusted with the responsibility of guiding learning experiences and building relationships. Younger students learn firsthand what it feels like to be known by someone they respect. Two classrooms are linked, and students form partnerships that remain constant for the year. For instance, a kindergarten class partners with a fourth-grade class, and among their many buddy activities is the "Kindergardening Project," a long-term science experiment. Buddies come together at regular intervals; the older ones help their younger partners to plant seedlings and record their observations as the plants grow. Related lessons involve identifying parts of the plant and conditions for growth. As the seedlings develop, parents join the effort, tilling a plot of ground and working with members of both classes as they come together to plant the garden and plan for its care. Buddy activities come in all shapes and sizes: field trips, story times, computer projects, service-learning experiences, geography

WHERE TO GO FOR MORE

CARING SCHOOL COMMUNITY PROGRAM

Training and manuals from the **Developmental Studies Center**
See Resources, page 313
Phone: (800) 666-7270 x239
www.devstu.org

lessons, math contests, fitness meets, mural painting, writing across the curriculum, plays and productions. Teachers determine the classroom pairings at the beginning of the year and set expectations for themselves, such as one buddy program a month. They look for ways to incorporate the model with required learning. When they occur often and regularly, the buddy relationships change the social context of the school. Genuine connections are fostered. Students get to know each other, they look out for each other, and they feel safe with each other.

CREATING CONDUITS FOR SIGNIFICANT CONNECTIONS

Each of the four components is designed as a conduit for significant connections. With that goal in mind, *schoolwide activities* are reshaped to increase the level of engagement for students, parents, staff and the community. For instance, Clearview modified the concept of a science fair. Members of each class developed an interactive, hands-on science demonstration drawn from some aspect of their curriculum. They presented it to audiences of fellow students, parents, staff and members of the community during a well-publicized evening event. The change in design converted an individual and competitive exercise into a cooperative learning experience. It drew parents to all of the classrooms, introducing them to students from different grade levels. Other activities suggested in *At Home in Our Schools* include Family Film Night, Family Math, a Heritage Museum and a Grandpersons Gathering.

The fourth component, *Homeside Activities*, involves parents and students in meaningful explorations around academic skills. First graders, for instance, play a "Sorting Game" with their parents, collecting 10 household items and brainstorming together about possible classifications (small/large, can be eaten/cannot be eaten). The child chooses one way to group the objects and determines where to place them, then draws a picture showing the two distinct groups. Second graders at Clearview, as part of a social studies unit on family traditions, interview their parents to learn the how and why behind their own names. Fifth graders put a practical spin on math, asking their parents where they apply computation skills at work and at home and what "short cuts" they use. A teacher expanded this approach to include home budgets and the development of individual student budgets. All of these exercises involve a sharing and reflective time back in the classroom.

SEE "EVERYDAY MATH" ON PAGES 287 & 288

These four components generate opportunities for getting to know each other and become the core for building a community of respect. The quality of this community in turn enhances learning. A number of measurable outcomes improved at Clearview, including a sustained increase in student attendance, a substantial decrease in disciplinary incidents and an increase in parent involvement. *Clearview Elementary, Washington School District*

Everyday Math

Dear Student,

You are in charge of this Homeside Activity, which means you are in charge of finding an adult to do it, explaining and "directing" the activity, making sure the adult signs it and bringing it back to class. Please find about 20 minutes that you can spend on the activity with a parent or other adult— a neighbor, grandparent, older brother or sister, or family friend. If you'd like, get a bunch of people involved!

One of the most important reasons for doing this activity is that you and the adult will learn things from each other about what you think, feel, know and want to know. In class we can then also learn from each other when we share what we have learned at home. Just be sure to ask the adults for permission to pass along what they say—and don't forget to thank them for contributing to our class's learning!

Use the questions on the back of this page to interview a parent or another adult about how he or she uses mathematics in everyday life. Also find out about how the adult learned math when he or she was in school. You can make up your own interview questions, too. Take notes in the space provided.

HOMESIDE ACTIVITY

INTERVIEW QUESTIONS

Can you think of two or three ways you commonly use math?

_____

_____

Do you have any quick tricks or mathematical "short cuts" that you use?
If so, can you explain them to me?

_____

_____

_____

Tell me a story about learning or doing math in school when you were a child.

_____

_____

_____

_____

• •

Comments

After you have completed
this activity, each of you
please sign your name and
the date below. If you have
any comments, please write
them in the space provided.

_____

_____

_____

Signatures

                                                                    date:

_____ _____ _____

BRINGING CHARACTER TO LIFE WITH A "LIVING MUSEUM"

Blueprints for building communities of peace and respect are found in our historical heritage, and as students study that heritage, they begin to see the powerful difference one person can make. A biographical study of a hero can inspire young people to effect changes in their current world. Long Elementary School took the idea of a biographical study one step further by creating a "Living History Museum" to help students identify with the strengths and characteristics that propelled African-American heroes to action.

GRADE: 5

STEPPING INTO AN HEROIC ROLE

The project, integrated into the language arts curriculum, involves all members of the fifth grade. Each student selects a historic figure from the teacher's suggested list, researching who they are and what they did. They write a report, then redraft the material in a first-person narrative for oral presentation. Students also create their own costumes, using body-length paper to draw the appropriate attire, color it and decorate it. They cut out circles for their faces and arms, don their costumes and become part of the show that takes place in a library that has been transformed into the "Living History Museum."

As fellow students enter the museum, they encounter a classmate emulating the presence of Harriet Tubman. She stands like a statue in a paper housedress and bandana until a token is dropped into the slotted box next to her. Then she comes to life, talking about her experience as a slave and the empathy she feels for those she works to free. She tells about her work as a nurse, guide and spy. From her story, students learn about the determination and courage that enabled 300 slaves to escape to freedom. This heroine is not the only one in the room. She is surrounded by notable people, including Thurgood Marshall, Booker T. Washington, Dr. May Jemison and Marion McLeod Bethune. Each one has a story to tell.

> THE PROCESS OF SHARING THESE STORIES WITH THE STUDENT BODY AND VISITING PARENTS ENHANCES A SCHOOLWIDE CLIMATE OF RESPECT.

MODELING RESPONSIBILITY, RESEARCH AND THE ABILITY TO TEACH OTHERS

The process of sharing these stories with the student body and visiting parents enhances a schoolwide climate of respect. Each fifth-grade class is responsible for the museum show for a block of time in a two-day period. To keep the flow of viewers manageable, the kindergarten through fourth-grade students are scheduled by class for particular viewing times. The chance to learn from their older classmates in such a novel setting invites their interest and respect. In turn, these fifth-graders model responsibility, creative use of academic research and their ability to teach others. In all, everyone gains an enriching appreciation of African-Americans whose character and actions helped to further peace and respect in their worlds. *Long Elementary, Lindbergh School District*

LAWS OF LIFE:
WRITING ABOUT WHAT REALLY MATTERS

"Love and respect yourself, and others have no choice but to do the same."

The essay of a high school student concluded with this "law of life." It speaks to the community-building dynamic at work within the international *Laws of Life* Essay Contest. Something self-affirming happens when young people are asked to write about values that are personally meaningful, stories of who and what shaped them, how they operate in their lives and the principles on which they intend to build their lives. When this is done within the context of peer support and public appreciation, it creates a community of people who honor what really matters in each other's lives.

GRADES: 6 - 8
9 - 12

"Getting past the potholes in life"

Growing up in St. Louis, my mother and father stressed to me that in order to succeed in life you must have patience. Take your time and observe all things, they said. . . .Writing this paper has caused me to think about slowing down and looking at the whole perspective of my life, not focusing on the tempting things, such as fancy cars, clothes and material things. Instead, I plan to focus on education . . .and other important things that will help me to become a well-spoken business-man in my city. — Kevin Holloway

excerpted from Writing from the Heart *(See box, page 292)*

More than 1500 students in the Hazelwood School District considered their own *laws of life*. The effort, introduced by the superintendent and organized by a district coordinator, involved English classes at three high schools and three middle schools. The essays revealed the writers' passionate voices, and although the topics were at times sad, they clearly expressed thoughtful analysis and deep convictions. A personal account by one student who was ridiculed illustrated her courage and belief in herself. Another student found a cherished heritage in his memories of a grandmother's joy for life. The Hazelwood teachers voluntarily joined in the process, writing about their own *laws of life*. As students and teachers safely shared their drafts during the peer editing process, the culture of the classroom warmed. People simply got to know each other better, and this fostered a deeper sense of belonging.

LAWS OF LIFE PROVIDES A FLEXIBLE, FIELD-TESTED FORMAT

The *Laws of Life* Essay Contest, initiated by the John Templeton Foundation, has a classroom and a community component. The classroom component involves the process of prewriting, peer editing and submitting the finished works. The community component involves organizations—civic, service or corporate—in the judging process and sponsorship of the awards ceremonies. This field-tested format:

- challenges young people to discover for themselves the core values that guide them and allows them to express their ideas in writing that is meaningful to themselves and others.

- encourages teachers and students, parents and children, schools and community members to think about what is important to them and their society.

- supports curriculum requirements and state standards for language arts.
- offers communities an opportunity to honor young people for articulating what they believe.
- builds strong ties as educators and community volunteers work side by side on an activity that encourages positive public impressions of students.

KEYS TO MAKING IT WORK

The reflective nature of the essay and the freedom to choose the focus engages each student's genuine voice. Students become involved emotionally and intellectually; they want to write well. At the same time, the community wants to hear what they have to say. The success of the contest lies in its ability to evoke the authenticity of students and involve the community in recognizing their voices. The process of creating the essays involves the following facets:

Prewriting: Directions for this contest are flexible. Students may write on any topic related to the *laws of life*, including personal narratives about events that illustrate their codes of living; expositions about principles that direct their daily lives; and descriptions of role models, real or fictional. Questions that help elicit essay ideas are suggested in the handout **"Thoughtful Questions" on page 293.**

Some teachers tie the assignment to literature, history or environmental issues. Hazelwood teachers use this writing to fulfill curriculum standards for essays and portfolios. They require submission of the essay for a class grade but make entry in the contest optional.

Peer Response and Peer Editing:
When students have created first drafts, they share them in small groups. It usually takes one class period, allowing supportive responses to the content and suggestions for clarification or development. Teachers guide students toward constructive rather than critical statements, focusing on such comments as, "What happened isn't clear to me." "You could give more details about what this person did next." "You might want to add some dialogue." Because students often write about sensitive and personal experiences, peer editors need to respond with compassion and confidentiality. A structured review list helps students to know what to expect and to focus on

---

TEACHING TIPS

Many students write about sensitive and personal experiences. They should choose something they feel they can share with others. Confidentiality is built into the submission and judging process, but sharing of one's work is part of the classroom dynamic and peer editing. Also the essays may be read at the awards ceremonies and published.

Give ideas of what others have written about, but avoid reading essays by previous winners. These essays can intimidate students and inhibit their originality.

Encourage students to use their personal experiences (either positive or negative) to generate ideas for their essays.

Discourage students from writing about their romantic relationships.

Be flexible. Students of all abilities and levels can write meaningful essays. Individualize your expectations for each student.

grammatical and mechanical improvements. After receiving a peer response, students revise and edit their own writing. A few days are usually sufficient for final revisions.

Judging Entries: Essays are submitted with an entry form so names remain anonymous. The form is included in the *Laws of Life Teacher's Guide* (see box). If the number of essays submitted is large, screeners may determine a smaller quantity to send to the judges. Hazelwood teachers from the next grade levels found screening essays increased their understanding of students they would work with the following year. Selection of finalists is based on the same criteria as the final judging: content that clearly states or illustrates a law of life, clarity of writing, the emotional involvement apparent in each essay, and specific and persuasive support. Judges are often volunteers from the organization that helps sponsor the contest. In Hazelwood, however, district administrators ranked the essays. Whatever the source, judges evaluate the essays for compelling content rather than mechanics, remain impartial and retain confidentiality. Suggestions for judging criteria and tally forms are included in the Contest Manual (see box).

Celebrating: Local sponsors often assist schools with prize money and awards celebrations. In Hazelwood, the local Rotary Club helped finance prizes and an evening ceremony. Finalists received framed certificates and monetary awards. Their teachers shared the stage with them. The winners from each grade level read their essays to an audience that was moved by their experiences and sincerity. The celebration—whether it is a school assembly, luncheon, evening reception or dinner—brings the community together to applaud the efforts of all essay writers and to recognize the winners.

> ### WHERE TO GO FOR MORE
>
> The **John Templeton Foundation** provides these materials free of charge:
>
> - Contest Brochure
> - Contest Manual
> - Teacher's Guide
> - *Essays from the Heart* Video
>
> (800) 245-1285 or (610) 687-8942
> Web site: www.lawsoflife.org
> Also see Resources, page 314
>
> A worldwide selection of essays are included in ***Writing from the Heart*** edited by Peggy Veljkovic
> See References, page 310
> This book is available from the John Templeton Foundation

Publishing: Schools have created booklets including the final submissions of all of their students. More polished editions have been printed with the support of sponsors and distributed throughout local areas. *Hazelwood School District*

Laws of Life: Thoughtful Questions

The laws of life are the core values and ideals by which we live. Honesty, perseverance, the Golden Rule, these are universal laws that transcend religious, cultural and national borders.

NOTE TO TEACHERS: *The following questionnaire is an effective tool to help students determine what they may want to write about in their essays.*

1. Who is someone that you admire? List three qualities that you admire about that person.

2. Describe an incident or event from which you learned a lesson "the hard way."

3. What could you change about yourself to become a better person?

4. What three qualities do you value in a friend, a teacher, a parent?

5. Describe a situation in which you went out of your way to help someone else.

6. Has life been good to you? Explain.

7. Describe a situation in your life in which someone went out of his or her way to help you.

8. Name three things for which you are thankful.

9. Who has been most important in your life in helping you establish your values? Explain.

10. Do you have a responsibility to help those who are less fortunate? Explain.

11. When you become a parent, what are the three most important values that you hope your children will have?

CONFRONTING THE REALITY OF BULLYING

The following section describes three comprehensive approaches to the issue of bullying that engage students in the issue, both emotionally and intellectually. Two provide a blueprint for an all-school approach. One draws students deeper into the subject through acting, another brings students from diverse schools together in videoconferencing dialogues.

CREATING A BULLY-FREE ENVIRONMENT

To make Claymont a place where every child and adult is safe and feels that they belong:
▲ *Hurtful teasing and bullying will not be allowed.*
▲ *Students and adults will help each other by speaking out against hurtful teasing and bullying.*
▲ *Students and adults will treat each other with respect and kindness.*

This mission statement and the bully-free mascot rivet the attention of those who walk through Claymont Elementary School. Together, they reflect the nature of a comprehensive response to bullying that engages both students and adults. The Claymont experience weaves several facets together to create an environment where students:
• know bullying behaviors will not be tolerated before, during and after school.
• are encouraged to be problem-solvers and seek out adult help.
• see themselves as positive change agents in their role as witnesses.

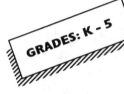

GRADES: K - 5

KEEPING THE ISSUE IN FOCUS AND ON TRACK
Committed leadership, administrative support and a unified focus provide the backbone behind the mission. The program is in its third year and continues to receive the full support of the principal. This support preserves visibility and continuity in the mission and the policies that support it. Consistent leadership from the counseling staff and a committee of faculty and parents keeps the issue in focus.

At the same time, the involvement of an inclusive community of adults closes the ranks on bullying. This community includes teacher aides, support staff, parents, lunch room and playground supervisors, bus drivers, coaches, scout and activity leaders, custodians and the nurse. It involves those who are with students before school starts and after it ends, those who are privy to persistent health complaints that can mask a fear of being in class or in school, and those who are stationed in such bully-prone areas as the bus and the playground. They are brought in on the ground floor in an initial series of meetings that provide access to information, current research and resources. Their input helps to formulate the mission statement and an action plan that recognizes the contribution people can make from their respective roles in the school.

INFORMING AND EMPOWERING WITH EDUCATION
Within such a framework of support, students are encouraged to own the problem. Whether they are bullies, targets or witnesses, they are the key players. An educational approach evolved at Claymont to inform and empower its students.

The educational approach includes:
- memorable dialogues between the students and a national expert;
- a foundation of consistent learning experiences provided by counselors in classroom presentations;
- the integration of "Don't Laugh at Me," a nationally available resource, into daily classroom learning;
- student involvement in resolving persistent teasing or bullying situations.

MEMORABLE DIALOGUES

"Biting." "Scratching." "Pulling hair." Fourth-graders quickly named these actions in response to a question posed by SuEllen Fried, co-author of *Bullies and Victims* and a national advocate for children. She asked her audience if the ways girls express physical bullying is different than the ways boys do, and if so, what it looks like. This group of 60 fourth-graders continued to identify actions that defined emotional, verbal and sexual bullying at their grade level.

Fried recognizes students as front-line authorities on the nature of bullying. They are living with it. She engages them in the issue with an approach that blends information, true stories, empathic sensitivity and direct questions. Students hear painful stories and hopeful stories. They are asked to vote on the kind of bullying that is most common among them and the form that is most harmful. They brainstorm safe responses to bullying situations and rank their level of safety. By the close of the session, Fried asks if anyone would like to take the courageous step of apologizing publicly to another person in the room. She handles this exchange with respect for both parties involved. The effect of the session is to cast students in the role of change agents.

FOR MORE ON THIS APPROACH
Contact The Bullying Prevention & Intervention Training Institute
(913) 362-2226
Also see Resources, page 313

This was the starting place for Claymont. Fried reached the entire student body, engaging two classes at a time. She also met with the community of adults in informative sessions that reinforced their understanding of the problem and the importance of their individual roles in confronting bullying.

CONSISTENT LEARNING EXPERIENCES

At school, a continuing stream of activities, story presentations, discussions, role-plays and skill-building sessions reinforce this initial experience and carry the momentum from one year to the next. These age-appropriate experiences provide awareness, an increased sense of empathy, a common language to talk about the issue, a chance to explore safe options of response and to problem-solve real situations.

The counseling team structures their regular schedule of classroom visits to provide age-appropriate learning experiences. It might be the story of *Andrew's Angry Words* and an activity that shows how to make mean words disappear. In third grade, it might be how to use humor or questions to deflect teasing. In the higher grade levels, units focus on decision-making and conflict resolution.

A NATIONAL RESOURCE: "DON'T LAUGH AT ME"

An emotional connection comes through a resource called "Don't Laugh at Me." With a music video of the song "Don't Laugh at Me," the program creates an immediate connection with the pain of ridicule and exclusion. This experience launches a progressive series of activities that enrich the relational skills of students and the culture of the classroom.

A third-grade teacher at Claymont integrated the activities into the daily learning of her students. It was the first thing they did each morning. The first few exercises moved students into the realm of feelings. An accepted language surfaced as they worked collectively on experiences like the "Torn Heart" and completing the sentence stem "How would I feel if...." They rated their feelings in a journal, becoming aware of changes from day to day and in response to different circumstances. The students moved from awareness to managing feelings as they discussed how to create a "peace place" within themselves and within their classroom. One student volunteered a teepee-shaped tent and the class determined the rules for its use. They set a time limit of five minutes and parameters that reinforced its purpose as a safe place to calm down and be with your feelings.

In like manner, the class set up a "ridicule-free zone" and created a constitution of caring. They brainstormed what could be done if the constitution was violated and these consequences were posted. As the activities progressed, students staged skits that exposed the troubling side of teasing. They literally stepped into each other's paper shoes to role-play a different perspective from their own. They worked with conflict de-escalation and conflict resolution techniques.

Then they strengthened their role as witnesses in bullying situations. An exercise that introduced an imaginary "bullying-buster machine" helped them to find and use their voice in mock bullying encounters. **See pages 299-301 for the complete lesson.** The concept of a "bullying buster" also made its way into their language and self-image. More than once, students returned from lunch or recess to tell the teacher they had been a bullying-buster. They told of standing up for someone who was being teased or reaching out to a classmate who had been excluded by other students.

The class invested an hour a day for eight weeks in the program. Although there was an increase in cooperation and caring, the real test occurred when the teacher brought a case of teasing out into the open. With the target away from class, she initiated a conversation about what was going on and brought the class together as problem-solvers to address their actions, their effect and what they could do to change. Students talked openly about feelings of guilt and peer pressure. Together, they suggested ways to correct hurtful behaviors and put them into action. The harrassment stopped.

DON'T LAUGH AT ME

This resource, through music and video, provides an emotional connection that sensitizes students to the issues of bullying and ridicule. The accompanying curriculum includes 14 sessions focused on developing the healthy expression of feelings, the appreciation of diversity, the creation of a caring classroom culture, and the resolution of conflicts.

Their web site provides ordering information for the video and CD and allows educators to download the curriculum for camp, grades 2-5 and grades 6-8.
Web site: www.dontlaugh.org
Also see Resources, page 314

STUDENTS IN ACTION

While extended explorations raise the awareness of students, real situations engage them. The learning moves from head to heart to action as they are enlisted in the process of confronting a bullying problem. The third-graders who completed the "Don't Laugh at Me" course responded as an entire class, but another technique involves the informal leaders of a class. When a target is identified, the counselor brings together a small group of positive student leaders from the class. They develop a plan and try it out, then come back together to see what worked and what did not. Meetings are called as needed, providing flexibility, ongoing problem-solving and a safe place to talk candidly about the realities of bullying. The nature of the teams, the fact that students are chosen because of their proximity to the problem, reinforces the sense that all students are seen as potential change agents and effective problem-solvers.

With all bullying situations, the counselors and teachers work closely with the administration and keep open lines of communication with the parents of all involved.

KEYS TO MAKING IT WORK

- A long-term, intentional focus and the commitment of the administration.

- A clear process for reporting and responding to teasing/bullying situations.

- A community of adults who connect with students: The definition of this community must be broad and inclusive, including bus drivers, custodians and those who work with students during lunch, recess and before and after school.

- A group that will keep the mission front and center: A dynamic committee of staff members and parents becomes a unifying force, getting the information out, keeping the community focused and reinvigorating the commitment each year.

- Student ownership: This is fostered through a combination of information, discussion, experiential learning, skills training and collaborative problem-solving.

- Ongoing communications: In specific bullying situations, open, clear communications among the administration, teachers, counselors, school Care Teams, parents and other adults that connect with students is essential. In a more general sense, messages supporting the anti-bullying approach are expressed in the principal's weekly calendar, school newsletter, reports home of positive student actions and p.a. announcements.

Claymont Elementary, Parkway School District

Be a Bullying Buster

Children look at the role of bystanders in instances of bullying and other unkind behavior and identify appropriate ways to respond.

Activity Level: Medium
Concentration Level: Medium
Activity Time: 50 minutes
Preparation Time: None

Objectives

- To identify ways to respond to unkind behaviors
- To practice assertion skills and "I" messages
- To learn boundaries for when to intervene and not intervene
- To be sensitized to the important role of bystanders

Materials

- VCR and "Don't Laugh at Me" video cued to the Peter, Paul & Mary version
- Chart paper
- A large paper heart or other symbol of caring

Gather Together (5 minutes)

- Pass a large heart around the circle and ask each person holding the heart to say something she likes about a friend or someone in the room. "I like when my friend helps me solve a problem," etc. Continue until everyone has contributed.

Explore Caring: The "Don't Laugh at Me" Video (10 minutes)

- Ask: What happy or hopeful images do you see in the "Don't Laugh at Me" video? (If a VCR isn't available, have the children listen to the song and record happy images that come to mind). Have students record their answers after they watch the video or listen to the song.

- Ask for some volunteers to share what they recorded. List the images on the chart paper and the positive feelings associated with those images.

- Discuss: What do these images have in common? (Many of the images include people showing caring—either by putting an arm around someone or giving someone an award, cheering for them, etc.) List all the ways that people show caring in the video. If children have difficulty remembering the images, return to the video for another showing.

Explore Bullying (10 minutes)

- Now explain that you are going to turn your attention to what we can do when we see someone being treated unkindly. Ask: What types of behavior constitute bullying? (Explain that someone is being bullied when he or she is repeatedly called names, made fun of, picked on, hit, kicked, shoved, pushed, pinched, threatened, or excluded from a group.) Ask for raised hands: How many of you have ever seen or heard about someone being bullied? Have students turn to a partner and tell each other about what they saw. Ask for a few volunteers to share.

- Now ask: Did anyone in this class ever do anything to help when someone was bullied? Or did any of you stand up for yourself when you were being bullied or treated badly? (If someone did, have him or her share what he or she did.)

- Brainstorm with students a list of things you can do when you or someone you see is being hurt or bullied. Record ideas on chart paper in two columns: ideas that mean confronting the bully and ideas that do not. Add to the children's ideas with suggestions from the following:

  - Refuse to join in (doesn't involve confrontation).

  - Report bullying you know about or see to an adult (doesn't involve confrontation).

  - Invite the person being hurt to join your group (might involve confrontation). Then ask the person who was bullied if it's okay to have the bully join your group if the bully apologizes (does involve confrontation).

  - Speak out using an "I" message. Say, "I don't like it when you treat him like that." "I want you to stop calling him that name." "I'm going to tell a counselor right now." (Does involve confrontation.)

  - Be a friend to the person who has been bullied by showing him you care about him: put an arm around him, give him a put-up, etc. (doesn't involve confrontation).

  - Distract the bully with a joke or something else so she stops the behavior (does involve confrontation).

- One important rule is that if students see someone being hurt physically or see an interaction that might escalate into physical violence, they should *not* confront the bully. Rather, they should quickly go and get help from an adult. Discuss with students signs that might indicate such a physical threat.

Intervene in Bullying: The Bullying Buster Machine (15 minutes)

- Introduce the next activity: It takes practice and courage to act strong without being mean when you or another child are being treated unkindly or bullied. Tell the students you would like them to pretend they are a Bullying Buster machine. To form the machine, have children break into two lines facing one another about three feet apart. They should imagine that they have switches on their arms. When you touch an arm, the Bullying Buster machine switches on. You will walk down the aisle between the students, pretending to be a bully. Once a child is "switched on," that child should give out a strong (but not mean) message to the bully.

- Walk along the aisle between the students. Recite a scenario from the ones listed below, or act it out if you are comfortable doing that. Then choose a child randomly and switch him or her on with a touch on the arm for a strong Bullying Buster response. Practice with several students before moving on to another scenario. Some possible situations:

  - Someone calls you a mean name (Possible Bullying Buster machine response: "I feel hurt and angry when you call me that name. Please don't do that.")

  - Someone tells you to do something you don't want to do.

  - Someone is calling someone else a bad name.

  - Someone is making fun of someone because she is blind.

  - Someone wants you to call someone else a bad name.

  - Someone tells you you can't play in the game.

  - Someone demands that you give him your afternoon snack.

  - Someone is teasing a friend of yours.

- Ask for a few volunteers to share: What are some feelings you had during this activity?

DON'T LAUGH AT ME TEACHERS GUIDE 2–5 © 2000 OPERATION RESEARCH, INC. AND EDUCATORS FOR SOCIAL RESPONSIBILITY

PAGE 300 • **FIELD-TESTED RESOURCES IN CHARACTER EDUCATION** • **COOPERATING SCHOOL DISTRICTS OF GREATER ST. LOUIS**

Close Together (10 minutes)

- Ask students to individually write a pledge to be a "Bullying Buster." What promises are they willing to make to the rest of the class today? What promises are they willing to make to the rest of the school today? They can begin their pledge with, "I promise to . . . "
- Do a go-round where each child reads his or her pledge.
- (Optional) Gather the pledges together in a Bullying Buster book to keep in your classroom or have students incorporate their pledges into a notebook or other personal item they carry often.

 Discuss with children that sharing an incidence of bullying with a teacher is not tattling. Explain that being in a caring classroom carries some rights and responsibilities. Say, "We all have the right to feel safe in this school and we all have the right to be protected. Your responsibility as a member of this community is to help ensure that sense of safety is possible for every child."

CURRICULUM CONNECTIONS (OPTIONAL)

Literature. Part of the popular Joshua T. Bates series, *Joshua T. Bates, Trouble Again* (Random House, 1998) by Susan Richards Shreve, is a good chapter book to discuss standing up to bullies with grades 2-5. Also use the book as a launching point to discuss the effects of peer pressure on our behaviors. Ask: Has there ever been a time that you did something like make fun of another kid, just to fit in? How can we make caring "cool" in our school? Use the book *King of the Playground* by Phyllis Reynolds Naylor to further discuss how to respond to bullies.

Geography. On chart paper taped together, have children draw one huge map of your school and its school grounds (perhaps teaming with other classrooms who would take certain zones of the school). As an extension of the Caring Being, have students create the "Caring School." Brainstorm a list of where they would most like to feel safe (the playground, the bus, the cafeteria, the library, home, etc.). Have them write in the words and ideas that they would like to see characterized in each place. Use this map as a launching point for discussion in "Take It to the Community."

Children's Conscious Acts of Caring

"When I was on a bus this boy was making faces at us. I [asked] him why he was making faces at us. He told me, 'Because I feel like it.' But I told him can you stop making faces at us. We shook hands and now we are friends." —from Vicky Leiva, elementary school student, San Francisco, California

---

LEARNING THROUGH THEATRE: PORTRAYING THE HUMAN COSTS OF BULLYING

There is something magical about the elementary school play. When the fifth-grade students at Glenridge Elementary used this forum to express their understanding of bullying, the effect was electric. They presented a drama that generated classroom discussions among the student body and left an audience of parents and siblings visibly moved.

The play highlighted a year of exploration that involved all grade levels, but the learning was intensified for fifth graders. Their experiences and feelings about bullying shaped the script of a play called "A Bully's Wish." They continued to engage the subject as they moved into auditions and, ultimately, performed a drama that portrayed the human costs of bullying.

GRADES: K - 5 WITH EMPHASIS ON 5TH GRADE

OBJECTIVES

The play was part of an ongoing, schoolwide effort designed to (1) heighten awareness of the damage bullying wreaks on both victims and bullies, and (2) prepare students to respond to bullying situations with compassion and courage.

THE PROCESS COMBINES COGNITIVE AND EXPERIENTIAL LEARNING

The process involved the collaborative efforts of the counselor, fifth-grade teachers, a playwright and director, the music director and the art teacher. It combined cognitive and experiential learning within these activities:

- seven once-a-week lessons on bullying
- two one-hour sessions of improvisations
- a writing assignment
- reflection and discussion throughout each phase
- auditions and rehearsals
- the performance
- classroom discussions and a writing assignment following the performance

BUILDING THE FOUNDATION

In seven weekly sessions with each classroom, the counselor built a foundation for understanding and talking about the subject. The roles of target, bully and witness were defined through real-life stories of positive student action from *Bullies & Victims: Helping your Child through the Schoolyard Battlefield.* A survey published in *Bully-Proofing Your School* was used to calibrate the extent of the problem. Students anonymously answered questions like, "How often do other children say mean things to you?" "In what grade is the student who bullies you?" "If you have been bullied this year, who have you told?" The results provided a view of the school culture from the students' perspectives and reinforced the need to address the issue in a meaningful way. The counselor focused on strategies for responding and confronting bullying situations in later sessions.

WHERE TO GO FOR MORE
Bullies & Victims
by SuEllen and Paula Fried
Bully-Proofing Your School
by C. Garrity, et al
See References, page 309

For several strategies that increase verbal response skills and confidence, see
"Be a Bullying Buster"
on pages 299-301

IMPROVISATIONS, WRITING AND DISCUSSION

The students drew from this foundation as they worked with the playwright. She met with each fifth-grade class in two one-hour sessions, coaching the students in the art of improvisation. Under her direction, they depicted the bullying of siblings, new students, students who excel and students who stumble academically, and students who look different or like different things. They enacted scenes where a clique targets a victim with taunts and name calling, where a victim tries to tell a parent what is happening, where a victim stands her ground and talks back, and where humor is used to defuse a bully.

Students were encouraged to fully enter the role of the character and make it believable. Empathy and unexpected insights surfaced as they moved out of themselves into another personality and set of circumstances. The playwright provided techniques for losing oneself in the role and for returning to one's own frame of reference. The teachers, knowing their students, facilitated discussions after each session. They helped individuals and the class as a whole to process what they had enacted. After the second session, they guided students through a written exercise with the assignment shown on the left, providing class time to share their writings and talk about them.

WRITING ASSIGNMENT

Write a piece about bullying. You have several options: You may write a narrative describing a scene where you were involved in a bully situation.
• You may be the person who was doing the bullying.
• You may be the victim.
• You may be a person who is a witness to the scene.

If you do not have any personal experience with bullying, you may write a story or a fictional scenario about a bully that describes what you know and feel about this topic.

The situation can be from home, school, playground, camp or wherever communities of people gather and interact. You may borrow ideas from the improvisations we have done in class. You may get an idea from your work with the counselor.

When writing, make sure that you use strong vocabulary to describe your characters, their actions and their speech.
• Include dialogue that is lively and realistic and shows what is happening in the scene.
• Be sure to include a conclusion to your scene that states your opinion about what has occurred.
• Be prepared to share your work in class if you can be comfortable doing so.

SCRIPTING THE PLAY

The playwright, influenced by themes that emerged in the improvisations and writings, scripted a play that reflected the pattern of bullying in the life of a 50-year-old man and the toll on his victims and himself. With seven monologues by the central character and six scenes that flash back to his school days, the play afforded speaking parts for two-thirds of the fifth-grade class. The remaining students had active roles as part of the chorus.

HOLDING AUDITIONS & REHEARSALS

Auditions were open to all fifth-grade students. They were held in their classrooms, providing an audience and a level of contagious excitement and peer support that encouraged more than 95% of them to try out. They teamed up with classmates to enact parts of the flashback scenes and, on the second run, read portions from one of the monologues. The playwright selected the cast, while the music director worked with students to develop a repertoire of songs that enhanced the scenes. The art teacher teamed with students to design and construct the set. Rehearsals were held daily for a four-week period. Most sessions took place during the school day as small groups of students were pulled from class to work on their specific scenes.

PERFORMING THE PLAY

The play was performed for the entire student body. Each teacher led a discussion of the themes when they returned to class. In an evening performance, the play was presented to families, reaching both parents and siblings with a powerful message. The fifth grade students later reflected on the entire experience in a four-part assignment that asked them to recount the story; describe the parts that came together to make the play possible, from the script to costumes to the lighting crew; analyze two problems that occurred and how they were resolved; and write about what they learned in producing the play.

KEYS TO MAKING IT WORK

- Access to a playwright is not a prerequisite. "A Bully's Wish" can be obtained and enacted. Another approach is to develop a script from the material generated by students. Some of the stronger improvisations can be refined and linked loosely with a narration. Students can also write material to be developed into a script. A two-part assignment is helpful. Ask them to write a monologue about what it feels like to be a bully or to be bullied. Ask them to create a scene, writing the actual dialogue between the characters.

> **WHERE TO GO FOR MORE**
> **"A Bully's Wish"**
> The script of this play and others are available from playwright Jamie Lefkowith • (314) 727-4318 or Jamcordrew@worldnet.att.net

- Use the play to involve the greatest number of students. It is written so that parts can be consolidated for a small cast or divided among a large cast.

- If the parts are divided among a large cast and multiple students represent a single character, the costumes can be color-coded so the audience can easily identify the role.

- Develop writing assignments that encourage reflection and application to life. Suggested topics: What did I learn about myself through this process? How would I like to change or improve my actions?

- Consider a facilitated discussion with parents and siblings following the evening performance.

- Consider performing the play for more audiences, especially younger students at other schools. Discussions should be a part of the play experience and can be facilitated by the actors.

Glenridge Elementary, Clayton School District

HIGH TECH DIALOGUES:
BRINGING STUDENTS TOGETHER TO CONFRONT BIAS

Thirty-six students—12 from each of three middle schools—experienced the kind of learning that breaks down barriers between people. They came together in a series of encounters, including videoconference dialogues, to confront bias and bullying. These students got "up close and personal," sharing their own experiences with name-calling, exclusion and their role in bullying situations. In their first videoconference session, they stumbled into their assumptions about each other, realizing that they were not divided by racial differences, but by school affiliations. Their schools evoked images—preppy, spoiled, indifferent, smart, rich, urban, poor, disadvantaged, stupid, dangerous, athletic, invisible—that did not fit the people they came to know through the dialogues.

GRADES: 6 - 8

MEETING THE CHALLENGE

These students met the challenge of the "NAMES Can Really Hurt Us" program. They looked at the bias and bullying in their own backyard, what they saw happening at school and after school. They looked at how they had been hurt by it, how they had hurt others and how they could make a difference. By the end of the year, and the program's well-designed encounters, this core group of students took a leadership role among their peers. Each team invited 50 of their classmates to a day-long exploration of the issue of name-calling. They met at a neutral site—150 students from three different schools—and kicked off the event with a video that disclosed their candid approach to the issue and their own vulnerability.

"NAMES Can Really Hurt Us"

The program is available through ADL'S
A WORLD OF DIFFERENCE® Institute
St. Louis Chapter
10420 Olive Street, Suite 208
St. Louis, MO 63141 • 314-432-6868
Contact: Kelley Shull • shulk@adl.org
See Resources
for national chapter, page 313

An eighth grade girl, for instance, described how she and her friends finally challenged students who were taunting a boy in their computer class. She concluded, somewhat remorsefully, "We should have stepped up for him right away instead of letting anything happen at all. But at least he knows now that someone cares." A boy spoke of a classmate who recruited 30 members to an "I-Hate-Alex" club. Another girl talked of being ridiculed by her peers because she liked to figure skate. Skating, they said, was a "white sport." The video set the tone for the day, encouraging the audience to risk their own experiences and feelings in the breakout sessions that followed.

MEETING OBJECTIVES

The day of breakout sessions was the culmination of the "NAMES Can Really Hurt Us" program, developed by the Anti-Defamation League's A WORLD OF DIFFERENCE® Institute. The program is designed to help students:

- address experiences with name-calling and develop the capacity to question their own ideas about culture, race, gender, and social differences.

- understand the complexity of the relationship between one's behaviors and one's values. (For example, if you value being an individual, do you respect and appreciate other people for their individual characteristics?)

- demonstrate an understanding of their own roles in making justice and equality a reality in the world around them.

- become leaders among their peers by creating an honest atmosphere where real experiences are shared.

St. Louis is the only city to pilot the middle school program using video-conferencing to connect students from geographically and sociologically diverse schools. This technological bridge, provided by Cooperating School Districts' Virtual Learning Center, eliminated the time and expense of travel. It also allowed the students to gain experience in using educational technology to accomplish their goals.

COMPONENTS OF DYNAMIC INTERACTION

The program involved a professional facilitator, 16 high school students who served as A WORLD OF DIFFERENCE® Peer Trainers, teacher advisors from each school and the coordinator of the videoconferencing center. It included several different encounters or meetings:

- a day-long peer leader retreat for each team of 12 students, guided by the professional facilitator;

- three one-hour videoconference dialogues and one in-person dialogue, guided by a professional facilitator;

- reflection sessions that follow each dialogue, guided by peer trainers;

- an assembly and a day of breakout sessions for a larger audience of peers.

Peer Leader Retreat: The retreat involved activities to help students understand that name-calling is connected to bullying and to the "isms"—racism, sexism, classism and able-ism. Students identified how they were victims as well as perpetrators of name-calling, and how they can move from being a bystander to an ally when they witness acts of name-calling.

Dialogues: The videoconference dialogues followed specific agendas that led students into an examination of their values and actions, the dynamics of bias and bullying, ways to counter negative messages, and ways to become an ally to others suffering from name-calling and bullying. In the second session, for instance, students at all three locations participated in a Value Line. They were given a series of word pairs and asked to quickly report the one that rated a higher priority: honesty/winning; family/friends; money/power; respect from others/self-respect. The dialogue focused on the difficulty of negotiating between competing values, real-world situations that create conflicts between values, and the self-awareness that actions do not always match one's personal values.

Reflection Sessions: These sessions were facilitated by the A WORLD OF DIFFERENCE® peer trainers. Two high school students were matched with each middle school and they worked with the same team of students throughout the year, building a base of trust. They described how they confront bias within their high school and helped the younger students identify areas they could address individually and collectively within their middle schools. They used role plays to introduce response skills and allow the chance to practice being an ally. The peer trainers also listened as the team members talked about what they learned from the dialogues, what they were willing to risk and what happened when they tried to address an injustice.

Assembly with Breakout Sessions: The concluding assembly was designed to involve the three student teams in an exploration of name-calling. The peer trainers facilitated the breakout sessions. The original 36 students set the tone for the day. Featured in a 14-minute videotape, they shared their experiences and feelings. Throughout the breakout sessions, their insightful participation helped fellow students make connections between bias and their own school environment.

KEYS TO MAKING IT WORK

- It is important to select candidates for the teams who have leadership potential and represent different constituencies within the school. Once trained, these students are called "peer leaders."

- Training for teacher and counselor facilitators ranges from 4 hours to 5 days, depending upon the commitment of the school to the program and the experience of faculty members with these issues.

- Training occurs before student teams are selected at each school. Training for adults and students alike stress listening skills, for unless participants feel that they are really being understood, they will not risk sharing their experiences and feelings. Learning to paraphrase, reflect back and remain silent are among the valuable techniques students learn.

- To extend the reach of the learning experience, multiple assemblies could be held at each of the three middle schools, involving the entire student body at each location.

Brittany Woods Middle School, University City School District;
Cross Keys Middle School, Ferguson-Florissant School District;
Ladue Middle School, Ladue School District;
Lindbergh High School, Lindbergh School District

RESOURCES

REFERENCES

The following publications and resources are referenced in the units of this book.
Apacki, Carol. *Energize!* Newark, OH: Quest International, 1991.
ISBN 1-56095-059-5

Bodine, Richard, et al. *Creating the Peaceable School: A Comprehensive Program for Teaching Conflict Resolution.* Champaign, IL: Research Press, 1994. ISBN 087822-346-0

Brousseau, Patricia. *Building Decision Skills,* Camden, ME: Institute for Global Ethics, 1995. *Contact: (800) 729-2615; www.globalethics.org*

Careers for the 21st Century. Catalogue of available videotapes. St. Louis, MO: Educational Excellence Inc., 1997. *Contact Take Off Multimedia: (800) 462-5232*

Character Matters. Activities and lesson plans for specific traits developed in a series of articles. St. Louis, MO: Newspapers in Education, 1996. *Contact Newspapers in Education: (314) 340-8875 or (800) 365-0820, x 8875*

Edelman, Marian Wright. *The Measure of Our Success.* Boston, MA: Beacon Press, 1992. ISBN 0-8070-3102-X

Fogarty, Robin. *The Mindful School: How to Integrate the Curriculum.* Palatine, IL: IRI/Skylight Publishing, Inc., 1991. *Contact IRI Skylight Publishing: (800) 348-4474*

Fried, Paula and SuEllen. *Bullies & Victims: Helping Your Child through the Schoolyard Battlefield.* New York, NY: M. Evans and Company, Inc., 1996. ISBN: 0-87131-840-7

Gallena, Jill. *Wackadoo Zoo.* Delaware Water Gap, PA: Wide World Music & Company. *Contact Wide World Music & Company, Box B, Delaware Water Gap, PA 1832.*

Garrity, Carla., et al. *Bully-Proofing Your School: A Comprehensive Approach for Elementary Schools.* Longmont, CO: Sopris West, 1998. ISBN: 0-944584-99-3

Granowsky, Alvin. *Robin Hood & The Sheriff Speaks.* Austin, TX: Steck Vaughn Publishing, 1993. *Contact Steck Vaughn Publishing: (800) 531-5015*

Granowksy, Alvin. *Jack and the Beanstalk & Giants Have Feelings Too.* Austin, TX: Steck Vaughn Publishing, 1996. *Contact Steck Vaughn Publishing: (800) 531-5015*

Hutchins, Pat. *Don't Forget the Bacon.* Pine Plains: Live Oak Media, 1992. ISBN: 0-87499-2524

Hyperstudio® (software). El Cajon, CA: Roger Wagner Publishing, Inc. *Contact Roger Wagner Publishing: (800) 497-3778*

Lachner, Dorothy. *Andrew's Angry Words*. New York, NY: North-South Books, 1995. ISBN 1 – 55858-435-8

McKay, Linda and Dave Lankford. *Ethical Decision-Making in the Workplace and Society for Young Adults.* Reston, VA: National Association of Secondary School Principals, 1988. Product number: 6619101 *Contact NASSP: (703) 860-0200*

McKay, Linda and Dave Lankford. *License to Lead.* Reston, VA: National Association of Secondary School Principals, 1996. Product number: 6209601 *Contact NASSP: (703) 860-0200*

Oh, the Places We'll Go—Traveling through the Year with PREP Themes. St. Louis, MO: Hazelwood School District, 1996. *Contact Dr. Tom Bick, Hazelwood School District: (314) 953-5000*

Pfefferkorn, Michael and Richard Rosenow. *Ethics: A View of Life. A Guide to Constructing an Ethics Course for the Secondary Schools.* St. Louis, MO: CSD, 1992. *Contact* **CHARACTER**plus: *(800) 835-8282*

Rich, Dorothy. *MegaSkills.* Boston, MA: Houghton Mifflin, 1988. ISBN 0-395-46849-3. *Contact MegaSkills Education Center: (202) 466-3633; www.megaskillshsi.org*

Tindall, J. *Peer Power: Strategic Professional Book I, Peer Power: Strategic Professional Book II.* Bristol, PA: Taylor and Francis Publishers, 1989, 1994. *Contact Taylor and Francis Publishers: (800) 821-8312; www.bkorders@tandfpa.com*

Reger, Terry and Carl Yochum. *The Portfolio: A Student Assessment Process.* St. Louis, MO: Ferguson-Florissant School District, 1994. *Contact Carl Yochum: (314) 831-4411*

United States. Department of the Treasury. Internal Revenue Service. *Understanding Taxes, High School Program.* Washington, D.C.: IRS, 1997. *Call the local IRS office to learn how to contact the Taxpayer Education Coordinator. Write or phone the coordinator to request Form 1742: Catalog Number 17697J*

Unnerstall, Joleene. **Project H.A.R.T.** St. Louis, MO: Women's Support & Community Services, 1995. *Contact: (314) 531-9100. www.womensupport.org*

Veljkovic, Peggy and Arthur J. Schwartz, Ed.D., eds. *Writing from the Heart: Young People Share Their Wisdom.* Radnor, PA: Templeton Foundation Press, 2000. ISBN 1-890151-48-3 *www.lawsoflife.org*

Vincent, Philip F., ed. *Promising Practices in Character Education: Nine Success Stories from around the Country.* Chapel Hill, NC: Character Development Group, 1996. ISBN 0-9653163-0-0 *Contact: (919) 967-2110*

Yochum, Carl. *Musical Definitions: Resources Indexed by Character Trait.* St. Louis, MO: Ferguson-Florissant School District, 1989.

FURTHER READING

Baldwin, Bruce A., Ph.D. *Beyond the Cornucopia Kids.* Wilmington, NC: Direction Dynamics, 1988. ISBN 0-933583-07-9

Boyer, Ernest L. *The Basic School.* Princeton, NJ: The Carnegie Foundation for the Advancement of Teaching, 1995. *Contact: (800) 777-4726*

Burrett, Kenneth and Rusnak, Timothy. *Integrated Character Education.* Phi Delta Kappa Educational Foundation, 1993. ISBN 0-87367-351-4

Curran, Lorna. *Cooperative Learning: Lessons For Little Ones.* San Clemente, CA: Kagan Cooperative Learning, 1992. ISBN 1-879097-09-5

Gauld, Joseph W. *Character First—The Hyde School Difference.* San Francisco, CA: ICS Press, 1993. ISBN 1-55815-262-8

Glenn, Stephen H. and Nelson, Jane, Ed.D. *Raising Self-Reliant Children in a Self-Indulgent World,* Rocklin, CA: Prima Publishing and Communications, 1989. ISBN 0-914629-92-1

Gibbs, Jeanne. *Tribes: A Process for Social Developmental and Cooperative Learning.* CA: Center Source Publications, 1987. ISBN 0-932762-08-5

Heath, Douglas H. *Schools of Hope: Developing Mind and Character in Today's Youth.* San Francisco, CA: Jossey-Bass Publishers, 1994.

Heath, Douglas H. *Lives of Hope: Women's and Men's Paths to Success and Fulfillment.* Haverford, PA: Conrow Publishing House, 1994. ISBN 0-9641727-0-4 (paper)

Huffman, Henry A. *Developing a Character Education Program: One School District's Experience.* Alexandria, VA: The Character Education Partnership, 1994.

Kidder, Rushworth W. *Shared Values in a Troubled World.* San Francisco,CA: Jossey-Bass Publishers, 1994. ISBN 1-55542-603-4

Kidder, Rushworth W. *How Good People Make Tough Choices. Resolving the Dilemmas for Ethical Living.* New York, NY: William Morrow Company, Inc., 1995. ISBN 0-688-13442-4

Lewis, Barbara A. *The Kids Guide to Service Projects: Over 500 Service Ideas for Young People Who Want to Make a Difference.* Minneapolis, MN: Free Spirit Publishing, 1995.

Lickona, Thomas. *Educating for Character. How Our Schools Can Teach Respect and Responsibility.* New York, NY: Bantam Books, 1991. ISBN 0-553-37052-9

Lickona, Thomas. *Raising Good Children. Helping your Child through the Stage of Moral Development.* New York, NY: Bantam Books, 1983, 1994. ISBN 0553-37429-X (paper)

Orlick, Terry. *The Cooperative Sports & Games Book.* New York, NY: Patheon Books, 1978. ISBN 0-394-73494-7

Rowen, Lawrence. *Beyond Winning.* Illinois: Fearon Teacher Aids, 1990. ISBN 0-8224-3380X

Saenger, Elizabeth B. *Exploring Ethics Through Children's Literature.* California: Critical Thinking Press & Software, 1993. ISBN 0-89455-485-9

Schulman, Michael. *Schools as Moral Communities: A Framework and Guide for School Administrators, Principals, and Teachers.* New York, NY: Jewish Foundation for Christian Rescuers, 1995.

Smedes, Lewis B. *Choices, Making Right Decisions in a Complex World.* New York, NY: Harper-Collins Publishers, 1991.

Urban, Hal. *20 Things I Want My Kids to Know.* Nashville, TN: Thomas Nelson Publisher, 1992. ISBN 0-8407-9153-4

U.S. Department of Education. *Helping Your Child* series. Office of Educational Research and Improvement, 1989.

Vincent, Philip F., (Editor). *Promising Practices in Character Eudcation: Nine Success Stories from across the Country, Volume II.* Chapel Hill, NC: Character Development Publishing, 1999. ISBN 1-892-056-02-X

RESOURCES (ORGANIZATIONS)

NATIONAL

A WORLD OF DIFFERENCE® Institute/National Chapter
A Program of the Anti-Defamation League
823 United Nations Plaza   Phone: (212) 885-7700
New York, NY 10017   Web site: www.adl.org

American Youth Foundation
2331 Hampton Avenue   Phone: (314) 646-6000
St. Louis, MO 63139   Fax: (314) 772-7542

Boy Scouts of America
1325 W. Walnut Hill Lane   Phone: (972) 580-2000
P.O. Box 152079   Fax: (972) 580-2502
Irving, TX 75015-2079   E-mail: bsa.scouting.org

Bullying Prevention & Intervention
Training Institute w/SuEllen Fried   Phone: (913) 362-2226
4003 Homestead Drive   Fax: (913) 362-2886
Shawnee Mission, KS 66208

Center for the 4th and 5th R's
Department of Education   Phone: (607) 753-2456
State Universty of N.Y./Cortland   Fax: (607) 753-5987
P.O. Box 2000   E-mail: c4n5rs@cortland.edu
Cortland, NY 13045

Character Counts! Coalition
4640 Admiralty Way #1001, Dpt. 50   Phone: (310) 306-1868
Marina del Ray, CA 90292-6610   Fax: (310) 827-1864
Web site: www.charactercounts.org   E-mail: cc@jiethics.org

The Character Education Partnership
1025 Connecticut Ave., Suite 111   Toll free: (800) 988-8081
Washington, D.C. 20036   Phone: (202) 296-7743
Web site: www.character.org   Fax: (202) 296-7779

CHARACTERplus™
Cooperating Schools Districts   Toll free: (800) 835-8282
8225 Florissant Road   Phone: (314) 835-8282
St. Louis, MO 63121   Fax: (314) 692-9700
    E-mail: characterplus@info.csd.org
Web site: http://info.csd.org/staffdev/chared/characterplus.html

Crisis Prevention Institute
3315-K North 124th St.   Toll free: (800) 558-8976
Brookfield, WI 53005   Phone: (262) 783-5787
Web site: www.execpc.com/~c   Fax: (262) 783-5906

Developmental Studies Center
2000 Embarcadero, #305   Toll free: (800) 666-7270 x239
Oakland, CA 94606-5300   Phone: (510) 533-0213 x240
Web site: www.devstu.org   Fax: (510) 464-3670

Don't Laugh at Me
2 Penn Plaza, 23rd Floor   Phone: (212) 904-5243
New York, NY 10121   Fax: (212) 904-3618
    Web site: www.dontlaugh.org

Educators for Social Responsibility
23 Garden Street
Cambridge, MA 02138

Toll free: (800) 370-2515
Fax: (617) 864-5164
Web site: esrnational.org

Efficacy Institute
182 Felton Street
Waltham, MA 02453
Web site: www.efficacy.org

Toll free: (800) 437-9081
Phone: (781) 547-6060
Fax: (781) 547-6077

Ethics Resource Center
1747 Pennsylvania Ave., #400
Washington, D.C. 20006

Phone: (202) 737-2258
Fax: (202) 737-2227

Freedom Forum First Amendment Center
1101 Wilson Blvd.
Arlington, VA 22209

Phone: (703) 284-2859
Fax: (703) 284-3519

Girl Scouts of the U.S.A.
420 Fifth Avenue
New York, NY 10018-2798

Toll free: (800) 478-7248

The Institute for Global Ethics
11-13 Main St, P.O. Box 563
Camden, ME 04843
Web site: www.globalethics.org

Toll free: (800) 729-2615
Phone: (207) 236-6658
Fax: (207) 236-4014

Jefferson Center for Character Education/Passkeys Foundation
P.O. Box 4137
Mission Viejo, CA 92690
Web site: www.jeffersoncenter.org

Phone: (949) 770-7602
Fax: (949) 450-1100
Fax: (207) 236-4014

Laws of Life/John Templeton Foundation
Five Radnor Corporate Center, #100
100 Matsonford Rd.
Radnor, PA 19087

Toll free: (800) 245-1285
Fax: (610) 687-8961
Website: www.lawsoflife.org

NASSP/National Association of Secondary School Principals
1904 Association Drive
Reston, VA 20191-1537
Web site: www.principal.org

Phone: (703) 860-0200
Fax: (703) 476-5432

NCCRE/National Center for Conflict Resolution
Illinois Bar Center
424 South Second Street
Springfield, MO 62701

Toll free: (800) 308-9419
Fax: (217) 523-7066
Web site: www.nccre.org

National Professional Resources, Inc.
25 South Regent St.
Port Chester, NY 10573
Web site: www.nprinc.com

Toll free: (800) 453-7461
Phone: (914) 937-8879
Fax: (914) 937-9327

PeaceJam Foundation
2427 West Argyle Place
Denver, CO 80211

Phone: (303) 455-2099
Web site: www.peacejam.org
E-mail: peacejam@aol.com

Quest International/Lions-Quest Programs
P.O. Box 304
Annapolis Junction, MD 20701
Web site: www.quest.edu

Toll free: (800) 446-2700
Fax: (240) 646-7023

INDEX

Adderholdt, Miriam, & Goldberg, Jan. *Perfectionism: What's Bad About Being Too Good?*
Minneapolis, MN: Free Spirit Publishing, 1999. $12.95

Beane, Allan L. *The Bully Free Classroom: Over 100 Tips and Strategies for Teachers K-8.*
Minneapolis, MN: Free Spirit Publishing, 1999. $19.95

Beedy, Jeffrey. *Sports Plus: Developing Youth Sports Programs that Teach Positive Values.*
Hamilton, MA: Project Adventure, Inc., 1997. $16.00

Begun, Ruth W. *Ready-to-Use Social Skills Lesson (4 levels: Pre K-K; 1-3; 4-6; 7-12).*
West Nyack, NY: Center for Applied Research, 1995. $29.95 each

Bennett, William J. *Book of Virtues.* New York, NY: Simon & Schuster, 1996. $16.00

Bennett, William J. *Moral Compass.* New York, NY: Simon & Schuster, 1996. $16.00

Benson, Peter L., Galbraith, Judy, & Espeland, Pamela. *What Teens Need To Succeed.*
Minneapolis, MN: Free Spirit Press, 1998. $14.95

Berman, Sally. *Service Learning for the Multiple Intelligences Classroom.*
Arlington Heights, VA: Skylight, 1999. $34.95

Bocchino, Rob. *Emotional Literacy: To Be a Different Kind of Smart.* Thousand Oaks, CA:
Corwin Press, 1999. $24.95

Boston University School of Education (Editor). *The Art of Loving Well.* Boston, MA: 1995.
$19.95

Brooks, B. David & Goble, Frank. *Case for Character Education.* Northridge, CA: Studio Four
Productions, 1997. $11.95

Canfield, Jack & Hansen, Mark V. *Chicken Soup for the Kid's Soul: 101 Stories of Courage,
Hope & Laughter.* Deerfield Beach, FL: Health Communications, Inc., 1998. $12.95

Character Connections Monthly Newsletter. National Professional Resources (Publisher). 1999.
$99.00 yearly subscription

Caroll, Jeri A. Gladhart, Marsha A. & Petersen, Dixie L. *Character Building/Literature-Based
Theme.* Carthage, IL: Teaching & Learning Company, 1997. $14.95

Charney, Ruth S. *Habits of Goodness: Case Studies in the Social Curriculum.* Greenfield, MA:
Northeast Foundation for Children, 1997. $18.50

Cohen, Jonathan. *Educating Minds & Hearts.* New York, NY: Teacher's College Press, 1999.
$21.95

Coles, Robert. *Moral Intelligence of Children.* New York, NY: Random House, Inc., 1997. $21.00

Delisle, Jim. *Growing Good Kids.* Minneapoli, MN: Free Spirit Publishing, 1996. $21.95

DeRoche, Edward F. & Williams, Mary M. *Educating Hearts & Minds.* Thousand Oaks, CA: Corwin Press, 1998. $22.95

Dotson, Anne C., & Dotson, Karen D. *Teaching Character/Parent's Guide.* Chapel Hill, NC: Character Development Publishing, 1997. $12.00

Dotson, Anne C., & Dotson, Karen D. *Teaching Character/Teacher's Guide.* Chapel Hill, NC: Character Development Publishing, 1997. $24.95

Duvall, Lynn. *Respecting Our Differences: A Guide to Getting Along in a Changing World.* Minneapolis, MN: Free Spirit Publishing, 1994. $12.95

Eberly, Don E. *America's Character.* Lanham, MD: Madison Books, 1995. $24.95

Espeland, Pamela & Verdick, Elizabeth. *Making Every Day Count: Daily Readings for Young People on Solving Problems, Setting Goals & Feeling Good About Yourself.* Minneapolis, MN: Free Spirit Publishing, 1998. $9.95

Espeland, Pamela & Wallner, Rosemary. *Making the Most of Today: Daily Readings for Young People on Self-Awareness, Creativity & Self-Esteem.* Minneapolis, MN: Free Spirit Publishing, 1998. $9.95

Etzioni, Amit. *New Golden Rule: Community & Morality.* New York, NY: Basic Books, 1996. $27.50

Garbarino, James. *Lost Boys.* New York, NY: The Free Press, 1999. $25.00

Garbarino, James. *Raising Children in a Socially Toxic Environment.* San Francisco, CA: Jossey-Bass, 1995. $27.95

Girard, Kathryn & Koch, Susan J. *Conflict Resolution in the Schools: A Manual for Educators.* San Francisco, CA: Jossey-Bass, 1996. $35.00

Glasser, William. *Building A Quality School: A Matter of Responsibility* (Video). National Professional Resources, 1998. $99.00

Glasser, William. *Choice Theory.* New York, NY: Harper Collins, 1998. $23.00

Glasser, William. *The Quality School: Managing Students Without Coercion.* New York, NY: Harper Collins, 1990. $12.00

Glenn, H. Stephen, *Raising Self-Reliant Children in a Self-Indulgent World.* Orem, UT : Empowering People, 1989. $12.95

Glenn, H. Stephen. *Seven Strategies for Developing Capable Students.* Orem, UT: Empowering People, 1998. $14.95

Goleman, Daniel. *Emotional Intelligence: Why It Can Matter More Than IQ.* New York, NY: Bantam Books, 1995. $13.95

Goleman, Daniel. *Emotional Intelligence: A New Vision For Educators* (Video).
National Professional Resources, 1996. $89.95

Harris, Pat, et al. *Character Education: Application in the Classroom, Secondary Edition*
(Video). National Professional Resources, 1998. $89.95

Healy, Jane M. *Failure to Connect.* New York, NY: Simon & Schuster, 1998. $25.00

Heath, Douglas. *Schools of Hope: Developing Mind & Character in Today's Youth.*
San Francisco, CA: Jossey-Bass, 1994. $34.95

Hillman, James. *Soul's Code.* New York, NY: Random House, 1996. $23.00

Hoffman, Judith B. & Lee, Anne R. *Character Education Workbook: for School Boards,
Administrators & Community Leaders.* Chapel Hill, NC: Character Development
Publishing, 1997. $12.00

Jackson, Philip W. Boostrom, Robert E., & Hansen, David T. *Moral Life of Schools.*
San Francisco, CA: Jossey-Bass, 1993. $30.95

Josephson, Michael & Hanson, Wes. *Power of Character: Prominent Americans Talk
about Life, Family, Work, Values & More.* San Francisco, CA: Jossey-Bass, 1998.
$23.50

Kagan, Miguel et al. *Classbuilding.* San Clemente, CA: Kagan Cooperative Learning, 1995.
$25.00

Kagan, Laurie, et al. *Teambuilding.* San Clemente, CA: Kagan Cooperative Learning, 1997.
$25.00

Kagan, Spencer. *Building Character Through Cooperative Learning* (Video). National
Professional Resources, 1999. $99.95

Kendall, John S. & Marzano, Robert J. *Content Knowledge K-12 Standards, Second Edition.*
Aurora, CO: Mid-continent Regional Educational Laboratory, Inc., 1997. $47.95

Kidder, Rushworth W. *How Good People Make Tough Choices: Resolving the Dilemmas
for Ethical Living.* New York, NY: William Morrow Company, Inc. 1995. $11.00

Kilpatrick, William and Gregory, & Wolf, Suzanne M. *Books That Build Character: A Guide to
Teaching Your Child Moral Values Through Stories.* New York, NY: Touchstone, 1994.
$11.00

Kohn, Alfie. *Punished By Rewards.* New York, NY: Houghton Mifflin Co., 1993. $13.95

Kohn, Alfie. *What to Look for in a Classroom and Other Essays.* San Francisco, CA:
Jossey-Bass, 1998. $25.00

Krovetz, Martin L. *Fostering Resiliency: Expecting All Students to Use Their Minds and
Hearts Well.* Thousand Oaks, CA: Corwin Press, 1999. $24.95

Lewis, Barbara A. *Kid's Guide to Service Projects.* Minneapolis, MN: Free Spirit Publishing, 1995. $10.95

Lewis, Barbara A. *Kid's Guide to Social Action.* Minneapolis, MN: Free Spirit Publishing, 1998. $16.95

Lewis, Barbara A. *What Do You Stand For? A Kid's Guide to Building Character.* Minneapolis, MN: Free Spirit Publishing, 1997. $18.95

Lewis, Catherine, et al. *Eleven Principles of Effective Character Education* (Video). National Professional Resources, 1997. $89.95

Lickona, Thomas et al. *Character Education: Restoring Respect & Responsibility in Our Schools* (Video). National Professional Resources, 1996. $79.95

Lickona, Thomas. *Educating for Character: How our Schools Can Teach Respect & Responsibility.* New York, NY: Bantam Books, 1992. $14.95

Lickona, Thomas. *Raising Good Children.* New York, NY: Bantam Books, 1994. $13.95

Live Wire Media (Publisher). *Character Way Learning Program* (3 module video set). 1995. $399.00

Lockwood, Anne T. *Character Education: Controversy & Consensus.* Thousand Oaks, CA: Corwin Press, 1997. $12.95

Macan, Lynn, et al. *Character Education: Application in the Classroom, Elementary Edition* (Video). National Professional Resources, 1998. $89.95

The MASTER Teacher, Inc. (Publisher). *Lesson Plans for Character Education, Elementary Edition.* Manhattan, KS: 1998. $59.95

The MASTER Teacher, Inc. (Publisher). *Lesson Plans for Character Education, Secondary Edition.* Manhattan, KS: 1998. $59.95

McCourt, Lisa. *Chicken Soup for Little Souls* (7 book set). Deerfield Beach, FL: Health Communications, Inc., 1998. $99.95

McKay, Linda et al. Service *Learning: Curriculum, Standards and the Community* (Video), National Professional Resources, 1998. $99.00

Murphy, Madonna M. *Character Education in America's Blue Ribbon Schools.* Lancaster, PA: Technomic Publishing, 1997. $44.95

Nelson, Jane. *Positive Discipline.* Orem, UT: Empowering People, 1996. $11.00

Packer, Alex J. *How Rude! The Teenagers' Guide to Good Manners, Proper Behavior, and Not Grossing People Out.* Minneapolis, MN: Free Spirit Publishing, 1997. $19.95

Perlstein, Ruth & Thrall, Gloria. *Ready-to-Use Conflict Resolution Activities for Secondary Students.* West Nyack, NY: Center for Applied Research in Education, 1996. $29.95

Pert, Candace. *Emotion: Gatekeeper to Performance—The Mind/Body Connection* (Video). National Professional Resources, 1999. $99.00

Pert, Candace. *Molecules of Emotion.* New York, NY: Simon & Schuster, 1999. $14.00

Pipher, Mary. *Shelter of Each Other: Rebuilding Our Families.* New York, NY: Ballantine Books, 1997. $12.95

Pollack, William. *Real Boys.* New York, NY: Henry Holt & Co., 1999. $13.95

Renzulli, Joseph. *Developing the Gifts & Talents of ALL Students* (Video). National Professional Resources, 1999. $99.95

Rimmerman, Harlan. *Resources in Cooperative Learning.* San Clemente, CA: Kagan Cooperative Learning, 1996. $25.00

Romain, Trevor. *Cliques, Phonies, & Other Baloney.* Minneapolis, MN: Free Spirit Publishing, 1998. $9.95

Rusnak, Timothy. *Integrated Approach to Character Education.* Thousand Oaks, CA: Corwin Press, 1998. $21.95

Ryan, Kevin A. & Bohlin, Karen E. *Building Character in Schools.* San Francisco, CA: Jossey-Bass, 1998. $25.00

Sadlow, Sarah. *Advisor/Advisee Character Education.* Chapel Hill, NC: Character Development Publishing, 1998. $24.95

Salovey, Peter, et al. *Optimizing Intelligences: Thinking, Emotion & Creativity* (Video). National Professional Resources, 1998. $99.95

Sapon-Shevin, Mara. *Because We Can Change The World: A Practical Guide to Building Cooperative, Inclusive Classroom Communities.* Needham Heights, MA: Allyn & Bacon, 1999. $29.95

Sergiovanni, Thomas J. *Leadership for the Schoolhouse.* San Francisco, CA: Jossey-Bass, 1996. $29.95

Sergiovanni, Thomas J. *Moral Leadership: Getting to the Heart of School Improvement.* San Francisco, CA: Jossey-Bass, 1992. $34.95

Shure, Myrna B. *Raising a Thinking Child.* New York, NY: Pocketbooks., 1994. $12.00

Sizer, Ted. *Crafting of America's Schools* (Video), National Professional Resources, 1997. $99.95

Soder, Roger. *Democracy, Education and the Schools.* San Francisco, CA: Jossey-Bass, 1996. $32.95

Teolis, Beth. *Ready-to-Use: Conflict Resolution Activities, Elementary Edition.* West Nyack, NY: Center for Applied Research in Education, 1998. $29.95

Urban, Hal. *Life's Greatest Lessons: 20 Things I Want My Kids to Know.* Redwood City, CA: Great Lessons Press, 1992. $14.00

Vincent, Philip F. *Developing Character in Students.* Chapel Hill, NC: New View Publications, 1994. $12.95

Vincent, Philip F. *Promising Practices in Character Education: Nine Success Stories from across the Country, Volume II.* Chapel Hill, NC: Character Development Publishing, 1999. $14.00

Vincent, Philip F. *Rules & Procedures for Character Education.* Chapel Hill, NC: Character Development Group, 1998. $14.00

Wiley, Lori Sandford. *Comprehensive Character-Building Classroom.* DeBary, FL: Longwood Communications, 1998. $19.95

Wynne, Edward & Ryan, Kevin. *Reclaiming Our Schools: Teaching Character, Academics & Discipline.* Old Tappan, NY: MacMillan Publishing Co., Inc., 1996. $31.00

ALL BOOKS AVAILABLE FOR PURCHASE FROM
NATIONAL PROFESSIONAL RESOURCES
1-800-453-7461
For additional current resources, see our web site
www.nprinc.com

Character Education: Restoring Respect & Responsibility in Our Schools

Thomas Lickona, a recognized leader in the character education movement, presents an insightful and compelling argument for the role of schools in the development of student respect, responsibility and moral education. In this video, specific classroom strategies, as well as school-wide approaches are outlined in a clear and forceful fashion. Children and youth with disabilities are included in the school population shown. Never before in our nation's history has the need to develop character in children been greater. With the changing role of families, lack of religious affiliation among our youth as well as a decaying moral climate depicted in our media and entertainment industry, schools must play a major role in character and moral development.   1996, VHS, 44 minutes, $79.95

Eleven Principles of Effective Character Education

Two of the country's prominent leaders in character education, Dr. Catherine Lewis and Dr. Thomas Lickona provide a compelling review of the critical principles essential to any effective character education program. Commissioned by the Character Education Partnership (CEP), this video presents a comprehensive guide to the development and assessment of character education programs in our nation,s schools. Visit schools in Maryland and New York where quality character education programs are being implemented by skilled and resourceful staff. This video is an invaluable resource ıor aıı schools that are developing or assessing their character education initiatives.

                    1997, VHS, 40 minutes, $89.95

Character Education: Application in the Classroom

Observe firsthand the application of Character Education in our nation's schools. Classroom teachers demonstrate specific lessons and describe practical instructional approaches that transform character education from a conceptual framework into an understandable series of learning activities.

The Elementary School version features the Principal, Lynn Lisy-Macan and instructional staff at the Brookside Elementary School in Binghamton, New York. This school was identified by *Business Week* and The Character Education Partnership (CEP) as a school of character. Observe lessons at various grade levels.

                    1998, VHS, 43 minutes, $89.95

The Secondary School version is an excellent staff development tool to assist educators who want to incorporate character education in their educational environments and still focus on subject content, and yet ensure mastery of academic standards. This video features Pat Harris, teacher, Chris Corley, principal, as well as teachers and staff of the Brentwood High School in Brentwood, MO. Also featured are teachers conducting service learning in the Kirkwood School as well as Linda McKay from the Cooperating School Districts in St. Louis, MO.

                    1998, VHS, 39 minutes, $89.95

Building Character Through Cooperative Learning

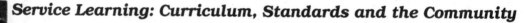

Dr. Spencer Kagan, internationally acclaimed researcher, trainer, and author, presents a powerful case for the use of Cooperative Learning in the building of character in today's youth. Cooperative learning is one of the best ways to develop core virtues, such as personal responsibility and respect, by fostering a classroom environment where social skills are practiced and nurtured.

Now, for the first time brought to video, Dr. Spencer Kagan outlines the value of cooperative learning in character education. This video illustrates how to incorporate proven strategies in cooperative learning into classroom instruction. Whether you are an experienced teacher in the use of cooperative learning, or a novice, you will find Dr. Kagan's instruction an invaluable resource. Observe classrooms, where cooperative learning is put into practice, emphasizing the character development and social skills so natural to this type of instructional approach. Achieve higher standards, both in academic and character education, through this insightful and instructional new video.

1999, VHS, 38 minutes, $99.95

Service Learning: Curriculum, Standards and the Community

One of the fastest growing educational initiatives sweeping our nation's schools is Service Learning. It is an approach that moves beyond the concept of "community service" to a higher, more academically-integrated type of instructional practice.

Through Service Learning, a comprehensive community-based experience unfolds. Students take responsibility to choose topics, develop plans and engage in meaningful community action. An essential part of this process involves student "reflection" which clearly sets it apart from the more traditional community service approach. This community-based learning is motivational and highly rewarding. Service Learning integrates academic curriculum, consistent with higher standards, with a strong character education component. Students learn how to apply their academic skills, while at the same time becoming contributory members of our society.

In this video, visit secondary schools, teachers, community leaders and settings (projects dealing with the homeless and community environments) throughout the United States as teachers and students develop Service Learning projects that promote academic, social and civic responsibility. Essential information is provided to help educators develop Service Learning experiences in their schools. A practical and valuable staff development resource for teachers and administrators committed to higher standards through authentic, community-based instruction.

1998, VHS, 35 minutes, $99.95

ALL VIDEOS AVAILABLE FOR PURCHASE FROM NATIONAL PROFESSIONAL RESOURCES
1-800-453-7461 • For additional current resources, see our web site: www.nprinc.com